Vedic Astrolo

A Textbook of

Varshaphala

Vedic Technique of the Tajika
or
Annual Horoscopy

Dr. K S Charak
M.S. (SURGERY), FRCS (UK)

UMA
Publications

A Textbook of
Varshaphala

First Edition	:	September 1993
Second Edition	:	August 1996
Reprinted	:	January 1999
Reprinted	:	July 2002
Third Edition	:	July 2006

ISBN 81-901008-1-5

Price:
Rs. 200/- US$ 20 £ 14

Published by:

UMA Publications
72 Gagan Vihar, Delhi - 110 051, INDIA
Phone: 91-11-2254 3563
E-mail: kscharak@gmail.com

Designed and Printed by:

SYSTEMS VISION
A-199 Okhla Ind. Area-1, New Delhi - 110 020, INDIA.

PREFACE TO THE FIRST EDITION

Ever since I started teaching astrology in the Bharatiya Vidya Bhawan, I felt the need to systematise my own knowledge and to organise it lesson by lesson for the students. Since I have been doing various branches of astrology now for over twenty years, I have gone through numerous books on the subject, reading and re-reading many of them, and find one essential difference between our method of teaching astrology and the style of writing in the books available. Since we face students with a high educational background (doctors, engineers, businessmen, lawyers, bureaucrats, retired officials, etc.), it becomes absolutely necessary for us to illustrate through actual horoscopes all the astrological points being taught, clarified and elaborated. To do it regularly, as we have to in the Bharatiya Vidya Bhawan, is a much tougher task than reading a paper in a seminar, answering some questions and later forgetting all about it. The available astrological texts are sadly deficient in actual horoscopic illustrations.

The subject of this book, the Tajika or the annual horoscopy, has been rather overwhelmingly dominated by the natal horoscopy. Recently, however, the need to resort to annual horoscopy has been increasing in our industrial society where career planning, travel planning, work planning and job planning are done within a specified time-table of one to, say, five years. In which of the next five years it would be more fruitful to start a venture is a question many people ask. This question is generally answered on the basis of the birth horoscope, the dasha periods and transits. The question is, whether such pinpointed guidance and counselling can be further refined and put in sharp focus astrologically? As a doctor, I am accustomed to employing series of tests for the diagnosis of a disease. As an astrologer, it appeals to me to foresee the same event by employing different astrological techniques to the birth chart, like the Vimshottari dasha, the Jaimini Chara dasha and, where necessary, even the Ashtakavarga. I have not seen a single instance where what is promised in the birth chart is not more clearly reflected in the Tajika concerned.

The Tajika takes care of all those areas that are covered by the natal horoscopy. Thus it can reveal about health and disease, marriage, child birth, income, expenditure, promotions, transfer, travel, rise and fall in career, imprisonment, death, etc. It is true to say that the Tajika cannot give what the birth horoscope does not promise. It is truer to say that the Tajika reveals, with greater clarity, the year in which the promise of the birth horoscope will be fulfilled. The Tajika is thus complimentary, supplementary and confirmatory in nature. What the Tajika reveals is vital not vast as the birth chart does, pivotal though not a plethora of details; and all this within the rigid time-frame of one year. It is an astrologer's precision instrument. The Tajika should be invariably made use of for giving important predictions though only after a thorough examination of the birth chart.

An incidental advantage of the Tajika could sometimes be to correct someone's birth time marginally.

While this book has been planned as explained in the summary at the end, it is relevant to point to a couple of ticklish areas, among others, which had to be tackled. The first was to explain the sixteen well-known Tajika yogas without which the entire edifice of the annual horoscopic reading collapses. These yogas have been dealt with in two ways: first, through definition, illustration and exhaustive comments, and later, through tabulation of all these in a chart form for an easy and clear understanding. No serious student of annual horoscopy can afford to miss these yogas as they reveal remarkably the nature of results that can be expected. Needless to say that this calls for a correct casting of the annual chart. *If in a particular year, the annual lagna falls on the borderline between two rashis, one has to be extra careful. Similarly, where the correct degrees of planets indicate a happy Ithasala, any miscalculation may make it look otherwise.* While there are some computer programmes that provide accurate annual horoscopes, one must be cautious in accepting any computer-cast chart as there are numerous computers which have been incorrectly programmed, and provide wrong data.

Another difficulty was to obtain the right horoscopes with specific events of specific years for illustrations. Fortunately our individual collection and mutual sharing of data helped overcome this problem.

This book covers all the relevant aspects of annual horoscopy and, at places, suggests areas of further research. It has been profusely illustrated. It is hoped that it effectively fills a long-felt void in the field of annual horoscopy. The list of illustrations appended in the beginning may be profitably gone through only after going through the relevant text.

The quotations for the various chapters have been taken from *The Vedic Experience* by Raimundo Panikkar, and *The Flute Calls Still* by Dilip Kumar Roy and Indira Devi.

September 1, 1993 DR K S CHARAK

CONTENTS

LIST OF ILLUSTRATIONS

CHAPTER I

INTRODUCTION

"O Thou who art the Root of the Tree of Life,
As also the last Asylum of repose,
When ends the cycle of Thy Cosmic play!
Who com'st as Grace to foster flowering prayer!
They are deluded by the Siren Maya
Who behold Thy Self as disparate : not so
Those blessed ones who have won through to vision.
For they in all that is see Thee alone
As the Everliving Sun-love - in whose light
All shines and the last mystery stands revealed."

'BHAGAVATA PURANA'

The Varshaphala, or the Annual Horoscopy as it may be called, is one of the scores of techniques of Vedic astrology employed to understand the occurrence of future events. While the Parashari system, which is more prevalent, is much more ancient, the Varshaphala in its present form is of relatively more recent origin. The Parashari system found its origin with the rishis of yore, those marvels of human beings whose intellectual excellence the best of present day computers cannot match. Therefrom, this system found its way to the King's court or the *durbar,* and eventually shrank into the family tradition as the kingships gradually waned. The Varshaphala originated in the *durbar* itself. It was developed as an offshoot of the Parashari system to provide a more spontaneous and quick answer to the usual problems of the kings, like conquests, prosperity, succession, etc. The *Prashna,* or the Horary astrology, is closely related to the Varshaphala and appears to have a similar origin and utility. The Varshaphala is more popular in northern India though it is used everywhere. The Urdu word *Tajika* for Varshaphala too signifies its popularity in northern India where Urdu has been the dominant language.

Inherent to the Vedic astrology is the construction of a chart of the heavens, with the placement of the *grahas,* poorly translated as planets, in different houses and signs in the chart. In the annual, or the progressed, horoscope (or the *Varsha-Kundali)* too, a chart is constructed and the special principles of Varshaphala employed to forecast events. The annual horoscopy differs from the rest in the fact that it picks up one particular year of a native's life and examines it in more minute details. Going into greater minuteness, each month of a particular year, and further, each day or half-a-day during a month, may be subjected to astrological scrutiny for the clearest view of events and their closest timing possible. Such a calculation would naturally demand greater labour on the part of the astrologer. The Varshaphala is thus capable of providing a magnified view of one particular year of a native's life, from one birthday to the next.

The usual horoscope is generally cast for *the time of birth* of a native. The Varshaphala, however, is solar-based. In other words, it is the position of the Sun that is of significance here. *The solar year for a native begins every time the Sun returns to the same longitude as it had at the time of the native's birth.* Between this time and the next solar return is the period covered by one annual chart or the Varsha-Kundali. The time of solar return is technically called *Varshapravesha,* which literally means 'entry of the year'. A Varsha-Kundali is a chart constructed for the Varshapravesha determined for a particular year of life. Such an annual chart is meant to be constructed for every year, and examined in details in order to derive maximum benefit from astrological foresight.

THE TAJIKA SYSTEM

There are three major systems of astrology as applied to individual charts.

(a) The Parashari

(b) The Jaimini

(c) The Varshaphala or the annual horoscopy.

The first two are called as the *Jataka* or the *Hora Shastra*. The last one is known as the *Tajika Shastra* (or the *Tajaka Shastra)*. The most popular of these is the Parashari system which forms the background against which the other systems are studied and evaluated. The Tajika or the annual horoscopy resembles the Parashari system in numerous ways. Thus, the houses and planets in the annual chart have the same significance as they have in the Parashari system. The detailed method involved in the casting of the horoscope, and constructing of the vargas or the divisional charts, like the Navamsha, the Drekkana, the Hora, the Saptamsha, the Dwadashamsha, the Trimshamsha, etc., is the same. The Tajika, like the Parashari, also has an elaborate system of 'dashas' or operational periods so necessary for the timing of events. These dasha systems are a remarkable feature of Vedic astrology.

Special Features of the Tajika

The Tajika system has certain special features which make it distinct. These may be briefly described below.

1. *Specified duration* : One Varshaphala or annual chart applies to a specified period of one year only, and extends from one solar return to the next, thus covering one solar year. For any subsequent year of life, another Varsha-Kundli has to be prepared.

2. *A transit chart* : The annual chart is basically a transit chart. What is considered here is the transit of various planets at the exact moment of solar return. This moment of solar return is highly significant. The position of various planets at this moment of time holds sway over events for the next one year.

Being a transit chart in essence, the Varshaphala does not apply independent of the birth chart. Any attempt to prognosticate events on the basis of the annual chart without first taking into consideration the analysis of the birth chart is, therefore, doomed to failure. It is mandatory to analyse the birth chart thoroughly before proceeding to analyse the annual chart. *What is not promised in the birth chart is not likely to materialise whether or not the annual chart indicates it.* The proper use of the Varshaphala is to see more clearly and more definitely the events promised in the birth chart. The special feature of this transit chart is that it holds true for a period of one year.

The Varshaphala is, however, also an improvement over a simple transit in that it involves the use of certain operational periods or dashas as are employed in relation to the birth chart for the timing of events. There are various dasha systems used in the Varsha chart, and these understandably apply to the one year in question. While the Mahadasha (MD), the Antardasha (AD) and the Pratyantar-dasha (PD) in the birth chart help in the timing of events fairly closely, the dashas in the Varshaphala ensure a still closer timing, reaching upto the nearest day an event is likely to take place.

It may, however, be added here that the annual horoscopy has been less often employed in the recent past. A lot of research needs to be done before some of its principles attain the same infallibility as those of the widely practised Parashari system. For example, *our understanding of the Tajika dashas and their application needs greater research before we obtain consistent results.* Several other aspects of the Tajika are, however, better understood and provide dazzling results.

3. *Aspects* : Planets not only exert influence over the house where they are located, they also extend their influence over the houses and planets which they aspect. In turn, they are influenced, favourably or otherwise, by the other aspecting planets. In the Tajika system, the aspects are different from those in the Parashari system. The Tajika aspects are of three types:

(a) *Friendly (Mitra Drishti)* : A planet exerts a friendly aspect on houses and planets placed in the houses 3, 5, 9, and 11 when counted from itself. In turn, it receives friendly aspect from planets located in these houses. In other words, *planets placed in the houses 3, 5, 9, and 11 from each other become friends.* The friendly aspect is further divided into two types :

(i) *Very friendly (Pratyaksha Mitra)* : Between planets located in 5/9 from each other.

(ii) *Semi-friendly or secretly friendly (Gupta Mitra)* : Between planets located in 3/11 from each other.

(b) *Inimical (Shatru Drishti)* : Planets become enemies of each other when they are located in kendras (houses 1, 4, 7 and

10)[1] from each other. The inimical aspects are also of two types:

(i) *Openly inimical (Pratyaksha Shatru)* : Between planets located in houses 1/7 from each other.

(ii) *Secretly inimical (Gupta Shatru)* : Between planets located in houses 4/10 from each other.

(c) *Neutral (Sama Drishti)* : Planets exert neutral influence (or no influence) on each other when they are placed in houses 2, 12, 6 or 8 from each other.

Similarly, the houses 2, 12, 6 and 8 from any planet receive no aspect from the planet in question.

As an example, in the chart[2] here, the Sun and Mercury, being located in the same house, are inimical towards each other[3]. They are also inimical towards the Moon and Mars which fall in kendras from them. With Jupiter they are friendly since Jupiter is placed in the third house from them. They are neutral toward Venus and Saturn, respectively in the second and eighth from them. For the Moon, Venus and Saturn are friends, the Sun,

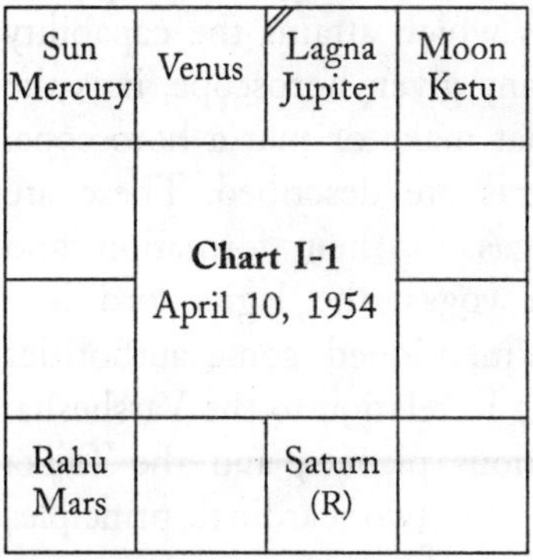

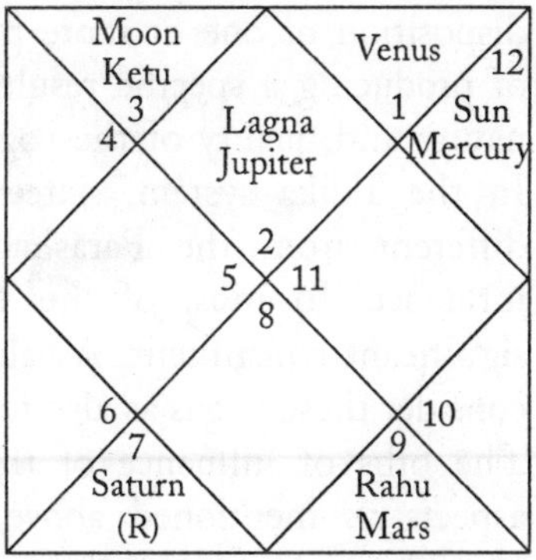

---

1. This is identical with the western method where kendra aspects are held inimical. The great Varahamihira, however, gives special importance to the kendras without holding the planets located in them as overtly inimical.

2. See next chapter for orientation about the north Indian and the south Indian charts.

3. This also is a standard method of interpreting the Vimshottari dasha-antardasha of planets located together.

Mercury and Mars are enemies, while Jupiter is neutral. Similarly, other planetary relationships can be worked out.

4. *Sex of planets* : According to the Tajika system, the male planets are the Sun, Mars and Jupiter, while the female planets are the Moon, Mercury, Venus and Saturn. This is at variance with the Parashari concepts. The male planets gain strength during day time, and in the masculine houses in the annual chart. The female planets gain strength during night time, and when they are located in the feminine houses. This knowledge will be used in a subsequent chapter dealing with the strength of planets.

5. *Lord of the year* : One of the seven planets (from the Sun to Saturn, excluding Rahu and Ketu) is supposed to hold rulership over the entire year. The events of the year are significantly influenced by the strength and disposition of this ruler, also called the *Varshesha* or the *Varsheshwara.* While analysing the special yogas in an annual chart, some authorities attach the same significance to the Varshesha as they do to the lagna lord. The determination of the Varshesha involves an elaborate method which is a characteristic of the annual horoscopy.

6. *The sixteen yogas :* A yoga in astrology is a specific disposition of one or more planets which attains the capability of producing a specific result. In any given horoscope, it is the nature and quality of the yogas that make or mar a horoscope. In the Tajika system, sixteen yogas are described. These are different from the Parashari yogas in their formation and influence. In most of the Tajika yogas, the lagna lord is a significant constituent. As already mentioned, some authorities consider these yogas as also forming in relation to the Varshesha. The orbs of influence of the various planets, and the Tajika aspects as mentioned above, are the two cardinal principles around which most of these yogas revolve. The countless yogas encountered in the Parashari system are generally not applied to the annual chart.

An understanding of the yogas in the Tajika is the key to successful predictions based on the annual chart. These very yogas are also applicable to the Prashna Kundali or the Horary chart which also makes use of the Tajika aspects as mentioned earlier.

7. *Sahams*: A unique feature of the Tajika system is the determination of certain sensitive points or *Sahams.* Each such sensitive point or Saham is meant to shed light on one particular aspect of life during the year in question. For example, there will be one Saham for marriage as there will be one for child birth. Similarly, there is a different Saham for each of the other such mundane events as love, sorrow, joy, success, foreign travel, education, monetary gains, disease, death, and the like. Practitioners of Varshaphala pick up for study only such Sahams in respect of a particular native during a particular year as are relevant.

8. *The Muntha*: Another sensitive and generally auspicious point in the annual chart is the Muntha. The location of the Muntha in the annual chart and the planets aspecting or associating with it, as also its sign lord, are all important in influencing the events during the year for which the annual chart is being considered.

9. *The Tri-Pataki map*: The Tri-Pataki map is another special feature of the Varshaphala. In this, the twelve rashis or signs are labelled on the twelve points of the Tri-Pataki, and the various planets marked on these rashis after working out their progression since birth. *In the Tri-Pataki, the benefic and malefic influences on the Moon are generally considered.*

Relation Between the Annual Chart and the Birth Chart

It has been already emphasised that the annual chart is essentially a transit chart and, therefore, cannot be taken into consideration in isolation. The annual chart can only shed more light on a promise indicated in the birth chart. What is not indicated in the birth chart cannot come to pass during the year in question even if the annual chart may indicate it. *This fact must be particularly borne in mind when the annual chart indicates such untoward events as death, disease or accidents.* The birth chart naturally takes precedence over transits.

That the annual chart is an ingenious projection of the birth chart only can be ascertained when the following factors are considered.

1. *The Sun's longitude*: The longitude of the Sun at birth forms the basis of the annual chart. The Sun thus retains the

same rashi position in the annual chart, as also in its divisional charts, as it does at the time of birth.

2. *The importance of birth lagna* : The disposition of the birth ascendant in the annual chart is significant in that it influences the events occurring during the year. Even more significant is the importance of the lord of the lagna in the birth chart. The lagna lord of the birth horoscope is one of the five office bearers in the annual chart; one of the five office bearers eventually qualifies for the post of the Varshesha or the year lord. The birth lagna lord is thus a regular claimant for the post of the Varshesha every year.

Also related to the birth ascendant is the Muntha which constitutes an important link between the birth chart and the annual chart. The Muntha is located in the lagna at the time of birth. It progresses by one sign during one solar year. It is thus *the birth ascendant in progression.* Important events happening during the year can be explained according to the disposition of the Muntha as well as that of the year lord.

3. *The Tri-Pataki* : The Tri-Pataki chart consists of placement of planets in relation to Varsha lagna, after working out their progression in relation to their position at birth. The Tri-Pataki thus makes use of the ascendant in the annual chart, and the planetary position in the birth chart.

4. *Nakshatra dashas* : The Parashari dashas are nakshatra-based. In other words, they depend upon the nakshatra or the constellation of the Moon in the birth chart. Some of these nakshatra dashas, when reduced to a period of one year, find their use in the annual chart. The sequence of these dashas during a given year of life depends on the nakshatra of the Moon at birth as also the age, in years, of the native at the time of casting the annual chart.

5. *Sahams* : As already mentioned, the Sahams are a special feature of the annual chart. However, *it is recommended that the Sahams be calculated for the birth chart as well.*[4] Only those Sahams which are strong in the birth chart can produce their results during the year if they are also strong in the annual chart. Those

4. See Chapter XI for the calculation of Sahams.

Sahams which are weak in the birth chart are incapable of producing results in the annual chart.

In summary, it may be stated that the Varshaphala provides an interesting and closer view of events pertaining to a given year of life of the native. It gives excellent results when integrated with a proper study of the birth chart. An understanding of certain special features of the Varshaphala (e.g., Yogas, Sahams, etc.) is imperative for successful predictions.

CHAPTER II

GENERAL CONSIDERATIONS

Then, as before, did the Creator fashion
the Sun and Moon, the Heaven and the Earth,
the atmosphere and the domain of light.

'RIG VEDA'

The Tajika system is only an extension of the Parashari system. A knowledge of the basics of the Parashari system thus becomes essential in order to understand and apply the Tajika system or the annual horoscopy. In the account that follows, some of these basics as applicable to the annual chart will be explained.

The Anatomy of the Chart

The Varshaphala or the annual horoscopy is a branch of astrology which has been mainly in vogue in the northern India. Thus, the chart as drawn for an annual horoscope invariably used to be the one used in the north India. With progressive exchange of late between the north and the south, the Tajika system is gradually finding favour with the south Indian practitioners of astrology as well. Thus, often the chart has to be drawn in the south Indian manner. Either method is as good, depending upon the convenience of the practitioner.

(a) **The north Indian chart :** Here, the *houses are fixed.* The houses are either triangular or rhomboid in shape. The upper central rhomboid represents the first house or the lagna or the ascendant, and the remaining houses follow regularly in order, in an *anti-clockwise direction.* The sign coinciding with the lagna is marked in the house fixed for the lagna, and the remaining signs marked in the remaining houses.

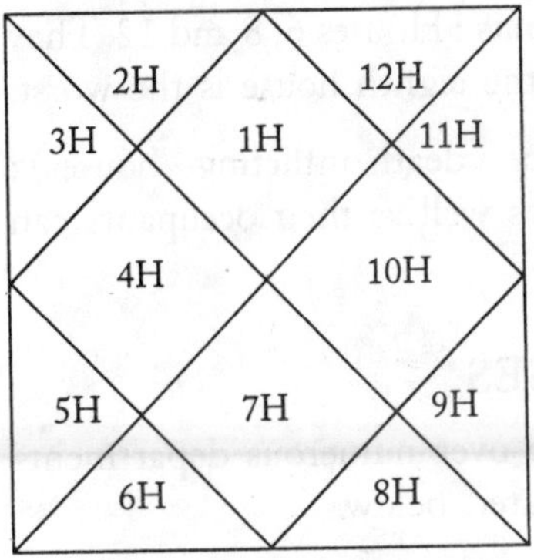

The North Indian Chart

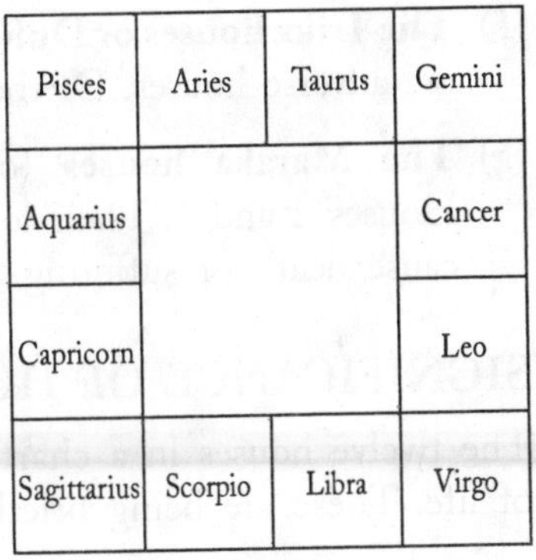

The South Indian Chart

b) **The South Indian chart :** In this type of chart, *the signs are fixed.* They proceed in a *clockwise manner* from Aries to Pisces. Each house is in the form of a square. The lagna is marked by two parallel lines across the top left corner in the sign where it falls, and the houses are counted from the lagna onwards.

THE HOUSES

A horoscope has twelve houses. The ascendant or the lagna is the first house. The remaining houses fall in regular order from it. The various houses have been classed into certain groups, as indicated below.

(a) **The Kendras** (or Quadrants) : Houses 1, 4, 7 and 10. They are the pillars of a horoscope.

(b) **The Panapharas** (or Successant houses) : Houses 2, 5, 8 and 11.

(c) **The Apoklimas** (or Cadent houses) : Houses 3, 6, 9 and 12.

(d) **The Trikonas** (or Trines) : Houses 1, 5 and 9. These are auspicious houses. House no. 1, i.e., the lagna or the ascendant, being both a kendra and a trikona, is the most important and beneficial house.

(e) **The Upachayas** : Houses 3, 6, 10 and 11. They indicate struggle, competition and activity.

(f) **The Trika houses or Duhsthanas** : Houses 6, 8 and 12. They are adverse houses. Of these, the eighth house is the worst.

(g) **The Maraka houses** (or the death-inflicting houses) : Houses 2 and 7. Their lords as well as their occupants can cause death or suffering.

SIGNIFICANCE OF HOUSES

The twelve houses in a chart rule over numerous departments of life. These are being briefly stated below.

1. **Lagna or the first house :** Body, health, appearance, complexion, longevity, beginning, queries, head, the present (time), details about birth.
2. **The second house :** Wealth, gains and losses, possessions, education, food, right eye, face, oral cavity, speech, family, death.
3. **The third house :** Siblings, courage, valour, shoulders, right ear, movement (short journeys), neighbourhood, business transactions, communication.
4. **The fourth house :** Home, fields, parental property, relatives, conveyance, mother, cattle, fragrance, comforts, clothes, ornaments, chest.
5. **The fifth house :** Progeny, wisdom, knowledge of the future, friends, riches, knowledge of the scriptures, upper abdomen.
6. **The sixth house :** Enemies, debts, quarrels, injury, thief (theft), fear, loss of honour, bad deeds, slavery, quadrupeds (pets), maternal uncles and aunts, waist.
7. **The seventh house :** Desires (pertaining to the matters of the heart), marriage, spouse, business partners, travel, path, death, lower abdomen and pelvis.
8. **The eighth house :** Longevity (and death), inheritance, wealth of the spouse, obstacles, discontinuity, interruption, worries, defeat, crevices, mutual conjugal adjustments, organ of excretion.

9. **The ninth house :** The guru (or the preceptor), gods, father, virtuous deeds, journey, grandson, hips and thighs.

10. **The tenth house :** The 'Karma', occupation, means of livelihood, status, promotions in job, administration, knees.

11. **The eleventh house :** Income, gains, procurements, *arrival,* praise, elder brother or sister, *good news,*[1] left ear, legs.

12. **The twelfth house :** Loss, expenditure, consequence, penury, pleasures of the bed, renunciation, moksha (or the final emancipation), left eye, feet.

THE PLANETS

The Vedic astrology makes use of nine *grahas* which, only for the sake of convenience, will henceforth be mentioned as planets. In regular order, they are: Ravi, Chandra, Mangala, Budha, Brihaspati, Shukra, Shani, Rahu and Ketu Their English equivalents, along with their symbols, are being tabulated below.

Table II-1

The Planets	The English Equivalent	Symbols
1. Ravi (Surya)	The Sun	☉
2. Chandra	The Moon	☽
3. Mangala	Mars	♂
4. Budha	Mercury	☿
5. Brihaspati	Jupiter	♃
6. Shukra	Venus	♀
7. Shani	Saturn	♄
8. Rahu	Rahu or Dragon's head	☊
9. Ketu	Ketu or Dragon's tail	☋

Of the above planets, the Sun and the Moon are the luminaries, while Rahu and Ken are shadowy planets having no material existence. It is these nine planets, moving in the twelve signs of the zodiac, equivalent to the twelve houses in a

1. The nature of the good news will depend upon a detailed analysis of the chart.

horoscope, that determine all the events, good or bad, occurring in the life of an individual.

THE ZODIAC

The zodiac represents the circular path followed by the planets round the earth. Its extent is 360 degrees (the circumference of a circle). It is divided into twelve equal parts (of 30 degrees each) labelled as rashis or signs. Each degree further consists of sixty minutes, and each minute of sixty seconds. The position of planets in the zodiac is represented in the rashi chart or the basic horoscope which consists of twelve houses equivalent to the twelve signs of the zodiac. Each house of the horoscope thus represents one particular rashi or sign.

THE RASHIS OR SIGNS

The twelve rashis, each of 30 degrees extent, are listed below, along with their English equivalents and symbols.

Table II - 2

The Rashis	The English Equivalent	Extent (degrees)	Symbol
1. Mesha	Aries	0-30	♈
2. Vrishabha	Taurus	30-60	♉
3. Mithuna	Gemini	60-90	♊
4. Karka	Cancer	90-120	♋
5. Simha	Leo	120-150	♌
6. Kanya	Virgo	150-180	♍
7. Tula	Libra	180-210	♎
8. Vrishchika	Scorpio	210-240	♏
9. Dhanu	Sagittarius	240-270	♐
10. Makara	Capricorn	270-300	♑
11. Kumbha	Aquarius	300-330	♒
12. Meena	Pisces	330-360	♓

SOME CHARACTERISTICS OF RASHIS

1. **Malefic/Male :** The odd signs (1, 3, 5, 7, 9, 11) are malefic in nature, and of male gender.

2. **Benefic/Female :** The even signs (2, 4, 6, 8, 10, 12) are benefic in nature and of female gender.
3. **Movable or otherwise :** Rashis 1, 4, 7 and 10 are movable in nature. They indicate change and mobility.

   Rashis 2, 5, 8 and 11 are fixed. They indicate fixity, stability as well as obstinacy.

   Rashis 3, 6, 9 and 12 are mixed or common, and represent a balance between mobility and fixity.
4. **Directions**

East	:	Rashis 1, 5 and 9
South	:	Rashis 2, 6 and 10
West	:	Rashis 3, 7 and 11
North	:	Rashis 4, 8 and 12

5. **Inherent nature**

Fiery	:	Rashis 1, 5 and 9
Earthy	:	2, 6 and 10
Airy	:	3, 7 and 11
Watery	:	4, 8 and 12

6. **Biological characteristics**

Quadrupeds	:	1, 2, 5, posterior half of 9, and anterior half of 10
Bipeds	:	3, 6, 7, anterior half of 9, and 11
Insect (or keeta)	:	4 and 8
Those inhabiting water (or Jalachara)	:	Posterior half of 10, and 12.

7. **Parts of the body**

   These roughly correspond to those ruled by the different houses.

Aries	:	Head
Taurus	:	Face, throat
Gemini	:	Shoulders, upper limbs
Cancer	:	Chest, lungs

Leo	:	Stomach, upper abdomen
Virgo	:	Intestines, waist
Libra	:	Lower abdomen
Scorpio	:	Private parts of the body (external genitalia)
Sagittarius	:	Thighs
Capricorn	:	Knees
Aquarius	:	Legs
Pisces	:	Feet

MORE ABOUT PLANETS

1. Planetary Lordship

All planets, excluding Rahu and Ketu, have lordship over the rashis. While the Sun and the Moon own a single rashi each, the rest of them each own two rashis. The planetary lordship over the various rashis is as follows:

The Sun	owns Leo
The Moon	owns Cancer
Mars	owns Aries and Scorpio
Mercury	owns Gemini and Virgo
Jupiter	owns Sagittarius and Pisces
Venus	owns Taurus and Libra
Saturn	owns Capricorn and Aquarius

II. Benefics and Malefics

Planets could be either natural benefits or natural malefics.

Jupiter, Venus, waxing Moon and a well-associated Mercury are natural benefics.

Waning Moon, ill-associated Mercury, the Sun, Mars, Saturn, Rahu and Ketu are natural malefics.

Planets, however, are subservient to the sign rising in the lagna. Thus, different planets behave differently for different lagnas. A natural malefic may become benefic for a particular lagna, while a natural benefic may acquire harmful propensities. In general, the benefic and malefic nature of planets for a given lagna may be decided by taking into consideration the following factors :

1. Benefics as lords of kendras shed their beneficence.
2. Malefics as lords of kendras shed their maleficence.
3. The trikona lords are ever benefic, whether or not they are natural benefics.
4. Lords of houses 3, 6 and 11 are ever malefic, more intensely so if they also own the eighth house.
5. Lords of houses 2, 12 and 8 may be treated as neutral, and they give benefic and malefic results depending upon their association with benefics or malefics. Lord of the eighth house, however, is particularly malefic unless it also owns a trikona.
6. A planet owning both a kendra and a trikona acquires exceedingly beneficial propensities.
7. Association of kendra and trikona lords produces highly beneficial results.
8. Lords of houses 2 and 7 are Marakas or death-inflicting.
9. Rahu behaves as Saturn and Ketu as Mars. In addition, Rahu and Ketu give results according to the sign in which they are located as also the planets they are associated with.
10. Rahu and Ketu in trikonas associated with kendra lords, or in kendras associated with trikona lords, acquire highly benefic properties.
11. In the annual chart, the relationship of various planets with each other and with the lagna lord must be additionally taken into account, not forgetting the special Tajika aspects that govern these relations.

III. Natural Mutual Relationship of Planets

In addition to the mutual relationship of planets in the annual chart, as decided by their friendly, inimical or neutral aspects, the natural relationship of planets as employed in the Parashari system must also be considered. This may be tabulated as follows:

Table II-3

Planets	Friends	Neutrals	Enemies
Sun	Mon, Mar, Jup	Mer	Ven, Sat
Moon	Sun, Mer	Mar Jup Ven, Sat	–
Mars	Sun, Mon, Jup	Ven, Sat	Mer
Mercury	Sun, Ven	Mar, Jup, Sat	Mon
Jupiter	Sun, Mon, Mar	Sat	Mer, Ven
Venus	Mer, Sat	Mar, Jup	Sun, Mon
Saturn	Mer, Ven	Jup	Sun, Mon, Mar

According to one view, in the Tajika system, there are some natural friends and enemies. The planets are divided into two groups: (A) Group I consists of the Sun, the Moon, Mars and Jupiter, who are mutually friendly, and have common enemies in Mercury, Venus and Saturn. (B) Group II consists of Mercury, Venus and Saturn which are mutually friendly, and jointly inimical towards the Sun, the Moon, Mars and Jupiter. *In practice, however, the planetary relationships based only on the nature of aspects in the Tajika are employed in analysing an annual chart.*

IV. Exaltation and Debilitation of Planets

Planets are strong when exalted, and devoid of strength when debilitated. The point of exaltation for each planet is fixed; six signs or 180 degrees away from the exaltation point is the debilitation point of the planet.

V. The Moola Trikona Signs

Planets are also strong when located in certain specially favourable signs called their Moola Trikonas.

Table II-4 lists the exaltation, the debilitation and the Moola Trikonas of the various planets.

Table II - 4
Exaltation, Debilitation and Moola Trikona Signs of Planets

Planets	Exaltation (signs - deg.)	Debilitation (signs - deg.)	Moola Trikona (signs -deg.)
Sun	Aries 10°	Libra 10°	Leo 0° to 20°
Moon	Taurus 3°	Scorpio 3°	Taurus 4° to 20°
Mars	Capricorn 28°	Cancer 28°	Aries 0° to 12°
Mercury	Virgo 15°	Pisces 15°	Virgo 16° to 20°
Jupiter	Cancer 5°	Capricorn 5°	Sagittarius 0° to 10°
Venus	Pisces 27°	Virgo 27°	Libra 0° to 15°
Saturn	Libra 20°	Aries 20°	Aquarius 0° to 20°

VI. Aspects

All planets aspect the seventh house or the planets located in the seventh house from their own position. In addition, there are special aspects allotted to Mars, Jupiter and Saturn. Mars aspects the fourth and eighth houses from its location, besides its seventh aspect. Jupiter's additional aspects are fifth and ninth. Saturn has additional aspects on the third and the tenth houses. These are the Parashari aspects and are at variance with the aspects generally employed in the Tajika.

VII. Combustion and Retrogression

Planets when too near the Sun lose their vitality and are said to be combust. Also, during their sojourn around the Sun, sometimes the planets appear to be moving in a backward direction when seen from the earth; such planets are called as retrograde. The Moon and the Sun do not become retrograde, while Rahu and Ketu are ever retrograde. Both the combust as well as the retrograde planets are considered weak and harmful in the Tajika.

VIII. Directions

The eight directions are ruled by the planets as follows : East: Sun; South East : Venus; South : Mars; South West : Rahu; West : Saturn; North West : Moon; North : Mercury; North East : Jupiter.

IX. Significations of Planets

Planets, like houses, also rule over various events or aspects of life. These are briefly summarised below.

1. **Sun :** Father, soul, glory, association with the rulers, energy, light, drive, journey in woods and hilly regions, patience, victory, courage, gold.
2. **Moon :** Mother, mind, mental happiness, white objects, fruits, flowers, silver, milk, beauty (of appearance).
3. **Mars :** Physical and mental energy, siblings, courage (boldness), battles, enemy, enmity, cruelty, weapons, sinful acts, injury, scars.
4. **Mercury :** Good speech, intelligence, adeptness, cleverness of speech, *Vidya* (higher or scriptural education), truthfulness.
5. **Jupiter :** Jnana (knowledge of the Real), good qualities, son, guru, knowledge of the scriptures, austerities, devotion, wisdom, esteem, control over senses, treasure.
6. **Venus :** Pleasures of the senses and of the bed, good clothes, ornaments, conveyance, fragrance, perfumes, flowers, riches, comforts, marriage, auspicious events.
7. **Saturn :** Longevity, death, fear, fall (from height or status), dishonour, ailment, misery, penury, defamation, sin, servility, slavery, stability, association with 'low' people, laziness, debts, imprisonment, agriculture.
8. **Rahu :** Paternal relations (grandfather, etc.), chronic and incurable disease, serpent bites, epidemics, mathematics.
9. **Ketu :** Maternal grandfather, undiagnosed disease, parasitic infestation, intrigues, occultism, spirituality, emancipation.

THE NAKSHATRAS

The zodiac is divided into twenty-seven nakshatras or constellations, each having an extent of 13 degrees and 20 minutes. Each nakshatra may be further divided into four equal parts of 3 degrees 20 minutes each, and called the padas or charanas or quarters. Thus there are 108 nakshatra charanas or quarters. Since there are twelve rashis in the zodiac as equivalent to twenty seven nakshatras, each rashi consists of two-and-a-quarter nakshatras or nine nakshatra charanas. The twenty-seven nakshatras, in three groups of nine each, are ruled by nine planets. The order of rulers over the first nine nakshatras is Ketu Venus, Sun, Moon, Mars, Rahu, Jupiter, Saturn and Mercury. This order repeats in the next group of nine nakshatras, and again in the last group of nine nakshatras.

The relation between the rashis, the nakshatras, and the nakshatra lords may be better understood from Table II-5.

THE VARGAS

Each sign or rashi is further subdivided into its vargas or specified divisions. These vargas are employed to make the varga charts or the divisional charts. A rashi chart in general only provides a broad overview of events. In order that more detailed and accurate analysis is performed, it is important to prepare the various divisional charts. Generally, astrologers make Shadvargas (six-fold divisions) or Saptavargas (seven-fold divisions) for routine analysis. These vargas are very briefly described below. They would again be referred to later.

1. **The Rashi chart :** This is the basic chart as cast generally.

2. **Hora :** Each sign is divided into two parts of 15 degrees each. The first part in an odd sign and the second part in an even sign belongs to the Hora of the Sun (or Leo). The second part of an odd sign and the first part of an even sign belongs to the Hora of the Moon (or Cancer).

3. **Drekkana :** Each sign is divided into three parts of 10 degrees each. The first part belongs to the sign itself; the second part to the sign fifth from it; the third to the sign ninth from it.

4. **Navamsha :** This is the most important of the vargas. Each sign is divided into nine equal parts of 3°20'. In movable signs, the first Navamsha belongs to the same sign, and the remaining Navamshas follow in order. In the fixed signs, the first Navamsha falls in the ninth house from itself. In the mixed signs, the first Navamsha falls in the fifth from itself.

Table II - 5

Rashis, Nakshatras and Nakshatra lords

Rashis	Nakshatras	Extent s	d	m	Pada	Lord
1. Aries	1. Ashwini	0	13	20	4	Ketu
	2. Bharani	0	26	40	4	Venus
	3. Krittika	1	0	0	1	Sun
2. Taurus	3. Krittika	1	10	0	3	Sun
	4. Rohini	1	23	20	4	Moon
	5. Mrigasira	2	0	0	2	Mars
3. Gemini	5. Mrigasira	2	6	40	2	Mars
	6. Ardra	2	20	0	4	Rahu
	7. Punarvasu	3	0	0	3	Jupiter
4. Cancer	7. Punarvasu	3	3	20	1	Jupiter
	8. Pushya	3	16	40	4	Saturn
	9. Ashlesha	4	0	0	4	Mercury
5. Leo	10. Magha	4	13	20	4	Ketu
	11. Poorva Phalguni	4	26	40	4	Venus
	12. Uttara Phalguni	5	0	0	1	Sun
6. Virgo	12. Uttara Phalguni	5	10	0	3	Sun
	13. Hasta	5	23	20	4	Moon
	14. Chitra	6	0	0	2	Mars
7. Libra	14. Chitra	6	6	40	2	Mars
	15. Swati	6	20	0	4	Rahu
	16. Vishakha	7	0	0	3	Jupiter
8. Scorpio	16. Vishakha	7	3	20	1	Jupiter
	17. Anuradha	7	16	40	4	Saturn
	18. Jyestha	8	0	0	4	Mercury
9. Sagitt.	19. Moola	8	13	20	4	Ketu
	20. Poorva Asadha	8	26	40	4	Venus
	21. Uttara Asadha	9	0	0	1	Sun
10. Capri.	21. Uttara Asadha	9	10	0	3	Sun
	22. Shravana	9	23	20	4	Moon
	23. Dhanishtha	10	0	0	2	Mars
11. Aquarius	23. Dhanishtha	10	6	40	2	Mars
	24. Satha Bhishaj	10	20	0	4	Rahu
	25. P. Bhadrapada	11	0	0	3	Jupiter
12. Pisces	25. P. Bhadrapada	11	3	20	1	Jupiter
	26. U. Bhadrapada	11	16	40	4	Saturn
	27. Revati	12	0	0	4	Mercury

5. **Dwadashamsha :** Each sign is divided into twelve equal parts of 2°30'. The first Dwadashamsha belongs to the same sign, the next one to the subsequent sign, and so on.

6. **Trimshamsha :** In odd signs, the first five degrees belong to Mars, the next 5° to Saturn, the next 8° to Jupiter, the next 7° to Mercury, and the last 5° to Venus. In the even signs, the order is reversed, i.e., Venus 5°, Mercury 7°, Jupiter 8°, Saturn 5°, and finally Mars 5°, in this order from the first to the fifth division.

7. **Saptamsha :** The above mentioned six divisions constitute the Shadvargas. When the Saptamsha too is included, it makes the Saptavargas. Each sign is divided into seven equal parts (of 4°17'8.5"). In odd signs, the first Saptamsha belongs to the same sign; the remaining ones follow in regular order. In the even signs, the first Saptamsha belongs to the sign in the seventh from itself.

The vargas have been more thoroughly dealt with subsequently, while dealing with planetary strength.

CHAPTER III

CASTING THE ANNUAL CHART

From Ocean with its waves was born the year
which marshals the succession of nights and days,
controlling everything that blinks the eye.

'RIG VEDA'

The longitude of the Sun at birth forms the basis of the annual chart. The annual chart for any given year of a native's life is the horoscope cast for the moment when the Sun attains, during that year, the same longitude as it had at the time of birth. All calculations of cusps and longitudes are done on the sidereal or Nirayana basis. The use of the Chitrapaksha ayanamsha (as employed in the *Lahiri's Indian Ephemeris)* has given us sound results.

The Solar Cycle

A solar year has a duration of three hundred and sixty five days, six hours, nine minutes and about ten seconds. In other words, the Sun takes this length of time to complete one round of the twelve signs of the zodiac. After this duration of time, the Sun will return to its original position; another sojourn for the same duration, and the Sun attains the same position again. This would go on repeating every year. Thus, if we add 365 days 6 hours 9 minutes and 10 seconds to the weekday and time of birth, we get the weekday and time next year when the Sun would regain the same longitude as it had at the beginning. *The time when the Sun after one sojourn returns to its original position is called the solar return or the Varsha-pravesha.*

If we ignore the completed weeks out of the above mentioned period of time (i.e., 365 d. 6 h. 9 m. 10 s.), we get a remainder of 1 d. 6 h. 9 m. and 10 s. This is a constant for one year. Double this figure would give us the constant for two years, and so on. This constant figure for any year or years is called *Dhruvanka* (literally, a 'fixed value' or a `numerical constant'). Thus, adding the Dhruvanka for any number of completed years to the weekday and time of birth would give us the weekday and time of Varshapravesha for the year to commence. The weekday thus obtained may be the same as that falling on the native's actual birthday as given by the calender during that year, or it may fall a day before or a day after the actual birthday.

A horoscope cast for this particular weekday, falling on or around one's natural birthday, and for the time obtained as above, is called as the annual chart or the Varsha Kundali (Varsha : year; Kundali : chart).

Steps involved in preparing an annual chart

The first requirement of an annual chart is the construction of the birth chart along with its dashas and antardashas. Next comes the determination of Varshapravesha. Finally, a chart is constructed for the Varshapravesha so obtained. The following steps must be gone through.

1. Note the weekday of the birth of the native along with his date, time and place of birth.
2. Calculate the ascendant, the tenth house, the longitudes of planets, and the Vimshottari Dasha/Antardasha, etc., as relevant to the birth horoscope.
3. Decide on the particular calender year for which the annual chart is to be prepared.
4. For the calender year in question, find the native's *completed years* of life by subtracting the year of birth from the current year.
5. Find out the Dhruvanka or the constant for the number of completed years (see Table III-1).
6. Add to the weekday (use 0 for Sunday, 1 for Monday, 2 for Tuesday, and so on) and the time of birth, the Dhruvanka for the completed years. The total will give the weekday and the time of Varshapravesha.

Table III - 1
Dhruvankas for completed years

Completed years	Dhruvanka d	h	m	s	Completed years	Dhruvanka d	h	m	s
1	1	6	9	10	31	3	22	44	1
2	2	12	18	19	32	5	4	53	11
3	3	18	27	29	33	6	11	2	21
4	5	0	36	39	34	0	17	11	30
5	6	6	45	49	35	1	23	20	40
6	0	12	54	58	36	3	5	29	49
7	1	19	4	8	37	4	11	38	59
8	3	1	13	18	38	5	17	48	9
9	4	7	22	27	39	6	23	57	19
10	5	13	31	37	40	1	6	6	29
11	6	19	40	47	41	2	12	15	38
12	1	1	49	57	42	3	18	24	48
13	2	7	59	6	43	5	0	33	58
14	3	14	8	16	44	6	6	43	7
15	4	20	17	26	45	0	12	52	17
16	6	2	26	36	46	1	19	1	27
17	0	8	35	45	47	3	1	10	37
18	1	14	44	55	48	4	7	19	46
19	2	20	54	5	49	5	13	28	56
20	4	3	3	14	50	6	19	38	6
21	5	9	12	24	55	6	2	23	55
22	6	15	21	34	60	5	9	9	43
23	0	21	30	44	65	4	15	55	32
24	2	3	39	53	70	3	22	41	20
25	3	9	49	3	75	3	5	27	9
26	4	15	58	13	80	2	12	12	58
27	5	22	7	22	85	1	18	58	56
28	0	4	16	32	90	1	1	44	35
29	1	10	25	42	95	0	8	30	23
30	2	16	34	52	100	6	15	16	12

7. Calculate the ascendant and the tenth house for this day and time. Also calculate the longitudes of planets as well as the mid-points of the houses for this moment. This gives us the Varsha chart proper.

Note: The longitude of the Sun as obtained for the moment of Varshapravesha may not be exactly the same as that at the time of birth. The two may differ by a few minutes. This difference, which is due to the disturbance of the Sun's longitude by the planets, may be safely ignored in the Varshaphala calculations.

Example : Native born on August 20, 1944 (Sunday), at 7 : 11 A.M. (IST)[1], at Bombay (Lat. 18°58'N; Long. 72°50'E). Calculate the annual chart for the year commencing August 1984. (This data refers to the late Mr. Rajiv Gandhi, the Prime Minister of India between 1984 and 1989.)

The birth chart calculated for this native is as follows:

Ascendant	Leo	14°36'
Sun	Leo	3°49'
Moon	Leo	17°08'
Mars	Virgo	1°11'
Mercury	Leo	28°33'
Jupiter	Leo	12°10'
Venus	Leo	18°39'
Saturn	Gemini	14°12'
Rahu	Cancer	4°09'
Ketu	Capricorn	4°09'
Tenth house	Taurus	14°56'

Balance of Vimshottari dasha of Venus at birth : 14 yrs. 3 m. 18 d. The MD/AD of Rahu-Jupiter : August 20, 1984 to January 14, 1987.

The Annual Chart

(a) Completed years : 1984 - 1944 = 40.

The annual chart is thus for the forty-first year of life of the native, commencing from August 1984.

1. Source Pupul Jayakar's biography of Mrs Indira Gandhi which gives the birth time as 8:11 AM (Wartime), equivalent to 7:11 AM (IST).

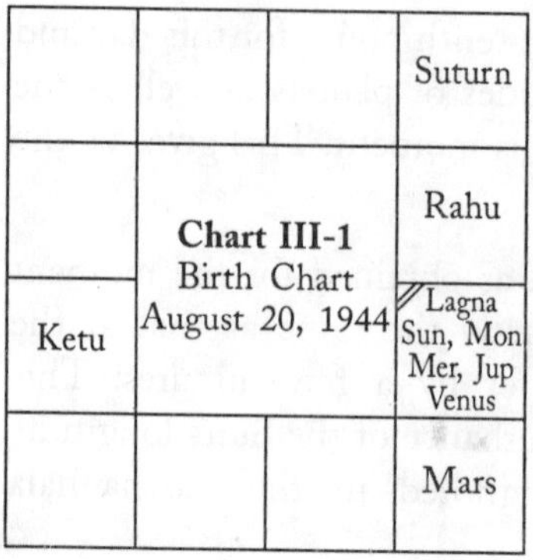

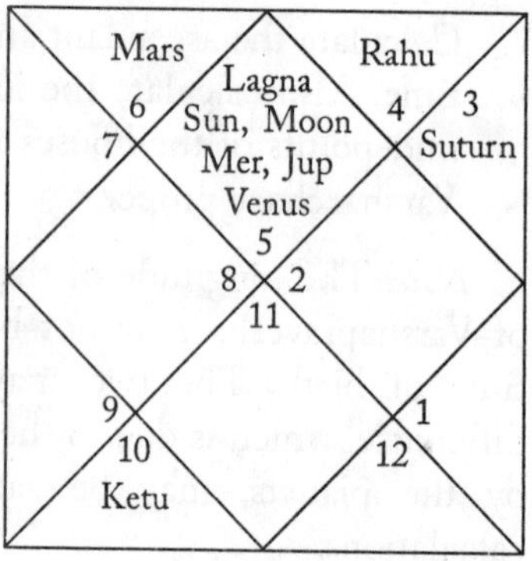

(b) Day and time of birth:

0 d (i.e., Sunday) 7h 11m 0s (IST).

(c) Dhruvanka for forty years : 1d 6h 6m 29s

(d) Varshapravesha :

Birth day and time	:	0d 7h 11m 0s (IST)
plus		
Dhruvanka for 40 years	:	1d 6h 6m 29s
		1d 13h 17m 29s

Thus the Varshapravesha for the forty-first year occurs on Monday at 13h 17m 29s (IST).

In the year 1984, Monday nearest to the English date of the native's birth falls on the same date, i.e., on August 20. Thus, the time of solar return or the Varshapravesha for the native's forty-first year of life is August 20, 1984 (Monday), at 13 hours, 17 minutes, 29 seconds (IST) for Bombay.

(e) *Ascendant and other houses* : From the Indian Standard Time of the Varshapravesha, find out the local mean time (LMT) for Bombay. Next calculate the ascendant and the tenth house for this LMT.

(f) *Calculating the remaining houses* : Adding six signs to the ascendant gives the mid-point of the seventh house. Similarly, adding six signs to the tenth house provides the mid-point of the fourth house. Houses 11 and 12 are equidistantly placed between houses 10 and 1 (i.e., lagna). If we divide the distance between the tenth house and the lagna into three equal parts and add one part to the mid-point of the tenth house, we get the mid-point of the 11th house. Adding the same one-third to the mid-point of the 11th house provides the mid-point of the 12th house. Similarly find out the mid-points of houses 2 and 3 between the lagna and the fourth house. Adding six signs to each of the houses 2, 3, 11, and 12, we get the mid-points of the houses 8, 9, 5 and 6 respectively. The mid-points of the various houses for the annual chart under consideration are being given below.

Ascendant	Scorpio	9° 26'
2H	Sagittarius	10° 41'
3H	Capricorn	11° 55'
4H	Aquarius	13° 10'
5H	Pisces	11° 55'
6H	Aries	10° 41'
7H	Taurus	9° 26'
8H	Gemini	10° 41'
9H	Cancer	11° 55'
10H	Leo	13° 10'
11H	Virgo	11° 55'
12H	Libra	10° 41'

(g) *The position of planets* : Several Indian ephemerides give the position of planets according to the Indian Standard Time. From any of these, which use the Chitrapaksha ayanamsha (e.g., the Lahiri's), calculate the position of planets for the IST of the Varshapravesha. For the annual chart in question, the position of planets is given as under:

Sun	Leo	3° 50'
Moon	Taurus	9° 40'
Mars	Scorpio	7° 42'
Mercury (R)	Leo	18° 20'
Jupiter (R)	Sagittarius	9° 38'
Venus	Leo	21° 45'
Saturn	Libra	17° 13'
Rahu	Taurus	8° 55'
Ketu	Scorpio	8° 55'

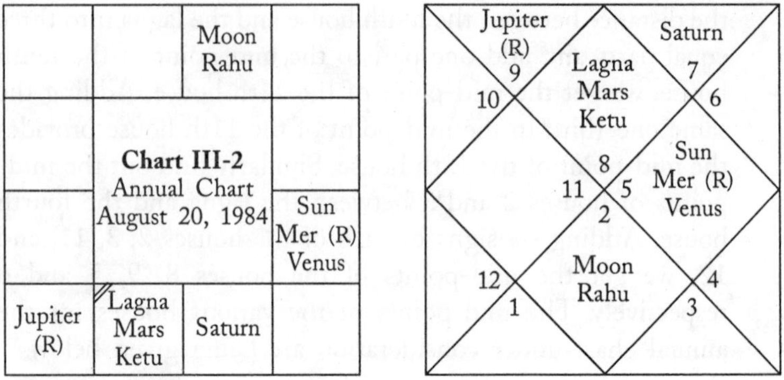

This chart will be referred to repeatedly in our subsequent discussions as the 'Example Chart'.

The Older Method for the Varshapravesha

It may be of relevance to mention here that the duration of the solar cycle as taken into account above is according to the modern astronomical concepts. The older Vedic method has been taking into consideration the value of the solar cycle as given in the *Surya Siddhanta*. This value differs from the modern scientific observations slightly.

According to the ancient method of computing time, a day is divided into sixty *Ghatis.*[2] Each Ghati consists of sixty *Palas* (or *Vighatis*) and each *Pala* of sixty *Vipalas*. Thus, one hour of our modern time is equivalent to two-and-a-half Ghatis. In other words, twenty-four minutes make a *Ghati*, twenty-four seconds make a *Pala*, and 0.4 seconds make a *Vipala*. The *Surya Siddhanta* lays down a span of three hundred and sixty-five days, fifteen Ghatis, thirty-one Palas and thirty Vipalas as the duration of one solar cycle. This will be equivalent to 365 days, 6 hours, 12 minutes and 36 seconds, giving us a constant or Dhruvanka of 1 d. 6 h. 12 m. and 36 s. for one year. A simple multiplication of this value would give us the Dhruvanka of any number of years required (see Table III - 2).

2. A Ghati is labelled as 'Danda' in Bengal and Orissa.

Table III - 2
Dhruvankas according to the ancient method

Completed Years	Dhruvanka d	h	m	s
1	1	6	12	36
2	2	12	25	12
3	3	18	37	48
4	5	0	50	24
5	6	7	3	0
10	5	14	6	0
15	4	21	9	0
20	4	4	12	0
30	2	18	18	0
40	1	8	24	0
50	6	22	30	0

In the charts and examples to be discussed, only the modern values of Dhruvanka will be employed

Casting the Annual Chart for the Subsequent Year

When the Varshapravesha for a particular year is known, the Varshapravesha for the subsequent year can be known by adding the Dhruvanka for one year to the known Varshapravesha.

1. In the Example Chart, the Varshapravesha for the 41st year is 1d. 13h. 17m. 29s.
2. Add to it the Dhruvanka for one year, i.e., 1d. 6h. 9m. 10s.
3. We get 2 d. (i.e., Tuesday) 19h. 26m. 39s., which falls on August 20, 1985.
4. A chart cast for the above Varshapravesha will be the annual chart for the forty-second year of the native.

CHAPTER IV

THE MUNTHA

Yet certain ones, though seeing, may not see her,
and other ones, though hearing, may not hear her.
But to some the Word reveals herself quite freely,
like fair-robed bride surrendering to her husband.

'RIG VEDA'

The Muntha is an important point in the annual chart. It is located in the lagna at the time of birth. Each year, the Muntha progresses by one rashi. Thus, when the second year of life begins (i.e., at the first birthday), the Muntha has progressed into the rashi falling in the second house from the birth lagna. At the commencement of the third year of birth, the Muntha is in the sign falling in the third house from the birth lagna, and so on. In the annual chart, the Muntha is located in the house where its rashi falls, after calculating this rashi considering the birth ascendant and the year of life in question.

Because of its progression by one sign each year, the Muntha has been termed as the progressed ascendant. *The lord of the Muntha is also of significance as it is one of the five office-bearers in the annual chart.* One of the office-bearers finally takes over as the lord of the year.

Calculating the Muntha

Add to the lagna sign in the birth chart the number of completed years of life. Divide the total by 12. The remainder gives the rashi or sign where the Muntha is located in the annual chart. When the remainder is zero, the Muntha would naturally be located in the sign Pisces, the twelfth rashi.

In the Example Chart (discussed in the previous chapter), the birth ascendant is Leo, signified by the number 5. Since the annual chart is for the forty-first year of the native's life, we have the number of completed years as forty. Adding five (the birth ascendant) to forty (the no. of completed years), we get a total of forty-five. Dividing forty-five by twelve (the total no. of rashis), we get a remainder of nine. The number nine stands for the ninth sign of the zodiac, i.e., Sagittarius. Thus the Muntha is marked in the sign Sagittarius in the annual chart, which here coincides with the second house of the annual chart.

Progression of the Muntha during the Year

Since the Muntha progresses by one sign or 30 degrees in a year, it progresses by 2°30' each month (30°÷12 = 2°30'). The daily motion of the Muntha may also be calculated by dividing 2°30' by 30 (the number of days in a month), giving a value of 5 minutes. These values are of importance if one intends to go into very close timing of events during a given year.

Results pertaining to the Muntha

The Muntha gives results according to its location in different houses, its association with different planets, and the disposition of the lord of the sign in which the Muntha is located. The results pertaining to the Muntha, as discussed hereunder, are mainly based on the *Tajika Neelakanthi*, the famous treatise of Sri Neelakantha, the celebrated authority on the Tajika Shastra.

THE MUNTHA IN DIFFERENT HOUSES

The location of the Muntha in houses 4, 6, 7 8 and 12 in the annual chart is considered inauspicious. It is particularly auspicious when placed in the houses 9, 10 and 11. In the remaining houses (houses 1, 2, 3, 5) it yields good results through the native's personal efforts.

The results ascribed to the Muntha on the basis of its location in different houses are briefly given below.

Ascendant or the first house : Dominance over opponents, dignity, favours from the government, good health, and acquisition of wealth and status through efforts. It may also indicate change of residence, displacement, transfer, and the birth of a child.

Second house : Efforts succeeding into acquisition of wealth, gains from business and trade, respect from one's associates, favours from the opposite sex, dainty dishes, and governmental favours ensuring livelihood (see Example Chart).

Third house : Courageous efforts yielding wealth, general comforts, favours from siblings, acquisition of name and fame, success in endeavours, inclination to do good to others, availability of sustenance from the ruler (a government service!).

Fourth house : Physical ailment, mental anguish, fear from foes, opposition from the near and dear ones, loss of wealth, disgrace, displeasure of the ruler.

Fifth house : Inclination towards good and pious deeds, birth of a child or happiness through the offspring, physical pleasures and comforts, rise in status.

Sixth house : Fear from foes, thieves and rulers, diminished body resistance causing proneness to illness, failure in undertakings, loss of wealth, perverted thinking, remorse, increase in the number of enemies, adverse results from well-intended deeds.

Seventh house : Physical ailment, perverted thinking, loss of wealth, disappointment arising from the spouse, the business partners and the enemies, inclination towards bad deeds, disappointment, likelihood of imprisonment.

Eighth house : The Muntha here produces extremely bad results in the form of incurable illness, loss of wealth, quarrels, loss of physical strength and stamina, inclination towards mean deeds, dominance by enemies, displeasure of the ruler, losses in litigation, distant travel, change in the place of residence, and varied worldly discomforts and set-backs.

Ninth house : Fulfilment of desires, inclination towards pious deeds, religious ceremony at home, favours from the ruler, happiness from the spouse and the offspring, increase in status and fortune, beneficial and fruitful journey.

Tenth house : Rise in status, promotion in job, increase in income and wealth, favours from the ruler, accomplishment of good deeds, gain in honour and dignity.

Eleventh house : Gains from all sides, happiness from children (birth of a child !), solution of outstanding problems, favours from superiors and rulers, gain in physical and mental health, fulfilment of desires.

Twelfth house : Loss of wealth, excessive expenditure, obstacles to profession, displacement/transfer, physical ailments, mental anguish, association with wicked people, irreligious inclinations, enmity with friends, and failure in undertakings.

Note:

1. The Muntha associated with or aspected by benefics and by its own lord produces benefic results pertaining to its location. An ill-associated/ill-aspected Muntha only produces bad results even if it is located in benefic houses.

2. The Muntha is not only productive of adverse results when placed in the houses 4, 6, 7, 8 and 12 from the lagna in the annual chart, it also yields bad results when placed in these houses as considered from the lagna in the birth chart.

3. When the Muntha is associated with or aspected by benefics or its own lord, the house where it is located prospers. Where this Muntha falls in the birth chart, that house also prospers during the year.

INFLUENCES ON THE MUNTHA

Besides its location in various houses, the Muntha is also under the influence of various planets which aspect or associate with it, and of various rashis in which it is placed. Thus, for example, the Muntha may be aspected by the Sun or be associated with it or be in the rashi[1] owned by the Sun (i.e., Leo). In each case, the influence of the Sun on the Muntha will manifest. Other planets too will affect it accordingly. The results of various planets

1. An important principle here is the influence of a planet through the sign owned by it. This principle holds true not only in the annual chart but also in the natal chart.

influencing the Muntha in any of the ways mentioned above are being described below.

Sun : The Muntha under the influence of the Sun ensures favours from the ruler, elevation of status (promotions in service), monetary gains, dominance over opponents, gainful journey. Ill effects accrue when the Muntha is ill-placed and ill-aspected.

Moon : Gain of health, wealth, name and fame, association with virtuous people, peace of mind, fulfilment of desires. When this Muntha is ill-aspected and ill-placed, there is mental agony.

Mars : Bilious disorders, accident, injury, surgical operation, blood disorders, quarrels, mental agony, and excessive expenditure.

If this Muntha is placed in favourable houses, under the influence of benefics like Jupiter and Venus, it ensures gain in wealth and success through personal effort and courage.

Mercury : Increased intellect, success in education, favours from women (marriage,), satisfaction in respect of children, gain in virtue, name and fame. Affliction to the Muntha produces adverse results.

Jupiter : Child birth, peace at home, sudden gain in wealth, rise in status, desired employment, gain of precious metals and stones. Affliction to such a Muntha adversely affects the name and fame of the native.

Venus : The good results obtained from the Muntha in the rashi of Venus or under aspect/association of Venus are similar to those that accrue from the influence of Mercury on the Muntha. In addition, there may be marriage, pleasures and comforts of all sorts, and gain in wealth. An afflicted Muntha gives rise to scandals and loss of honour.

Saturn : Physical ailments, disappointments, inclination towards unbecoming deeds, loss of honour and wealth. These ill effects are nullified if Jupiter also exerts its influence on the Muntha. Influence of Mars on this Muntha may lead to proneness to accidents, surgical operations, blood disorders, fear from fire and foes, and loss of money.

Rahu and Ketu[2] **:** The Muntha gives favourable results during the first half of the year, and unfavourable ones during the second half, if associated with Rahu. The reverse holds true when it is associated with Ketu.

THE MUNTHA LORD

The lord of the sign in which the Muntha is located is called the Muntha lord. In the annual chart, the Muntha lord yields desirable or adverse results according to its location, strength, and other planetary influences on it. The results accruing from the Muntha lord depending on its location are briefly described below.

First house : The Muntha lord in the lagna, especially when strong and aspecting the Muntha, ensures flow of money, good health, fulfilment of desires, elevated status, and general comforts.

Second house : Monetary gains, comforts of home and vehicles, satisfaction in respect of near and dear ones, and fulfilment of desires.

Third house : Comforts from brothers and sisters, increase in valour, accomplishments through success of efforts.

Fourth house : Loss of money, anxiety, disgrace, displeasure of superiors, ill health, and loss of comforts at home.

Fifth house : Success over opponents, fulfilment of desires, comforts from wife and children, gain of status and dignity.

Sixth house : Fear from opponents, excessive expenditure, loss from theft, association with the wicked, and ill health.

Seventh house : Ill health to the native and to the spouse, excessive travel, losses in travel, displeasure of the near and dear ones.

Eighth house : Ill health, displeasure of superiors, obstacles to profession, loss of money, disappointments, and generally adverse results throughout the year.

---

2. The results pertaining to Rahu and Ketu, as mentioned here, need further testing.

Ninth house : Noble thoughts, religious deeds, good health, inflow of money, and fulfilment of desires.

Tenth house : Promotion in job, elevated status, acquisition of vehicle or land, success over opponents, and fulfilment of desires.

Eleventh house : Inflow of money, promotion or elevation of status, co-operation and help from siblings, general comforts, and association with important people.

Twelfth house : Loss of health and wealth, excessive travel (foreign travel), disappointment from children, and loss of status.

It will be seen that, like the Muntha itself, the Muntha lord also gives adverse results in the houses 4, 6, 7, 8 and 12. In the rest, it is favourable. It will also be seen that in the same chart, the Muntha and its lord may indicate contradictory results. In such a situation, a balance in interpretation is called for. It is further necessary to consider several other factors in the chart as have been discussed elsewhere. The Muntha, as already stated, represents the birth lagna in progression. Considering the Muntha in the analysis of the annual chart is extremely important though it may not be taken as the final word.

CHAPTER V

THE DASHA SYSTEM

Toward whom does the rising Flame aspire?
Toward whom does the Wind eagerly blow?
On whom do all the compass points converge?
Tell me of that Support — who may he be?

'ATHARVA VEDA'

The most outstanding feature of the Vedic system of astrology is its application in the timing of events. One of the methods employed for such a timing is the consideration of *Gochara* or the transit of planets. But by far the most dependable and accurate method involves the use of dashas or operational periods. Primarily belonging to the Jataka or natal horoscopy, these dasha systems have been extended to the annual chart also. The planets are allotted certain periods of time over which they exert their influence on the native. The various events unfold in the life of an individual in accordance with the changing dashas.

Several dashas have been described as of relevance to the annual chart. Of these, three are more popular. They are:

(a) The Mudda Dasha (or the Vimshottari-Mudda Dasha)

(b) The Yogini Dasha

(c) The Patyayini Dasha

The Mudda dasha and the Yogini dasha are nakshatra-based dashas, and depend on the birth nakshatra. They are the equivalents of similar dashas (the Vimshottari and the Yogini) in the birth horoscope, with the difference that their period of operation is reduced to one year. The Mudda dasha is the most popular of the three dashas mentioned above.

THE MUDDA DASHA

For a given year of life, the order of dasha is calculated thus:

Add to the completed years of life, the Moon's nakshatra at birth; subtract two; divide the value thus obtained by nine. Ignore the quotient. The remainder gives the Mudda dasha operating at the time of commencement of the year.

The first dasha will be that of the Sun, the Moon, Mars, Rahu, Jupiter, Saturn, Mercury, Ketu, or Venus, as the remainder after the above operation is 1, 2, 3, 4, 5, 6, 7, 8 or zero. This order is the same as that of the Vimshottari dasha in the natal chart. After deciding the first dasha operating at the time of the Varshapravesha, the subsequent dashas follow the regular order.

Example Chart

(Completed years plus the Moon's nakshatra at birth minus two) divided by nine

$$\text{or } \frac{40 + 11 \text{ (Poorva Phalguni)} - 2}{9}$$

or 49 ÷ 9. We get Q : 5; R : 4.

Ignoring the quotient, we get the remainder of 4, which means that the dasha operating at the time of commencement of the year was that of Rahu. The subsequent dashas will follow the order Jupiter, Saturn, Mercury, Ketu, Venus, Sun, Moon and Mars.

The duration in the Mudda dasha

The duration of each dasha *in days* is obtained by multiplying its duration in years as allotted in the Vimshottari dasha by three. Thus, in the annual chart, the duration of various periods under the Mudda dasha will be as given in Table V-1.

Working out the balance of dasha

After finding the dasha operating at the time of Varshapravesha, it is required to find out the balance of this dasha. For this

Table V-1

Dasha	Duration	
Sun	18 days	(6×3)
Moon	30 days	(10×3)
Mars	21 days	(7×3)
Rahu	54 days	(18×3)
Jupiter	48 days	(16×3)
Saturn	57 days	(19×3)
Mercury	51 days	(17×3)
Ketu	21 days	(7×3)
Venus	60 days	(20×3)
Total	360 days	(120×3)

purpose, it is necessary to find out the exact longitude of the Moon at the time of birth. This will give us the nakshatra at the time of birth as well as the extent of this nakshatra traversed by the Moon. The extent of the nakshatra yet to be traversed will give us the balance of the dasha at the time of Varshapravesha.

Example Chart

The longitude of the Moon at birth is $4^s17°8'$. The nakshatra Magha ends at $4^s13°20'$. Of the 13°20' of the next nakshatra, i.e., Poorva Phalguni, the Moon has already traversed 3°48'. The remaining portion of the nakshatra is 9°32'.

We have already seen that it was the Rahu dasha operating at the commencement of the forty-first year of the native. The total duration of Rahu dasha as already indicated is 54 days.

If 13°20' (the extent of a nakshatra) indicates a Rahu dasha of 54 days, then 9°32' (i.e., the part of the nakshatra yet to be traversed by the natal Moon) would indicate a balance of Rahu equal to 38.61 days [i.e., (54 × 9°32') ÷ 13°20'] or 1 month and 8.61 days. After these many days of Rahu, the next dasha of Jupiter will start. Subtracting these 38.61 days from the total duration of Rahu of 54 days, we get 13.39 days which will be Rahu's dasha toward the end of the year.

The dasha periods for the native of the Example Chart for his forty-first year starting w.e.f. August 20, 1984 may be tabulated as below.

Table V-2
The Mudda dasha

Dasha	Duration		Ends on		
	m	d	d	m	y
1. Rahu	1	8.61	29	9	1984
2. Jupiter	1	18	17	11	84
3. Saturn	1	27	14	1	85
4. Mercury	1	21	5	3	85
5. Ketu	0	21	26	3	85
6. Venus	2	0	26	5	85
7. Sun	0	18	14	6	85
8. Moon	1	0	14	7	85
9. Mars	0	21	5	8	85
10. Rahu	0	15.39	20	8	1985

The View of Kalidasa

The celebrated author of the *Uttara Kalamrita* advocates that, in the calculation of the Mudda dasha, the position of the Moon in the annual chart, and not in the birth chart, is to be considered. According to this view, the balance of dasha at the time of the Varshapravesha is calculated from the nakshatra of the Moon in the annual chart. The first dasha during the year will be that of the Moon's nakshatra lord. The order of dashas and their duration according to this system are mentioned below.

The Planet	Duration (days)
Sun	110
Moon	60
Mars	32
Mercury	40
Jupiter	48
Venus	56
Saturn	4
Rahu	5
Lagna	10
Total	365

This method of the Mudda dasha calculation is not in popular use. It may be noted here that this dasha takes into account 365 days instead of the 360 usually considered in the nakshatra dashas of annual chart. When 360 days are taken to represent one year, they represent 360 'solar days', each of which would indicate the movement of the Sun by one degree. The duration of such a 'solar day' would be different from our usual day of twenty-four hours. One could accurately spread the 360 days of the Tajika dashas over the 365 days of the year by proportionately increasing the dasha periods. Generally, however, it is more convenient to round off the dasha periods to enable them to spread over the 365 days of the year, with a negligible, and acceptable, error.

Note: Ketu's period has not been mentioned here though the Moon could well be in Ketu's nakshatra. Should Ketu be taken to be equivalent to Rahu, or to Mars? This needs to be tested!

Sub-periods in the Mudda Dasha

For a closer timing, after deciding the major periods, one should go into the calculation of the sub-periods. In a given major period, or Mahadasha (MD), the first sub-period, or Antardasha (AD), belongs to the same planet. The remaining sub-periods follow in the order of the Vimshottari dasha. The duration of the sub-periods in each major period is proportionate to each planet's major period. See Table V-3 for the duration of sub-periods in the major periods of various planets.

THE YOGINI DASHA

To the sum of the birth nakshatra and the completed years of life, add three. Divide the total by eight. The remainder gives the Yogini dasha at the commencement of the year as follows:

Remainder	Yogini Dasha
1	Mangala
2	Pingala
3	Dhanya
4	Bhramari
5	Bhadrika
6	Ulka
7	Siddha
8	Sankata

Table V-3
Sub-periods in Vimshottari Mudda Dasha

Antardasha	Mahadasha					
	Sun -18 d		Moon - 30 d		Mars - 21 d	
	Days	Hours	Days	Hours	Days	Hours
Sun	0	21.6				
Moon	1	12.0	2	12.0		
Mars	1	1.2	1	18.0	1	5.4
Rahu	2	16.8	4	12.0	3	3.6
Jupiter	2	9.6	4	0.0	2	19.2
Saturn	2	20.4	4	18.0	3	7.8
Mercury	2	13.2	4	6.0	2	23.4
Ketu	1	1.2	1	18.0	1	5.4
Venus	3	0.0	5	0.0	3	12.0
Sun			1	12.0	1	1.2
Moon					1	18.0
	Rahu - 54d		Jupiter - 48d		Saturn - 57d	
Rahu	8	2.4				
Jupiter	7	12.0	6	9.6		
Saturn	8	11.0	7	14.4	9	0.6
Mercury	7	13.6	6	19.2	8	1.8
Ketu	3	3.6	2	19.2	3	7.8
Venus	9	0.0	8	0.0	9	12.0
Sun	2	16.8	2	9.6	2	20.4
Moon	4	12.0	4	0.0	4	18.0
Mars	3	3.6	2	19.2	3	7.8
Rahu			7	12.0	8	11.0
Jupiter				I	7	14.4
	Mercury - 51d		Ketu - 21d		Venus - 60d	
Mercury	7	5.4				
Ketu	2	23.4	1	5.4		
Venus	8	12.0	3	12.0	10	0.0
Sun	2	13.2	1	1.2	3	0.0
Moon	4	6.0	1	18.0	5	0.0
Mars	2	23.4	1	5.4	3	12.0
Rahu	7	13.6	3	3.6	9	0.0
Jupiter	6	19.2	2	19.2	8	0.0
Saturn	8	1.8	3	7.8	9	12.0
Mercury			2	23.4	8	12.0
Ketu					3	12.0

Example Chart

(Completed years 40 + Birth nakshatra 11 + 3) ÷ 8
= 54 ÷ 8; Q : 6; R : 6.

Thus we get a quotient of 6, which is to be ignored, and a remainder of 6, which shows that the first dasha in the year will be Ulka.

Lords of Yogini Dashas and their Duration

The above-mentioned eight Yogini dashas are ruled by their lords. These, along with the duration of these dashas, are tabulated in Table V-4.

Table V-4

Dasha	Lord	Duration (days)
1. Mangala	Moon	10
2. Pingala	Sun	20
3. Dhanya	Jupiter	30
4. Bhramari	Mars	40
5. Bhadrika	Mercury	50
6. Ulka	Saturn	60
7. Siddha	Venus	70
8. Sankata	Rahu/Ketu	80

It will thus be seen that alternating Yogini dashas belong to benefics and malefics, and are, therefore, alternatively good or bad.

Balance of Yogini Dasha

As in the case of the Mudda dasha, the balance of Yogini dasha at the beginning of the year must also be determined.

In the Example Chart, where we have already seen that the Ulka dasha operates at the time of the commencement of the year, the balance of the Ulka can be determined from the untraversed part of the Moon's nakshatra at birth. The formula for this is:

(Total duration of Ulka, i.e., 60 days × The un-traversed portion of the Moon's nakshatra at birth, i.e., 9°32' in our case)÷ the total duration of a nakshatra, i.e., 13°20'.

This gives us a value of 42.9 days. Thus the year starts with an Ulka balance of 42.9 days. The remaining part of the Ulka, of 17.1 days, will operate toward the end of the year.

The Yogini dasha periods for the native, for his forty-first year starting from 20th August 1984, are shown in table V-5.

Table V-5

Dasha	Duration		Ends on		
	m	d	d	m	y
1. Ulka	1	12.9	3	10	1984
2. Siddha	2	10.0	13	12	1984
3. Sankata	2	20.0	3	3	1985
4. Mangala	0	10.0	13	3	1985
5. Pingala	0	20.0	3	4	1985
6. Dhanya	1	0.0	3	5	1985
7. Bhramari	1	10.0	13	6	1985
S. Bhadrika	1	20.0	3	8	1985
9. Ulka	0	17.1	20	8	1935

The sub-periods in the Yogini dasha may also be worked out proportionately.

THE PATYAYINI DASHA

This dasha, unlike the Mudda and the Yogini, is not nakshatra-based. It depends on the degrees of longitude of a planet after deleting the completed rashis or signs. The seven planets, from the Sun to Saturn, and the lagna, participate in this system.

The Krishamshas : The longitudes of the seven planets, from the Sun to Saturn, and the mid-point of the lagna, are noted down in signs, degrees, minutes (and seconds). The signs are ignored. The remaining degrees and minutes (and seconds) in each case constitute the *Krishamshas* of the various planets and the lagna. The Krishamshas are then tabulated in the ascending order. For the Example chart, the Krishamshas are tabulated in Table V-6.

Table V-6

Example Chart: The Krishamshas in ascending order

Planets	Sun	Mar	Asc	Jup	Mon	Sat	Mer	Ven
Krishamshas	3°50'	7°42'	9°26'	9°38'	9°40'	17°13'	18°20'	21°45'

This ascending order of the Krishamshas determines the dasha order in the Patyayini dasha system.

The Patyamshas: The dasha lord with the minimum Krishamshas has the same value for its Patyamshas. Thus, in the above example, the value for the Sun's Patyamshas is the same as its Krishamshas in the above table, i.e., 3°50'.

To find out the Patyamshas of the next planet, i.e., Mars, in the dasha order, subtract the Krishamshas of the preceding planet, in this case the Sun, from the Krishamshas of the planet concerned. Thus, in the Example Chart, the Patyamsha value for Mars will be 3°52' (7°42' - 3°50' = 3°52').

The next dasha in order in the above example is that of the ascendant whose Patyamsha will be determined by subtracting the Mars' Krishamshas from those of the ascendant. Thus, by successively subtracting the Krishamshas of one dasha lord from those of the next higher in order, we get the Patyamshas of all the eight dasha lords (i.e., the seven planets and the lagna).

The Patyamshas of the various dasha lords in respect of the Example Chart are tabulated in table V-7.

Table V-7

Example Chart : the Patyamshas

Dasha lords	Sun	Mar	Asc	Jup	Mon	Sat	Mer	Ven
Krishamshas	3°50'	7°42'	9°26'	9°38'	9°40'	17°13'	18°20'	21°45'
Patyamshas	3°50'	3°52'	1°44'	0°12'	0°02'	7°33'	1°07'	3°25'

When the Patyamshas of all the dasha lords are totalled, they are equal to the Krishamshas of the last dasha lord, i.e., the dasha lord with the highest Krishamsha value.

Calculating the Duration of Dashas

The highest value of Krishamsha expressed in degrees, minutes, etc., is equivalent to one year (365 days). The Patyamshas represent the proportional periods of time (i.e., the Patyayini dasha) for the various dasha lords. For example, in the above case, the Patyayini dasha of the Sun will be obtained by the formula:

$$\frac{365 \text{ days} \times 3°50' \text{ (i.e., the Patyamshas of the Sun)}}{21°45' \text{ (the highest Krishamsha value, that of Venus here)}}$$

Table V-8 gives the Patyayini dasha duration for the year in the case of the native of our Example Chart.

Table V-8
Example Chart : The Patyayini dasha

Dasha	Duration (days)	Ends on d	m	y
1. Sun	64.33	23	10	1984
2. Mars	64.89	27	12	1984
3. Ascendant (Lagna)	29.09	25	1	1985
4. Jupiter	3.36	28	1	1985
5. Moon	0.56	29	1	1985
6. Saturn	126.70	5	6	1985
7. Mercury	18.74	23	6	1985
8. Venus	57.34	20	8	1985

It may be noted here that instead of considering 365 days in a year while calculating this dasha, it may be found convenient to consider 360 days as in the nakshatra dashas, without much appreciable error.

The Sub-periods or the Antardashas

For each dasha (or MD) as calculated above, it is possible, and appropriate, to calculate the sub-periods (or AD) using the formula

(Dasha duration of MD lord × Dasha duration of AD lord) ÷ 365

The result will be the AD in days.

Let us, for example, calculate the sub-periods during the MD of the Sun in the above example.

Total duration of the Sun MD = 64.33 days.

The AD of:

Sun	=	(64.33 × 64.33) ÷ 365	= 11d	8.11 h
Mars	=	(64.33 × 64.89) ÷ 365	= 11d	10.48 h
Ascendant	=	(64.33 × 29.09) ÷ 365	= 5d	3.05 h
Jupiter	=	(64.33 × 3.36) ÷ 365	= 0d	14.21 h
Moon	=	(64.33 × 0.56) ÷ 365	= 0d	2.37 h
Saturn	=	(64.33 × 126.70) ÷ 365	= 22d	7.93 h
Mercury	=	(64.33 × 18.74) ÷ 365	= 3d	7.27 h
Venus	=	(64.33 × 57.34) ÷ 365	= 10d	2.54 h

Table V-9 shows the sub-periods in the major period of the Sun (August 20, 1984 to October 23, 1984)

Table V-9
Sub-periods in the major period of the Sun

Sub-period	Duration		Ends on		
	days	hours	d	m	y
1. Sun	11	8.11	31	8	1984
2. Mars	11	10.48	12	9	1984
3. Ascendant	5	3.05	17	9	1984
4. Jupiter	0	14.21	18	9	1984
5. Moon	0	2.37	18	9	1984
6. Saturn	22	7.93	10	10	1984
7. Mercury	3	7.27	13	10	1984
8. Venus	10	2.54	23	10	1984

CHAPTER VI

OF PLANETARY STRENGTHS

You in your sturdy strength hold fast the forests,
clamping the trees all firmly to the ground,
when rains and lightning issue from your clouds.

'RIG VEDA'

Planets give favourable or adverse results depending upon their strength or weakness in the annual chart. Three different methods are employed for determining the planetary strength in the annual chart. Of these, the most elaborate though less often employed method is the *Dwadashavargiya Bala* or the twelve-fold strength of a planet. The simplest to determine is the *Harsha Bala*. But the one that is most popular and useful is the *Panchavargiya Bala* or the five-fold strength of a planet. This last method is the one that will be most often referred to in the discussion of various charts. These methods are being discussed below.

THE HARSHA BALA

Harsha literally means 'happiness'. Planets are comfortable or 'happy' in certain situations which provide them with *bala* or strength. In the determination of strength by this method, four factors are considered. They are:

(a) Position of a planet in a specific house;

(b) Placement in its exaltation sign or in its own house;

(c) Placement in a house belonging to its own sex; and

(d) Strength depending upon the Varsha-pravesha being during the daytime or night-time.

These factors are individually considered below.

1. **Sthana Bala (Positional strength) :** Planets get strength when placed in certain specific houses in the annual chart. This is also referred to as the *Prathama Bala* (the 'First' strength, or the first state of being in 'Harsha'). According to this, the Sun in the ninth house of the annual chart, the Moon in the third house, Mars in the sixth house, Mercury in the lagna, Jupiter in the eleventh house, Venus in the fifth house, and Saturn in the twelfth house, are said to acquire Harsha Bala because of their location.

   In the Example Chart, only Saturn, located in the twelfth house of the annual chart, gets this strength.

2. **Uchcha-Swakshetri Bala (Strength from exaltation or own sign) :** This, the *Dwitiya Bala* (the 'Second' strength), is granted to a planet which is either exalted or located in its own house.

   In the Example Chart, this strength is granted to the Sun (own house), the Moon (exalted), Mars (own house), Jupiter (own house), and Saturn (exalted).

3. **Stri-Purusha Bala (Strength from gender) :** In the annual chart, the houses 1, 2, 3, 7, 8, and 9 are feminine houses. The remaining ones, i.e., houses 4, 5, 6, 10, 11, and 12 are masculine houses. Female planets (Moon, Mercury, Venus and Saturn) get this *Tritiya Bala* (the 'Third' strength) by their location in the feminine houses, while the male planets (Sun, Mars and Jupiter) obtain this strength by their location in the masculine houses.

   In the Example Chart, of the male planets, the Sun gets strength by its location in the tenth (a masculine) house. Of the female planets, the Moon gets strength by its location in the seventh (a feminine) house.

4. **Dina-Ratri Bala (Strength from 'day' and 'night') :** Male planets acquire the *Chaturtha Bala* (the 'Fourth' strength) when the year commences during day time. The female planets get it when the Varshapravesha occurs during night time.

In the Example Chart, the Varshapravesha being during day-time, the male planets (Sun, Mars and Jupiter) get strength.

Charting the Harsha Bala

Each of the above mentioned four factors yields a strength of five units to a planet which is appropriately located in the annual chart. For each of the seven planets (Sun to Saturn, excluding Rahu and Ketu), the total of all the four 'strengths' gives the Harsha Bala for the planet. Table VI-1 shows the Harsha Bala of planets in respect of the Example Chart.

Table VI-1
Example Chart : the Harsha bala of planets

	Sun	Mon	Mar	Mer	Jup	Ven	Sat
1. 'First Bala	0	0	0	0	0	0	5
2. 'Second' Bala	5	5	5	0	5	0	5
3. 'Third' Bala	5	5	0	0	0	0	0
4. 'Fourth' Bala	5	0	5	0	5	0	0
Total	15	10	10	0	10	0	10

Interpreting the Harsha Bala

A planet can have a maximum of twenty units of Harsha Bala, but it is rather unusual for it to do so. Generally, the maximum strength acquired by the planet is 15 units. Depending upon the Harsha Bala acquired by a planet, it may be allotted one of the four categories as follows:

(a) *Nirbala* (no strength), when the score is zero.

(b) *Alpabali* (weak), when the score is five.

(c) *Madhya Bali* (of medium strength), when the score is ten.

(d) *Poorna Bali* (fully strong), when the score is fifteen.

As mentioned above, in unusual circumstances, a planet may possess a strength of twenty units, in which case it may be labelled as *extra-ordinarily* strong. Such a situation may occur, for example, in a case of Varshapravesha at night with an exalted Moon in the third house.

In the Example Chart, the maximum strength has been acquired by the Sun, the planet indicating official status and matters concerning the government.

THE PANCHA-VARGIYA BALA

The Pancha-vargiya Bala refers to five sources or divisions of strength. This is the most important 'Bala to be determined since on this depends the selection of the *Varshesha* or the ruler of the year. This method yields numerical values of strength for different planets. In the annual chart, whenever the relative strength of planets is referred to, it is the Panchavargiya Bala that is generally meant.

The Planetary Relationships

An understanding of the mutual relationship of various planets is essential in order to arrive at the Pancha-vargiya Bala of planets. The mutual relationship as applicable to the annual chart has already been discussed. It is being briefly reiterated here.

A friendly relationship exists between planets located in houses 3, 5, 9 and 11 from each other. An *inimical relationship* exists between those located in houses 1, 4, 7 and 10 from each other. A *neutral relationship* exists between planets in houses 2, 6, 8 and 12 from each other. The mutual relations in respect of the Example Chart have been depicted in Table VI-2.

Table VI-2

Mutual relationship of planets in the example chart

	Friends	Enemies	Equals
Sun	Jup, Sat	Mon, Mar, Mer, Ven	
Mon		Sun, Mar, Mer, Ven	Jup Sat
Mar		Sun, Mon Mer, Ven	Jup Sat
Mer	Jup Sat	Sun, Mon, Mar, Ven	
Jup	Sun, Mer Ven, Sat		Mon, Mar
Ven	Jup, Sat	Sun, Mon, Mar, Mer	
Sat	Sun, Mer, Jup, Ven		Mon, Mar

The Pancha Vargas (the five divisions)

In the determination of the Pancha-vargiya Bala, the following five factors are considered.

1. *Griha Bala or Kshetra Bala :* This is the strength of a planet as indicated by its location in its own house, or in the house of another planet, depending upon the relationship between the two.
2. *Uchcha Bala :* Depends on how close (or how far removed) a planet is located from its point of exaltation (or debilitation).
3. *Hudda Bala :* A special feature of the Tajika system.
4. *Drekkana Bala :* Another special feature, since the Drekkana considered here is peculiar to the Pancha-vargiya Bala.
5. *Navamsha Bala :* Depends on the placement of a planet in the Navamsha chart.

The Measure of Bala

The strength of planets in the Pancha-vargiya Bala is expressed in units called the *Vishwa Bala* or the *Visheshanka Bala (VB)*. The VB is arrived at by adding up the total strength of a planet obtained after considering the above mentioned five factors, and then dividing this total by four. A planet in its own sign gets a strength of 30 units, in its deep exaltation *20* units, in its own Hudda 15 units, in its own Drekkana 10 units, and in its own Navamsha 5 units. Thus a planet can get a maximum of 80 units of strength, equivalent to a VB of 20 (80 ÷ 4 = 20).

When a planet is not in its own sign, its own Hudda, its own Drekkana, or its own Navamsha, its strength is appropriately reduced. This reduction is effected to three-fourths in the house of a friend, to one-half in the house of an equal or neutral, and to one-fourth in the house of an enemy. Table *VI-3* gives the strength of a planet in units, depending on its location in different houses, and on its consideration in various vargas.

One unit of strength consists of sixty sub-units. For example, when a planet in the Navamsha is placed in its own house, its strength is 5 units; when it is in the house of a friend, its strength

Table VI-3
Strength of a Planet in units depending on its placement in a particular house

Vargas \ Houses	Own	Friend	Neutral	Eenemy
1. Rashi	30	22	15	07
(Kshetra)	00	30	00	30
2. Hudda	15	11	07	03
	00	15	30	45
3. Drekkana	10	07	05	02
	00	30	00	30
4. Navamsha	05	03	02	01
	00	45	30	15

is 3:45 units; in the house of an equal, its strength would be 2:30 units; and in the house of an enemy, it would be 1:15 units. While the strength of planets is customarily measured as indicated above, it is perfectly all right to translate it in the decimal fraction. The above values would then correspond to 5.0, 3.75, 2.5 and 1.25 units respectively.

We now proceed to calculate individually the five-fold strength of planets.

I. Griha Bala or Kshetra Bala

It will be of help to consider the Example Chart.

(i) *The Sun* is in its own house (Leo), so its Griha Bala is 30 units.

(ii) *The Moon* is in the house of Venus, an enemy here. So, the Moon's strength is 7:30 units.

(iii) *Mars* in its own house gets 30 units.

(iv) *Mercury* in enemy's house gets 7:30 units.

(v) *Jupiter* in its own house gets 30 units.

(vi) *Venus* in the house of an enemy gets 7:30 units.

(vii) *Saturn* in the house of a friend gets 22:30 units.

II. Uchcha Bala

A planet in deep exaltation gets 20 units of Uchcha Bala. The one in deep debilitation gets zero units. In between the exaltation and debilitation points, a span of 180 degrees, the strength of planets gets correspondingly changed. Thus, 180 degrees are equivalent to 20 units of Uchcha Bala. In other words, each arc of nine degrees (180/20 = 9) accounts for one unit of Uchcha Bala. The method of calculating the Uchcha Bala consists of finding out how far away a planet is located from its debilitation point (where the Uchcha Bala is zero); dividing this distance from its debilitation point by 9 gives us the units of Uchcha Bala for the planet in question.

Method of calculating the Uchcha Bala : Subtract the debilitation point of a planet from its longitude in the annual chart. The debilitation point of a planet is situated 180° (or six signs) from its exaltation point. The exaltation and debilitation points of planets have already been described in the chapter on 'General Considerations'. For ease of reference the debilitation points of the various planets are again given here : Sun: 190° (6^s:10°); Moon: 213°(7^s:3°); Mars : 118°(3^s:28°); Mercury: 345° (11^s:15°); Jupiter: 275°(9^s:5°); Venus: 177°(5^s:27°); Saturn: 20° (0^s:20°). Subtracting the debilitation point from the longitude of a planet will give the distance in degrees and minutes by which the planet is located away from its 'zero' strength.

(i) If the longitude of the planet in question, in the annual chart, does not have sufficient rashis to subtract the planet's debilitation point, add 12 to the rashis of longitude and then subtract.

(ii) If the result from (i) above yields a value of more than six rashis, subtract this from 12 rashis. Convert the resulting value into degrees and minutes. Dividing this by nine gives us the Uchcha Bala of the planet.

Example

(i) The longitude of the Sun : 4^s:3°:50'.

(ii) Minus the debilitation point of the Sun, i.e., 6^s:10°:0'.

Since there are not sufficient rashis in the longitude of the Sun to effect a subtraction of the Sun's debilitation point, we add 12 rashis to the Sun's longitude, which now becomes 16^s:3°:50'.

Subtracting the Sun's debilitation point, we get : 9^s:23°:50'.

(iii) The result from step (ii) yields more than 6 rashis. So we subtract it from 12 rashis.

12^s - 9^s:23°:50' = 2^s:6°:10' or 66°:10'

(iv) Now we divides 66°:10' by nine. First we divide the degrees (i.e., 66) by nine and get a quotient of 7, which gives the units of Uchcha Bala. We also get a remainder of 3. Multiply this remainder by sixty (3 × 60 = 180), and add the minutes (10') as obtained above. This gives us a value of 190. Dividing this by nine, we get a quotient of 21. This gives the sub-units of the Uchcha Bala. Ignore the remainder from the second division.

Thus, the Uchcha Bala of the Sun is 7:21 units.

The Uchcha Bala of the remaining planets as calculated by the above method would be as follows :

Moon	19:15 units
Mars	11:04 units
Mercury	17:02 units
Jupiter	02:49 units
Venus	03:55 unit;
Saturn	19:41 units.

III. Hudda Bala

The Hudda is a special feature of the annual horoscopy and does not find its use elsewhere in astrology. It is a sort of energy for a graha or planet. In each sign, of thirty degrees, a specified number of degrees is allotted to five planets, from Mars to Saturn, barring the Sun and the Moon. Thus, each sign is divided into five parts or Huddas, each having its specific lord. The Sun and the Moon do not own any Hudda. The number of degrees allotted to different planets in different signs do not follow any regular pattern (see the table of Huddas, Table VI-4). Depending upon its longitude in the annual chart, a planet falls in its own Hudda, or that of a friend, a foe, or a neutral, and its strength is accordingly determined.

Charting the Hudda Bala in the Example Chart: Let us deal with the Sun first. Referring to Table VI-4, we find that the longitude of the Sun (Leo 3°50') falls in the first Hudda of Leo which is ruled by Jupiter. The Sun has a friend in Jupiter. Hence, the Sun gets a Hudda Bala of 11:15 units. The Hudda Bala of all the planets is tabulated in Table VI-5.

Table V1-4
Table of Huddas

Sl. No.	Signs →	1	2	3	4	5	6	7	8	9	10	11	12
1	Degrees	6	8	6	7	6	7	6	7	12	7	7	12
	Lord	Jup	Ven	Mer	Mar	Jup	Mer	Sat	Mar	Jup	Mer	Ven	Ven
2	Degrees	6	6	6	6	5	10	8	4	5	7	6	4
	Lord	Ven	Mer	Ven	Ven	Ven	Ven	Mer	Ven	Ven	Jup	Mer	Jup
3	Degrees	8	8	5	6	7	4	7	8	4	8	7	3
	Lord	Mer	Jup	Jup	Mer	Sat	Jup	Jup	Mer	Mer	Ven	Jup	Mer
4	Degrees	5	5	7	7	6	7	7	5	5	4	5	9
	Lord	Mar	Sat	Mar	Jup	Mer	Mar	Ven	Jup	Mar	Sat	Mar	Mar
5	Degrees	5	3	6	4	6	2	2	6	4	4	5	2
	Lord	Sat	Mar	Sat	Sat	Mar	Sat	Mar	Sat	Sat	Mar	Sat	Sat

Table VI-5
The Hudda Bala of planets in the Example Chart

Planet	Longitude	Hudda lord	Relation	Bala (units)
1. Sun	Leo 3°:50'	Jupiter	Friend	11:15
2. Moon	Taurus 9°:40'	Mercury	Enemy	3:45
3. Mars	Scorpio 7°:42'	Venus	Enemy	3:45
4 Mercury	Leo 18°:20'	Mercury	Self	15:00
5. Jupiter	Sagittarius 9°:38'	Jupiter	Self	15:00
6. Venus	Leo 21°:45'	Mercury	Enemy	3:45
7. Saturn	Libra 17°:13'	Jupiter	Friend	11:15

Note: The Hudda of the Tajika system, as mentioned above, does not conform to any regular pattern. It is somewhat like the Trimshamsha of Parashara where a sign is divided into five parts, and each part is allotted the lordship of a planet other than the Sun and the Moon. However, the regular system of Parashara is nowhere in evidence here. The Hudda thus offers an interesting area for further research.

IV. Drekkana Bala

The Drekkana lords for the consideration of the Panchavargiya Bala are different from those in the Parashari system (see Table VI - 6). Here the lord of the first Drekkana in Aries is Mars. The lords of the first Drekkana in the successive rashis are the planets that fall in regular order from Mars onwards (i.e., Mars, Mercury, Jupiter, Venus, Saturn, Sun, Moon, Mars, Mercury, Jupiter, Venus and Saturn). Begin the second Drekkana of Aries from the Sun, and proceed in the same order. The cycle continues through the third Drekkana of Aries, with its lord Venus, successively until the third Drekkana of Pisces whose lord happens to be Mars. This method of determining the Drekkana lord is only applicable to the Pancha-vargiya Bala.

The Drekkana Bala as applicable to the Example Chart is charted in Table VI-7.

Table VI-6

The Drekkana Chart for the Panchavargiya Bala

Signs → Drekkana ↓	1	2	3	4	5	6	7	8	9	10	11	12
1st 0-10°	Mar	Mer	Jup	Ven	Sat	Sun	Mon	Mar	Mer	Jup	Ven	Sat
2nd 10-20°	Sun	Mon	Mar	Mer	Jup	Ven	Sat	Sun	Mon	Mar	Mer	Jup
3rd 20-30°	Ven	Sat	Sun	Mon	Mar	Mer	Jup	Ven	Sat	Sun	Mon	Mar

V. Navamsha Bala

Unlike the Drekkana as mentioned above, the Navamsha for the Panchavargiya Bala is the same as in the Parashari system (see Table VI-8). The Navamsha Bala of various planets in the Example Chart has been tabulated in Table VI-9.

Table VI-7
The Drekkana Bala of planets in the Example Chart

Planet	Drekkana	Drekkana lord	Relation	Bala (units)
1. Sun	Leo - 1	Saturn	Friend	7:30
2. Moon	Taurus - 1	Mercury	Enemy	2:30
3. Mars	Scorpio - 1	Mars	Self	10:00
4. Mercury	Leo - 2	Jupiter	Friend	7:30
5. Jupiter	Sagittarius - 1	Mercury	Friend	7:30
6. Venus	Leo - 3	Mars	Enemy	2:30
7. Saturn	Libra - 2	Saturn	Self	10:00

Table VI-8
The Navamsha Chart

Signs → Navamsha ↓	1	2	3	4	5	6	7	8	9	18	11	12
1. 3°20'	1	10	7	4	1	10	7	4	1	10	7	4
2. 6°40'	2	11	8	5	2	11	8	5	2	11	8	5
3. 10°00'	3	12	9	6	3	12	9	6	3	12	9	6
4. 13°20'	4	1	10	7	4	1	10	7	4	1	10	7
5. 16°40'	5	2	11	8	5	2	11	8	5	2	11	8
6. 20°00'	6	3	12	9	6	3	12	9	6	3	12	9
7. 23°20'	7	4	1	10	7	4	1	10	7	4	1	10
8. 26°40'	8	5	2	11	8	5	2	11	8	5	2	11
9. 30°00'	9	6	3	12	9	6	3	12	9	6	3	12

Table VI-9
The Navamsha Bala of planets in the Example Chart

Planet		Navamsha lord	Relation	Bala (units)
1.	Sun	Venus	Enemy	1:15
2.	Moon	Jupiter	Neutral	2:30
3.	Mars	Mercury	Enemy	1:15
4.	Mercury	Mercury	Self	5:00
5.	Jupiter	Mercury	Friend	3:45
6.	Venus	Venus	Self	5:00
7.	Saturn	Jupiter	Friend	3:45

Tabulating the Pancha-vargiya Bala

The five-fold strength as calculated above is finally tabulated in the form of what is called as the *Brihat-Pancha-vargiya Chart.* Table VI-10, shows the Panchavargiya Bala of planets in respect of the Example Chart, tabulated under the Brihat-Panchavargiya Chart.

Table VI-10
The Panchavargiya Bala (Example Chart)

Planets → Bala ↓	Sun	Mon	Mar	Mer	Jup	Ven	Sat
Griha Bala	30	07	30	07	30	07	22
	00	30	00	30	00	30	30
Uchcha Bala	7	19	11	17	02	03	19
	21	15	04	02	49	55	41
Hudda Bala	11	03	03	15	15	3	11
	15	45	45	00	00	45	15
Drekkana Bala	07	02	10	07	07	02	10
	30	30	00	30	30	30	00
Navamsha Bala	01	02	01	05	03	05	03
	15	30	15	00	45	00	45
Total	57	35	56	52	59	22	67
	21	30	04	02	04	40	11
Vishwa Bala	14	08	14	13	14	05	16
(V.B.)	20	52	01	00	46	40	47
	15	30	00	30	00	00	45

Note : In calculating the V.B. it is preferable to do so up to sub-sub units.

The above table shows Saturn to be the strongest of all planets with its V.B. amounting to 16 units 47 sub-units and 45 sub-sub-units (also expressed as 16 : 47 : 45 units). Similarly, Venus is the weakest planet with its V.B. being 5 : 40 : 00 units.

While it is customary to express the Panchavargiya Bala in units, sub-units and sub-sub-units, as above, it is equally appropriate to express it in decimal fractions. The corresponding V.B. figures, in decimals, for the various planets will then be as follows:

Sun	:	14.337
Moon	:	8.875
Mars	:	14.016
Mercury	:	13.008
Jupiter	:	14.766
Venus	:	5.666
Saturn	:	16.796

The interpretation of the strength of a planet on the basis of the Panchavargiya Bala may be made as follows:

- A planet is said to be *Parakrami* ('Extra-ordinarily' strong) when its strength (i.e., the Vishwa Bala) is more than 15 units.
- A planet is *Poorna-Bali* (in 'Full' strength) when its V.B. is 10 to 15 units.
- A planet is *Madhya-Bali* (of 'Medium' strength) when its V.B. is 5 to 10 units.
- A planet is *Alpa-Bali* ('Weak') when its V.B. is less than 5 units.

It is noteworthy that in the Example Chart, all the planets (except the Moon and Venus) are very strong; Saturn is extra-ordinarily so.

THE DWADASHAVARGIYA BALA

The Dwadashavargiya Bala represents the twelve-fold strength of planets. This is arrived at by taking into consideration the location of a planet in twelve different vargas or divisions of a rashi. The twelve components of the Dwadashavargiya Bala are:

1. Rashi or the complete sign comprising 30°.
2. Hora or half the sign (15°) : Table VI-11.
3. Drekkana or one-third (10°) : Table VI-12.
4. Chaturthamsha or one-fourth (7°:30') : Table VI-13.
5. Panchamamsha or one-fifth (6°) : Table VI-14.
6. Shashtamsha or one-sixth (5°) : Table VI-15.
7. Saptamsha or one-seventh (4°:17':8.5") : Table VI-16.
8. Ashtamamsha or one-eighth (3°:45'): Table VI-17.
9. Navamsha or one-ninth (3°:20') : Table VI-8.
10. Dashamamsha or one-tenth (3°) : Table VI-18.
11. Ekadashamsha or one-eleventh (2°:43':38") : Table VI-19.
12. Dwadashamsha or one-twelfth (2°:30') : Table VI-20.

In each of the vargas or divisions mentioned above, the planet's position is noted, depending upon its longitude. A planet situated in its own house, in exaltation or in a friend's house is considered strong. One in an enemy's house or in debilitation is considered weak. And the one in an equal's house is taken as having average strength. A strong planet is beneficial while a weak one is harmful or malefic. After considering all the twelve divisions, the relative strength or weakness, in other words the relative beneficence and maleficence, of a planet is determined.

The Method of Casting the Vargas or the Divisional Charts

1. The *Rashi chart* is represented by the annual chart, and represents the first division of the Dwadashavargas. The mutual relationship of planets here determines whether a planet is a benefic or a malefic or a neutral.
2. The *Hora* or the second division is arrived at thus:
   (a) The first 15 degrees in an odd sign belong to the Sun, the second 15 degrees to the Moon.

(b) In an even sign, the first 15 degrees belong to the Moon while the second 15 degrees belong to the Sun.

Whether a planet is located in a benefic Hora, or a malefic or a neutral one, is decided by its relationship with the Hora lord (the Sun or the Moon).

3. The *Drekkana* or the third division: In a given sign, the first 10 degrees belong to the same sign, the next 10 degrees to the sign fifth from it, and the last 10 degrees to the sign placed in the ninth from it. The lords of the respective signs become the Drekkana lords. A planet's relationship with its Drekkana lord decides whether it is a benefic or a malefic or a neutral in effect according to its Drekkana position.
4. The *Chaturthamsha* or the fourth division: In a given sign, the first 7°:30' belong to the same sign, the next (7°30' to 15°) to the sign falling in the fourth house from it, the next (15° to 22°30') to the sign in the seventh from it, and the last (22°30' to 30°) to the sign falling in the tenth from it. The planets behave as benefics or malefics or neutrals depending on their disposition toward their Chaturthamsha lords.
5. The *Panchamamsha* or the fifth division: In an odd sign, the first six degrees belong to Mars, the next six degrees to Saturn, the next to Jupiter, the next to Mercury, and the last six degrees belong to Venus. In the even signs, this order of lordship is reversed with Venus, Mercury, Jupiter, Saturn and Mars, in this order, owning the six successive degrees in a sign. Note that the planetary allotment here is exactly like the Trimshamsha of the Parashari system though the degree-wise division is not the same.
6. *The Shashtamsha, the Saptamamsha, the Ashtamamsha, the Navamsha, and the Ekadashamsha* (the sixth, the seventh, the eighth, the ninth and the eleventh divisions) : Any of these divisions for a planet may be obtained in the following manner.

(a) Step one:

$$\frac{\text{Longitude of the planet} \times 6 \text{ or } 7 \text{ or } 8 \text{ or } 9 \text{ or } 11}{30}$$

(b) Step two: Add one to the quotient obtained above.

(c) Step three: Divide the value obtained after step two by 12. The remainder gives the sign in which the planet falls in the respective division or Varga.

For example, the longitude of the Sun is Leo 3°50' or 123°50'. The Shashtamsha or the sixth division for the Sun can be worked out thus:

(i) $$\frac{123°50' \times 6}{30}$$

(ii) The quotient obtained from step one is 24. Adding one, we get 25.

(iii) Dividing 25 by 12, we get a remainder of 1. Thus, the Sun falls in the sign Aries (signified by the remainder 1) in the Shashtamsha. Aries belongs to Mars, which is an enemy of the Sun in the Example Chart. Hence the Sun could be considered a malefic in the Shashtamsha. However, the Sun gets exalted in Aries and must be considered a benefic. Exaltation and debilitation should take precedence over normal mutual relationship. In the same manner, other Vargas indicated above can be worked out.

7. *The Dashamamsha* or the tenth division: In odd signs, the first three degrees belong to the same sign, the next three degrees to the sign next in order, and so on. In even signs, the first three degrees belong to the sign falling in the *ninth* from itself, the next three degrees to the next (or the tenth) sign, and so on.

8. *The Dwadashamsha* or the twelfth division : Each sign is divided into twelve divisions of 2°30' each. The first part belongs to the same sign, the next to the sign next in order, and so on.

In the Example Chart, the Sun is in its own rashi, hence strong or benefic. It is in its own Hora, in its own Drekkana, and in its own Chaturthamsha, hence benefic in each case. It falls in the Panchamamsha of Mars as also in the Shastamsha of Mars. In both these cases, it is exalted, hence a benefic. In

Table VI-11
The Hora Chart

Signs → Degree ↓	**1**	**2**	**3**	**4**	**5**	**6**	**7**	**8**	**9**	**10**	**11**	**12**
1. 0°-15°	Sun	Mon	Sun	Mon	Sun	Mon	Sun	Mon	Sun	Mon	Sun	Mon
2. 15°-30°	Mon	Sun	Mon	Sun	Mon	Sun	Mon	Sun	Mon	Sun	Mon	Sun

Table VI-12
The Drekkana Chart

Signs → Drekkana ↓	**1**	**2**	**3**	**4**	**5**	**6**	**7**	**8**	**9**	**10**	**11**	**12**
1st 0°-10°	1	2	3	4	5	6	7	8	9	10	11	12
2nd 10°-20°	5	6	7	8	9	10	11	12	1	2	3	4
3rd 20°-30°	9	10	11	12	1	2	3	4	5	6	7	8

Table VI-13
The Chaturthamsha Chart

Signs → Chaturthamsa ↓		**1**	**2**	**3**	**4**	**5**	**6**	**7**	**8**	**9**	**10**	**11**	**12**
1st	0°-7°30'	1	2	3	4	5	6	7	8	9	10	11	12
2nd	7°30'-15°0'	4	5	6	7	8	9	10	11	12	1	2	3
3rd	15°0'-22°30'	7	8	9	10	11	12	1	2	3	4	5	6
4th	22°30'-30°0'	10	11	12	1	2	3	4	5	6	7	8	9

Table VI-14
The Panchamamsha chart

Serial No	Degrees	Odd Signs (1, 3, 5, 7, 9, 11) Lords	Even Signs (2, 4, 6, 8, 10, 12) Lords
1.	0°- 6°	Mar	Ven
2.	6°-12°	Sat	Mer
3.	12°-18°	Jup	Jup
4.	18°-24°	Mer	Sat
5.	24°-30°	Ven	Mar

Table VI-15
The Shashtamsha Chart

Sl. No.	Signs → Shashtarnsha ↓	1	2	3	4	5	6	7	8	9	10	11	12
1.	0°- 5°	1	7	1	7	1	7	1	7	1	7	1	7
2.	5°-10°	2	8	2	8	2	8	2	8	2	8	2	8
3.	10°-15°	3	9	3	9	3	9	3	9	3	9	3	9
4.	15°-20°	4	10	4	10	4	10	4	10	4	10	4	10
5.	20°-25°	5	11	5	11	5	11	5	11	5	11	5	11
6.	25°-30"	6	12	6	12	6	12	6	12	6	12	6	12

Note : The 1st Shashtamsha in odd signs starts from Aries and in even signs from Libra.

Table VI-16: The Saptamsha Chart

Sl. No.	Signs → Saptamsha ↓	1	2	3	4	5	6	7	8	9	10	11	12
1.	4°17'08"	1	8	3	10	5	12	7	2	9	4	11	6
2.	8°34'17"	2	9	4	11	6	1	8	3	10	5	12	7
3	12°51'25"	3	10	5	12	7	2	9	4	11	6	1	8
4.	17°8'34"	4	11	6	1	8	3	10	5	12	7	2	9
5.	21°25'43"	5	12	7	2	9	4	11	6	1	8	3	10
6.	25°42'51"	6	1	8	3	10	5	12	7	2	9	4	11
7.	30°0'0"	7	2	9	4	11	6	1	8	3	10	5	12

Table VI-17: The Ashtamamsha Chart

Sl. No.	Signs → Ashtamamsha ↓	**1**	**2**	**3**	**4**	**5**	**6**	**7**	**8**	**9**	**10**	**11**	**12**
1.	3°45'	1	9	5	1	9	5	1	9	5	1	9	5
2.	7°30'	2	10	6	2	10	6	2	10	6	2	10	6
3.	11°15'	3	11	7	3	11	7	3	11	7	3	11	7
4.	15°0'	4	12	8	4	12	8	4	12	8	4	12	8
5.	18°45'	5	1	9	5	1	9	5	1	9	5	1	9
6.	22°30'	6	2	10	6	2	10	6	2	10	6	2	10
7.	26°15'	7	3	11	7	3	11	7	3	11	7	3	11
8.	30°0'	8	4	12	8	4	12	8	4	12	8	4	12

Table VI-18 : The Dashamamsha Chart

Sl. No.	Signs → Dashamamsha ↓	**1**	**2**	**3**	**4**	**5**	**6**	**7**	**8**	**9**	**10**	**11**	**12**
1.	0°-3°	1	10	3	12	5	2	7	4	9	6	11	8
2.	3°-6°	2	11	4	1	6	3	8	5	10	7	12	9
3.	6°-9°	3	12	5	2	7	4	9	6	11	8	1	10
4.	9°-12°	4	1	6	3	8	5	10	7	12	9	2	11
5.	12°-15°	5	2	7	4	9	6	11	8	1	10	3	12
6.	15°-18°	6	3	8	5	10	7	12	9	2	11	4	1
7.	18°-21°	7	4	9	6	11	8	1	10	3	12	5	2
8.	21°-24°	8	5	10	7	12	9	2	11	4	1	6	3
9.	24°-27°	9	6	11	8	1	10	3	12	5	2	7	4
10.	27-30°	10	7	12	9	2	11	4	1	6	3	8	5

Table VI-19
The Ekadashamsha Chart

Sl. No.	Signs → / Ekadashamsha ↓	1	2	3	4	5	6	7	8	9	10	11	12
1.	0°0'0"-2°43'38"	1	12	11	10	9	8	7	6	5	4	3	2
2.	2°43'38"-5°27'16"	2	1	12	11	10	9	8	7	6	5	4	3
3.	5°27'16"-8°10'54"	3	2	1	12	11	10	9	8	7	6	5	4
4.	8°10'54"-10°54'32"	4	3	2	1	12	11	10	9	8	7	6	5
5.	10°54'32"-13°38'11"	5	4	3	2	1	12	11	10	9	8	7	6
6.	13°38'11"-16°21'49"	6	5	4	3	2	1	12	11	10	9	8	7
7.	16°21'49"-19°5'27"	7	6	5	4	3	2	1	12	11	10	9	8
8.	19°5'27"-21°49'5"	8	7	6	5	4	3	2	1	12	11	10	9
9.	21°49'5"-24°32'44"	9	8	7	6	5	4	3	2	1	12	11	10
10.	24°32'44"-27°16'22"	10	9	8	7	6	5	4	3	2	1	12	11
11.	27°16'22"-30°0'0"	11	10	9	8	7	6	5	4	3	2	1	12

Table VI-20
The Dwadashamsha Chart

Sl. No.	Signs → / Dwadashamsha ↓	**1**	**2**	**3**	**4**	**5**	**6**	**7**	**8**	**9**	**10**	**11**	**12**
1.	0°0'-2°30'	1	2	3	4	5	6	7	8	9	10	11	12
2.	2°30'-5°0'	2	3	4	5	6	7	8	9	10	11	12	1
3.	5°0'-7°30'	3	4	5	6	7	8	9	10	11	12	1	2
4.	7°30'-10°0'	4	5	6	7	8	9	10	11	12	1	2	3
5.	10°0'-12°30'	5	6	7	8	9	10	11	12	1	2	3	4
6.	12°30'-15°0'	6	7	8	9	10	11	12	1	2	3	4	5
7.	15°0'-17°30'	7	8	9	10	11	12	1	2	3	4	5	6
8.	17°30'-20°0'	8	9	10	11	12	1	2	3	4	5	6	7
9.	20°0'-22°30'	9	10	11	12	1	2	3	4	5	6	7	8
10.	22°30'-25°0'	10	11	12	1	2	3	4	5	6	7	8	9
11.	25°0'-27°30'	11	12	1	2	3	4	5	6	7	8	9	10
12.	27°30'-30°0'	12	1	2	3	4	5	6	7	8	9	10	11

the Saptamsha as well as the Ashtamamsha, it falls in its own sign and the sign of a friend (Saturn) respectively, being benefic in either case. It falls in the Navamsha of Venus, an enemy (hence malefic), the Dashamamsha of Mercury, another enemy (hence malefic), in the Ekadashamsha of Saturn, a friend (hence benefic), and in the Dwadashamsha of Mercury (again malefic). Thus, out of the twelve factors considered, the Sun is a benefic in nine and a malefic in three. The Sun thus behaves as a benefic. The Dwadashavargiya Bala of all the planets can thus be worked out. The relevant tables may be referred to for convenience. The Dwadashavargiya Bala of planets in the Example Chart has been presented in Table VI-21.

Table VI-21
The Dwadashavargiya Bala of Planets

The Division		Sun	Mon	Mar	Mer	Jup	Ven	Sat
1.	First	B	B	B	M	B	M	B
2.	Second	B	B	M	M	B	M	N
3.	Third	B	B	B	B	B	M	B
4.	Fourth	B	M	N	B	B	B	N
5.	Fifth	B	M	M	B	B	M	B
6.	Sixth	B	M	B	M	B	M	N
7.	Seventh	B	N	M	B	B	B	B
8.	Eighth	B	N	N	M	B	B	B
9.	Ninth	M	N	M	B	B	B	B
10.	Tenth	M	M	M	B	B	B	B
11.	Eleventh	B	M	B	B	N	M	M
12.	Twelfth	M	M	N	M	B	M	M
Total :	B :	9	3	4	7	11	5	7
	M :	3	6	5	5	0	7	2
	N :	0	3	3	0	1	0	3

B : Benefic, M : Malefic, N : Neutral

The above elaborate method of taking into consideration the twelve different sources of strength is very useful. However, the Panchavargiya Bala has the advantage of providing the exact numerical strength of a planet. In the subsequent discussions, whenever the strength of a planet is referred to, it will be the Panchavargiya strength that will be meant.

INTERPRETATION OF THE DASHAS

Depending upon the strength of various dasha lords according to their Panchavargiya Bala, the different dashas produce good or bad results. A very general indication is being given here of the nature of results that may issue forth in different dashas. These must be interpreted along with other important factors in the annual chart as also the promise in the birth chart.

The Lagna

1. *Strong* : Good health, monetary gains, respect from near and dear ones.
2. *Of medium strength* : Foreign travel (displacement), loss of fame, un-desirable expenditure.
3. *Weak* : Bad health, loss of money, even death.

Note : The strength of the lagna depends upon the strength of its lord as well as the association of the lagna with its lord and with natural benefics.

The Sun

1. *Very strong* : Vehicles, high status, authority.
2. *Strong* : All the above to a slightly lesser extent; generally favourable.
3. *Of medium strength* : Struggles, opposition at the place of work, biliary ailments.
4. *Weak* : Fear from the ones in authority and from enemies, loss of wealth, ill health, loss of discrimination.

Note : The Sun in the houses 3, 6, 10 and 11 produces favourable results even when it is weak.

The Moon

1. *Very strong* : Increased wealth, association with women, acquisition of precious stones.
2. *Strong* : Generally good results pertaining to the above indications.

3. *Of medium strength* : Loss of wealth, opposition from near and dear ones, phlegmatic ailments.

4. *Weak* : Defamation, loss of wealth and virtue, chest diseases.

Mars

1. *Very strong* : Position of authority (in Army/Police), victory in war, fulfilment of desires.
2. *Strong* : Wealth, status, favours from the ruler.
3. *Of medium strength* : Fear from enemies, inflammatory diseases, biliary ailments.
4. *Weak* : Quarrels, strife at home and at the place of work, fear from foes, blood disorders, fever.

Note : Favourable results accrue when Mars is in houses 3, 6 and 11.

Mercury

1. *Very strong* : Gain of knowledge and learning, attainment of status, increase of fame, and appointment as an ambassador or a minister.
2. *Strong* : Gain of wealth through friends, guru or writings, comforts from the near and dear ones.
3. *Of medium strength* : Loss of fame, ill temper, injury from fall, fear of ill health.
4. *Weak* : Distorted reasoning, loss of wealth, fear of imprisonment, foreign travel.

Jupiter

1. *Very strong* : Favours from the ruler, guru, friends and elders, attainment of fame, wealth and virtue, child birth.
2. *Strong* : Virtuous deeds, favours from the superiors, increased enthusiasm, success in undertakings.
3. *Of medium strength* : Illness, poverty, ear ailment, loss of wealth and virtue.
4. *Weak* : Varied troubles and ailments, domestic strife, loss of wealth.

Venus

1. *Very strong*: Gain of wealth, comforts, vehicles, and wife, good health, general contentment.
2. *Strong*: Gains from business, good food and drinks, good clothes, favours from friends and women.
3. *Of medium strength*: Altered thinking, loss of wealth, ill health, opposition from the fair sex.
4. *Weak*: Opposition from the near and dear ones, ill health to wife, distorted reasoning, foreign travel.

Saturn

1. *Very strong*: New house, new clothes, acquisition of new land, increased wealth from association with the ruler.
2. *Strong*: Association with older women, acquisition of cattle and vehicles.
3. *Of medium strength*: Fear from foes and thieves, penury, ill health.
4. *Weak*: Varied calamities and disappointments, domestic strife, death.

Note:

(i) Saturn, like the Sun and Mars, is particularly favourable when located in houses 3, 6 and 11.

(ii) There is no such calculation for Rahu or Ketu though their dashas are considered. It is likely that Saturn's strength is representative of Rahu's, and Mars' strength of Ketu's. This requires elaborate testing before practical application.

CHAPTER VII

THE LORD OF THE YEAR

His comrades all rejoice when their friend returns
covered with glory, proclaimed victor in the assembly.
He frees them from their sin, provides them with food.
Prepared is he, fit for the competition.

'RIG VEDA'

The lord of the year, also called the *Varshesha* or the *Varsheshwara*, is an important planet in the annual chart. It is supposed to significantly influence the events that take place during the year. A strong Varsha lord (or the Varshesha) ensures success, prosperity and good health throughout the year in question, while a weak one indicates the reverse. The Varsha lord is selected out of the five planets which hold special significance during the year.

THE FIVE OFFICE-BEARERS (PANCHADHIKARIS)

In the annual chart, there are five office-bearers which hold a special significance. These office-bearers hold five different portfolios. One of these eventually qualifies for the post of Varshesha or the year lord. These five office-bearers are:

1. *Muntha Pati* (or the Munthesha), i.e., the lord of the sign in which the Muntha is located.
2. *Janma Lagna Pati* (or the Janmesha), i.e., the lord of the ascendant in the birth chart.
3. *Varsha Lagna Pati* (or the Varsha Lagnesha), i.e., the lord of the ascendant in the annual chart.
4. *Tri-Rashi Pati*, i.e., the lord of the Tri-Rashi; this is to be described separately.

5. *Dina-Ratri Pati* : This is the lord of the Sun sign in the case of Varshapravesha occurring during day time (hence called the *Dina Pati* or the lord of the day), and the lord of the Moon sign in the case of Varshapravesha occurring during nighttime (hence called the *Ratri Pati* or the lord of the night).

The Tri-Rashi Pati

The lord of the 'Tri-Rashi' varies from sign to sign, and also as the Varshapravesha occurs during the day time (i.e., from sunrise to sunset) or during the nighttime (i.e., from sunset to sunrise). Table VII-1 shows the various Tri-Rashi lords for different lagnas.

Table VII-1
The Tri-Rashi Patis

S. No.	Varsha Lagna	Tri-Rashi Pati for Varshapravesha during	
		Day time	Night time
1.	Aries	Sun	Jup
2.	Taurus	Ven	Mon
3.	Gemini	Sat	Mer
4.	Cancer	Ven	Mar
5.	Leo	Jup	Sun
6.	Virgo	Mon	Ven
7.	Libra	Mer	Sat
8.	Scorpio	Mar	Ven
9.	Sagittarius	Sat	Sat
10.	Capricorn	Mar	Mar
11.	Aquarius	Jup	Jup
12.	Pisces	Mon	Mon

In the Example Chart under consideration, the five office-bearers for the year will be as follows :

1. Muntha Pati : Jupiter
2. Janma Lagna Pati : Sun
3. Varsha Lagna Pati : Mars
4. Tri-Rashi Pati : Mars
5. Dina-Ratri Pati : Sun

DETERMINATION OF THE YEAR LORD

One of the above mentioned five office-bearers is now selected as Varshesha or the lord of the year. As is evident from the above example, there is no bar to one planet holding more than a single portfolio. The qualifications for the Varsha lord are :

(a) It should be the strongest of the five office-bearers.

(b) It should, at the same time, aspect the Varsha lagna.

While considering the above qualifications for the ruler of the year, it may be noted that:

(i) the relative strength of the planets is to be judged from the Panchavargiya chart; and

(ii) generally, no distinction is to be made between a friendly aspect and an inimical aspect between the lagna and the planet while deciding the Varshesha.

The Method of Selection

The Varshesha is selected out of the five office-bearers, keeping the following points in view.

1. If the strongest of the office-bearers does not aspect the lagna, choose the one that is next lower in strength, but aspecting the lagna. Aspect on the Varsha lagna is an essential requirement of the year lord, except under special circumstances.

2. When more than one office-bearers aspect the lagna, the strongest of them becomes the lord of the year.

3. When the office-bearers have equal strength, and all of them aspect the lagna, the one holding the greater number of portfolios qualifies to become the year lord.

   Note : The above mentioned condition generally does not arise since there is always some variation in the relative strength of different planets. If the Vishwa Bala has been calculated in the traditional manner, one should go not only up to units, but also to sub-units and sub-sub-units, in order to clearly differentiate between planets which are close to each other in strength. If the decimal system is employed, it is desirable to determine the Vishwa Bala to the third decimal.

4. The Muntha lord as the year lord:
   (a) When no office-bearer aspects the lagna, the Muntha lord assumes the lordship of the year.
   (b) When the strength of the office-bearers is less than 5 units in the Panchavargiya chart, the Muntha lord is to be taken as the Varshesha.
   (c) When the five office-bearers are equal in strength, aspect and the number of portfolios they hold, then also the Muntha lord assumes the lordship of the year. However, see the note to article 3, vide supra.
5. Miscellaneous views:
   (a) When no office-bearer aspects the lagna, some authorities bestow the year lordship upon the lord of the lagna in the annual chart.
   (b) Still others attribute the Varsha lordship to the Dina-Ratri Pati in case of otherwise equal claim (in respect of strength, aspect and number of portfolios) of the office-bearers on the year lordship.

In the Example Chart, the five portfolios are held among themselves by Jupiter, Mars and the Sun. Of these, Jupiter is the strongest, with a Panchavargiya Bala of 14:46:0 units (14.766 units). Being located, however, in the second house from the lagna, it does not aspect the lagna and, therefore, does not qualify for Varsha lordship.

Of the remaining two, Mars is placed in lagna while the Sun aspects the lagna from the tenth house. Of these two, according to the Panchavargiya Bala, the Sun is stronger (V.B. 14:20:15 units/ 14.337 units) than Mars (V.B. 14:1:0 units/ 14.016 units). *Hence, the Sun becomes the Varsha lord or the Varshesha. A strong Sun, the planet of royal dignity, in the tenth house, the house representing the government, also being the year lord, justifies the shape the events took during the year. The native, at the young age of forty, became the Prime Minister of India during this year.*

THE MOON AS THE YEAR LORD

The lord of the year is supposed to dominate the events during the year in question. The Moon, however, is considered to be mild in nature and, therefore, unable to 'govern' unless extra-ordinarily strong and well-positioned. In general, therefore, the Moon is not to be considered as Varshesha even though:

(a) it may be the strongest of the five office-holders; and
(b) If more than one planet establish Ithasala with the Moon, the strongest of them becomes the year lord.
(c) it may be aspecting the lagna as generally required of the Varshesha.

In such a situation, find out the planet next lower in strength, out of the five office-bearers, which also aspects the lagna. This planet will be the Varsha lord.

If the Moon is the strongest of the five office-bearers and aspects the lagna also, while no other office-bearer aspects the lagna, it still does not become the year lord. Under such a circumstance, the following method is employed:

(a) Find out the planet with which this Moon establishes an Ithasala yoga. That planet becomes the year lord.
(b) If more than one planet establish Ithasala with the Moon, the strongest of them becomes the year lord.
(c) If the Moon does not form Ithasala with any planet, then the lord of the Moon sign assumes the year lordship.

Note: The Ithasala, to be dealt with in the chapter on yogas, briefly means that the two planets participating in this yoga are in mutual aspect and the faster of the two is behind the slower one. An Ithasala is supposed to be favourable in general. When the faster-moving planet is ahead of the slower one, a generally unfavourable yoga, the Ishrafa yoga, is the result. An Ishrafa occurring between two benefics is generally not bad.

In Chart VII-1, three planets (the Moon, Mercury, and Venus) share among themselves the five portfolios. The Moon happens to be the strongest (V.B. 12:28:15 units/12.471 units) of the three but does not have to be considered for the year lordship. The next lower in strength is Mercury (V.B. 10:49:15

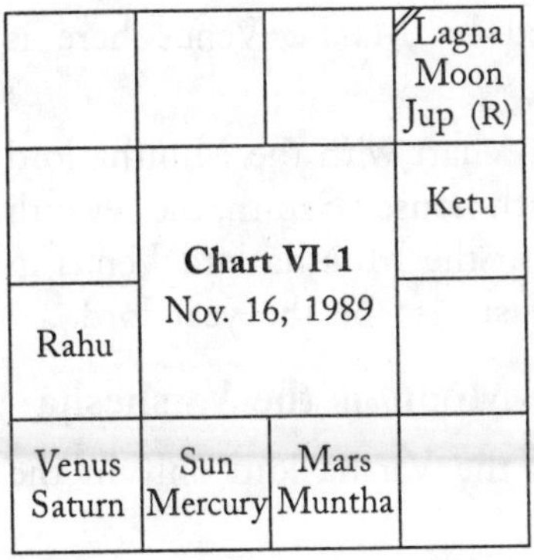

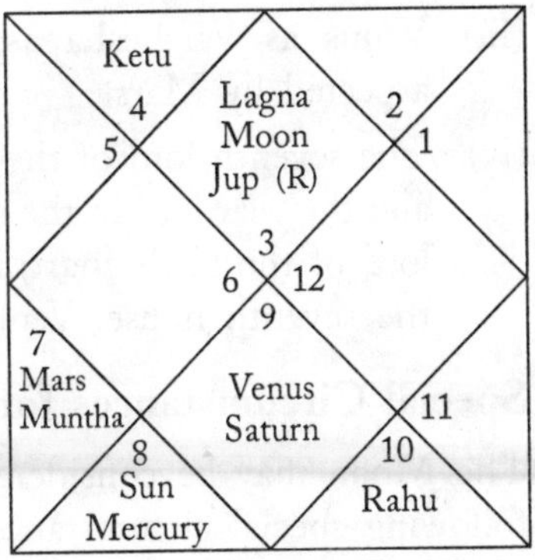

Lagna	12°53'	Mars	14°43'	Venus	17°28'
Sun	00°40'	Mercury	04°08'	Saturn	16°57'
Moon	18°57'	Jupiter (R)	16°35'	Rahu	26°54'

units/10.821 units), but Mercury does not aspect the lagna and, therefore, goes out of the competition. Venus, with the lowest strength (V.B. 9:6:30 units/9.108 units), becomes the Varsha lord on account of its aspect on the lagna.

Some authorities do not look for a planet falling next lower in strength to the Moon. They advocate to install the planet in Ithasala with the Moon as the year lord in the first place. In the above example, the Moon has just moved ahead of Venus leading to an Ishrafa yoga between the two. There is no longer any Ithasala there. An Ishrafa between two natural benefics is, however, not considered bad. If we do not grant the favourable quality to the Ishrafa, then the next consideration falls on the lord of the Moon sign, which is Mercury. However, Mercury as the year lord will not justify the one important event during the year, that of marriage. Some of the combinations for marriage as applicable here are:

(i) Seventh lord of the birth chart in the seventh house, with Venus as the year lord. With Cancer as his birth ascendant, the native has his natal seventh lord, Saturn, in the seventh house along with Venus in the annual chart.

(ii) Jupiter in the sign of one of the office-bearers. Jupiter here is in Gemini, the sign of Mercury, the lord of the lagna in the annual chart as also the Tri-Rashi Pati and the Dina-Ratri Pati.

(iii) Venus as Varshesha aspected by Mars : Venus here is aspected by Mars.

(iv) The seventh lord of the birth chart with the Muntha lord and the year lord in the seventh house : Saturn, the seventh lord of the birth chart, is with the Muntha lord Venus in the seventh house. Venus must also be the year lord.

Special Circumstances for the Moon as the Varshesha

The Moon may be considered as the Varsha lord only in the following special circumstances :

(a) Cancer rising as Varsha lagna, with the Moon in it, and the Moon happening to be the strongest office-bearer.

(b) The Moon being the strongest of the office-bearers, fully aspecting the lagna, the Varshapravesha occurring at night, and the Moon also being the Tri-Rashi Pati.

INTERPRETING THE YEAR LORD

The year lord is the most important planet in the annual horoscope. It holds sway over events that take place during the year. While interpreting the results indicated by the year lord, the following points must be borne in mind

1. Placement of the year lord in houses 6, 8 and 12 reduces its beneficence. Elsewhere it produces results without hindrance.
2. Combustion and retrogression of the year lord are the other deterrents to its beneficence.
3. A year lord in full strength according to the Panchavargiya Bala produces benefic results to the fullest extent; one in medium strength brings in mediocrity in benefic results; a weak year lord only produces bad results, disappointments and obstacles. An extra-ordinarily strong year lord produces excessively beneficial results during the year.
4. It is also important to take into consideration the strength of the year lord in the birth horoscope.
5. The year lord has dominance over the whole year. Its effects are generally felt throughout the year.
6. The results of the year lord also depend on the significatorship of the year lord. Thus, the Sun signifies royal dignity, and

the Sun as the year lord influences one's status and dignity, favourably or otherwise, during the year. The Moon signifies comforts and liquids, Mars signifies valour, Mercury signifies intellect, Jupiter signifies virtue and wisdom, Venus signifies physical pleasures, while Saturn signifies labour, lands and servants. The various year lords affect their significations variously.

7. The year lord in the annual chart has been ascribed the same importance as the lagna lord. Thus, the involvement of the year lord in the formation of various Tajika yogas must also be considered while analysing an annual chart.

The general results of different planets as year lords, depending upon their strength on the basis of the Panchavargiya Bala, are being described below.

1. The Sun as the Year Lord

(a) *In full strength* : Gain in wealth, name, fame and reputation, attainment of a position of authority, dominance over opponents, and fulfilment of desires. Particularly beneficial in houses 3, 6, 10 and 11.

(b) *Of medium strength* : The above results are obtained to a lesser extent. In addition, there is loss of vitality, risk of opposition from those in authority, likelihood of illness, change of place of work or residence, and obstacles in undertakings.

(c) *Weak* : Long-lasting illness, mental anguish, loss of wealth, disappointments, disgrace, enslavement, aimless wandering, and disagreement with the near and dear ones.

2. The Moon as the Year Lord

(a) *In* full *strength*: Increased wealth, gain from business, acquisition of physical pleasures and articles of comfort, attainment of rightful status, benefit from dealing in things white in colour, birth of a daughter.

(b) *Of medium strength*: *Loss* of money, decline in physical pleasures, decreased vitality, wrath of those in authority. If such a Moon forms Ishrafa yoga with a malefic planet, it leads to phlegmatic ailments.

(c) *Weak* : Phlegmatic illness (Pulmonary Tuberculosis!), fall in status, obstacle to profession, opposition from friends and relatives, distant travel, lack of conjugal bliss.

3. Mars as the Year Lord

(a) In full *strength* : Dominance over opponents, success in litigation, elevation of status, service in Army or Police, increase in income and wealth.

(b) *Of medium strength* : The above results are obtained to a lesser degree. In addition, it may lead to physical injury, loss of blood, excessive anger, etc.

(c) *Weak* : Fear from foes, thieves and fire, loss of fame, money and property, opposition from near and dear ones, change of residence, or long travel.

4. Mercury as the Year Lord

(a) *In full strength* : Recognition through intellectual deeds (writing, reading, research, study of scriptures), elevation in professional status, benefit from new undertakings, co-operation from near and dear ones.

(b) *Of medium strength* : The above mentioned results are available only to a lesser degree. Additionally, there may be problems due to intemperance in speech and argument.

(c) *Weak* : Loss of wealth, lack of discrimination, throat ailments, quarrels with relatives, untruthfulness.

5. Jupiter as the Year Lord

(a) *In full strength* : Comforts at home, inclination towards religious and virtuous pursuits, clarity of thought, increase in earnings, wealth and reputation, co-operation even from opponents, and acquisition of hidden wealth.

(b) *Of medium strength* : The above mentioned results accrue to a lesser extent. In addition, there is association with those in authority, and inclination towards study of books (and scriptures!). If Jupiter is involved in an Ishrafa (q.v.) with a malefic, there is loss of wealth.

(c) *Weak* : Loss of wealth and comforts, decline of virtue, disgrace, separation from spouse and children, physical ailment.

6. Venus as the Year Lord

(a) *In full strength* : Good health, plenty to earn, eat and enjoy, inclination towards study of scriptures, elevation of professional status, conjugal bliss, and varied comforts.

(b) *Of medium strength* : Mediocre earnings, increase of opponents, loss of fame, undisclosed anguish or ailment.

(c) *Weak* : Mental anguish, disgrace, obstacle to profession, opposition from friends and children, failure in undertakings, illness to wife or conjugal unhappiness.

7. Saturn as the Year Lord

(a) *In full strength* : Success in litigation, acquisition of new house, land or property, gains from the western direction (from the "Yavanas"), good health, leadership of fellow-beings.

(b) *Of medium strength* : The above mentioned results are obtained to an ordinary extent only. There is decrease in earnings, and benefit from servants, camels, buffaloes, etc.

(c) *Weak* : Failure in all undertakings, varied problems, fear from foes, opposition from friends, spouse, children and relatives, and general deprivation.

The results as described above are fairly general in nature. They must be interpreted keeping in mind such varied factors as the location of the year lord in the annual chart, the influence of other planets on the year lord, the involvement of the year lord in the various Tajika yogas, etc. Needless to stress that any results issuing forth from the annual chart will be dependent on a similar promise in the birth chart.

CHAPTER VIII

THE TRI-PATAKI CHAKRA

On all sides eyes, on all sides face,
on all sides arms, on all sides feet,
he, God, the One, creates heaven and earth,
forging them together with arms and wings.

'SVETASVATARA UPANISHAD'

The Tri-pataki Chakra (or the Tri-pataki map) consists of a special charting of various *planets as located in the birth chart in relation to the ascendant in the annual chart.* The planets are progressed by one sign every year starting from their position at birth.

The application and analysis of the Tri-pataki gives a very broad overview of the nature of events likely to dominate one particular year. While the *vedha* to any planet or to the lagna can be determined by charting the planets on the Tri-pataki, it is customary only to consider the various planetary influences on the Moon, or sometimes on the ascendant.

THE TRI-PATAKI CHAKRA

Three parallel lines are drawn vertically. Across these are drawn three parallel lines horizontally. The ends of these lines are joined as shown in Fig. VIII-1. On top of the three vertical lines, customarily, small flags are drawn. The word *Pataka* means 'a flag'; the pre-fix *Tri* means 'three'. This forms the Tri-pataki map.

Marking the Rashis

The central flag (marked 'a') represents the ascendant in the annual chart. The sign rising at the time of Varshapravesha is

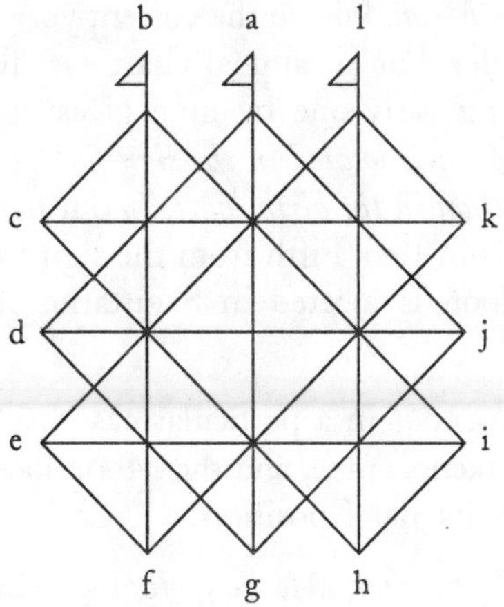

Figure VIII-1

marked here. The remaining signs are marked in order, in an anti-clockwise fashion, along the points 'b', 'c', 'd', etc. This forms the skeleton on which the progressed planets will be located.

The Concept of Vedha

The word *vedha* means to pierce. On the Tri-pataki map it will be noted that three lines converge on each of the twelve points, from 'a' to 'l'. For example, we have lines 'ad', 'ag' and 'aj' converging at point 'a'. For a planet situated at 'a', any planet located at points 'd', 'g' or 'j' will cause the *vedha.* Similarly, for a planet located at point 'b', planets located at points 'c', 'f' or 'i' will cause the *vedha.* Thus, the *vedha* is caused by planets situated at the other ends of the three lines converging at any one point. It is natural to assume that a planet is also under the influence of another planet located on the same point in the Tri-pataki chakra; for all practical purposes this may also be considered as the *vedha.*

Locating the Planets on the Tri-Pataki

For this purpose, it is *the current year* (i.e., completed years + 1) which is taken into account. In the Example Chart, the current year (for which the annual chart has been cast) is forty-one.

(i) *Locating the Moon.* Divide the current year by nine and find the remainder. For an annual chart cast for the forty-first year, dividing forty-one by nine gives us a remainder of five. *The Moon is located in the sign falling in the fifth house from its location in the birth chart. In* our native's birth chart, the Moon is in Leo. Fifth from the sign Leo is Sagittarius. So, the Moon is located in Sagittarius in the Tri-pataki chart.

Note : If the remainder in a particular case happens to be zero, it is to be taken as nine, and the Moon located in the ninth house from its natal position.

(ii) *Location of the Sun, Mercury, Jupiter, Venus, and Saturn.* Divide the current year by four and find the remainder. Locate the above mentioned planets on the Tri-pataki by counting from their position in the natal chart upto as many houses as indicated by the remainder. In our example, dividing forty-one by four, we get a remainder of one. So, the above mentioned planets are placed in the first house counted from their natal position. That is, they are located on the same signs on the Tri-pataki map as they occupy in the natal chart.

Note : If the remainder after the division is zero, it is to be taken as four, and the planets located in the fourth sign from their natal position.

(iii) *Location of Mars, Rahu and Ketu.* Divide the current year by six. The remainder determines the location of Mars, Rahu and Ketu in relation to their natal positions. For Rahu and Ketu, the location is decided by counting in the reverse order. Here, a 'zero' remainder means six. In the Example Chart, forty-one divided by six yields five as the remainder. Thus, the positions of Mars, Rahu and Ketu are marked in the rashis falling in the fifth from their natal positions. The positions of Rahu and Ketu, as mentioned above, are counted in the reverse order. Fig. VIII-2 shows the Tri-pataki chart for the forty-first year of our native according to the method described above.

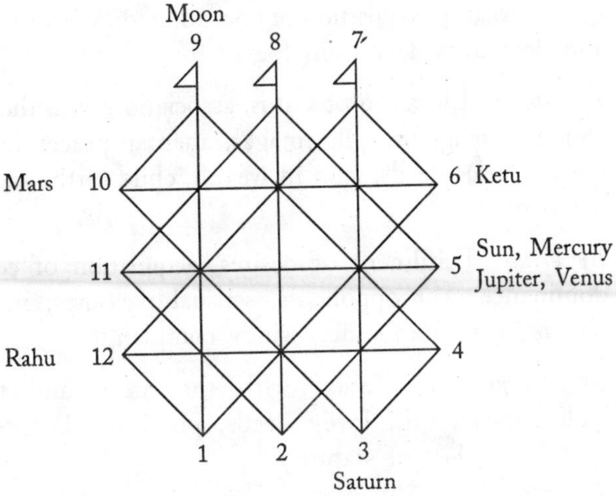

Figure VIII-2

Interpreting the Tri-pataki

Astrologers generally consider the vedha of the Moon in the Tri-pataki chakra. The vedha to the lagna, however, may also be suitably considered. When malefics cause the vedha to the Moon (or lagna), there are troubles and tensions during the year. When the benefics do so, the results are beneficial and desirable. Both malefics and benefics causing the vedha yield mixed results. When one malefic afflicts the Moon (or the lagna), the year produces troubles and obstacles of various sorts. When two malefics do so, there is likelihood of physical ailment. When three or more malefics cause the vedha, there may be intense trouble or even death. Benefic association or influence reduces the affliction correspondingly.

The following results have been ascribed to the vedha of the Moon by different planets.

1. *By the Sun*: High fever, bilious ailments, disappointments, mental tension.
2. *By Mars*: Fear from enemies, quarrels, blood disorders (including septicaemia, etc.), shortness of temper, pain and injury to the body, punishment, proneness to accidents.
3. *By Mercury*: Sharp intellect, association with good people,

gain of wealth, acquisition of education, differences with near and dear ones, fear from foes.

4. *By Jupiter* : Elevation of status, association with the virtuous and the religious, pilgrimages, mental peace, inclination toward pious deeds, gain in wealth, child birth, and general prosperity.
5. *By Venus* : Fulfilment of desires, acquisition of education, dominance over opponents, sensual pleasures, increase in income, fear from water, windy complaints.
6. *By Saturn* : Association with the mean and the low, inclination toward lowly deeds, physical ailments, windy complaints, loss of stature.
7. *By Rahu* : Severe illness, loss of honour and wealth, phobias, and generally undesirable results.
8. *By Ketu* : Ill health, poor digestion, depression.

The results of the vedha of the Moon or lagna as described above are too generalised and must be applied with great circumspection. They tend to occur during the dasha or the antardasha of planets causing the vedha. It is perhaps important to bear in mind not only the benefic or malefic nature of the planets but also their lordship, strength and signification.

In the Example Chart, the Moon has the vedha caused by an exalted Mars which is also the lagna lord of the annual chart. The lagna has the vedha caused by the Sun in Leo, its own sign, along with the three benefics Mercury, Jupiter and Venus. The native became the prime minister of India in his forty-first year of life, and, during this year, displayed a dignity and grace no less than the most distinguished leaders of his time in the world.

It will be interesting to have a look at the Tri-pataki chart cast for the forty-seventh year (extending from August 1990 to August 1991) of the same native, with Gemini rising in the lagna in the annual chart (See Fig. VIII-3). The ascendant and the Moon are both under the vedha caused by Rahu and Ketu, without any relief from benefics. The native met a violent end during this year. It cannot, however, be stressed too strongly here that such an analysis should always be correlated with a proper

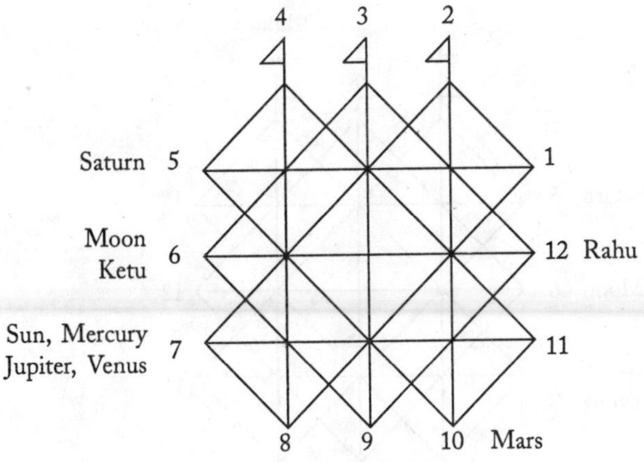

Figure VIII-3

analysis of the annual chart in the light of several other principles being described here, as also with the promise indicated in the natal chart.

Note: Some authorities, while locating the planets on the Tripataki, do not differentiate between Mars, Rahu and Ketu on the one hand, and the remaining planets (except the Moon) on the other. They divide the current year by four and locate all the planets (except the Moon for which the division is done by nine) depending upon the remainder obtained thus. Figs. VIII-4 & 5

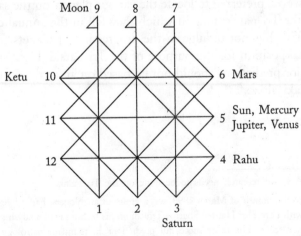

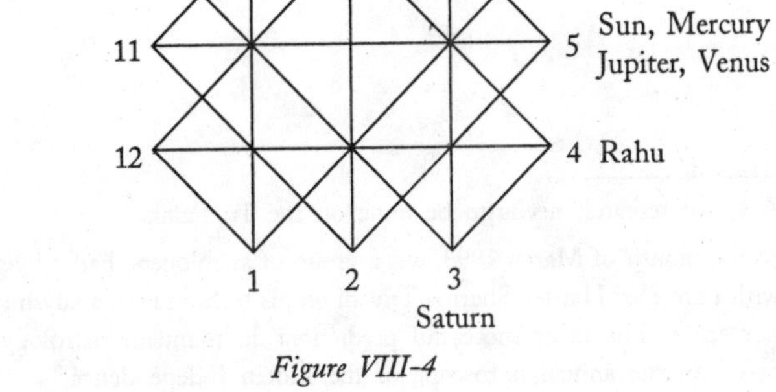

Figure VIII-4

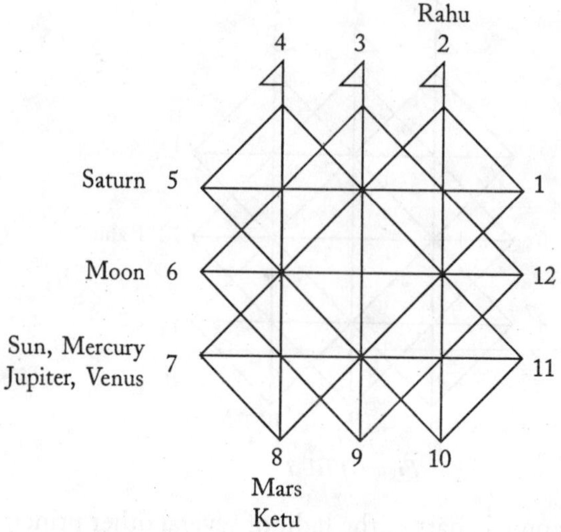

Figure VIII-5

show the Tri-pataki charts cast for the above native for the same years (forty-first and forty-seventh) by this latter technique.

We have not found the results obtained from the Tri-pataki to be very consistent.[1] Late Shri Hardev Sharma Trivedi, the erstwhile famous astrologer of north India well known for the publication of his celebrated Hindi almanac, the *Vishwa Vijaya Panchanga,* for almost the last fifty years, agrees with us. He, however, preferred to locate the various planets on the same signs in the Tri-pataki map in which they fell in the annual chart. He would thus not indulge in the progression of planets from their natal position for the purpose of the Tri-pataki. He insisted that major predictions should not be based on an analysis of the Tri-pataki alone.[2]

1. A lot of research needs to be done on the Tri-Pataki.

2. In the month of March 1993, we, a group of astrologers, had a long discussion with Late Shri Hardev Sharma Trivedi on his technique of analysing the annual horoscope. His most successful predictions in mundane astrology have been based on the annual horoscope of the Indian Independence.

CHAPTER IX

PLANETS IN DIFFERENT HOUSES

She carries in her lap the foolish and also the wise.
She bears the death of the wicked as well as the good.
She lives in friendly collaboration with the boar,
offering herself as the sanctuary to the wild pig.

'ATHARVA VEDA'

Planets by their location in different houses produce certain results. These results are very generalised since they get vastly modified by the nature of the lagna as also by the sign in which the planets are located. However, these results give important clues to the analysis of a chart. They are briefly described below.

THE SUN

The Sun is particularly favourable when located in houses 3, 6, 10 and 11.

1. **Lagna :** Situated alone in the lagna, or when aspected or associated with malefics, it leads to physical ailment, fever, headache, excessive expenditure, illness to wife, laziness, travel, proneness to anger, and trouble from enemies. Influence of benefics reduces the suffering.

2. **Second House :** Alone, or under the influence of malefics, it leads to excessive expenditure, strife with family members, financial troubles, diseases of the throat or eye, and varied disappointments. When under benefic influence, it leads to acquisition of wealth.

3. **Third House :** Increase in enthusiasm and valour, gain of name and fame, dominance over opponents, favours from

superiors, and good health. Brothers suffer when the Sun here is under malefic influence.

4. **Fourth House :** Suffering to mother, crops and cattle, fear of injury from quadrupeds and vehicles, strife with the higher-ups, suffering in journey, and proneness to ill health.
5. **Fifth House :** Strife with children and wife, loss of money, excessive expenditure, illness to children, fear from superiors, mental anguish, and abdominal discomfort. Benefic influences (by association or aspect) reduce the suffering and may lead to child birth.
6. **Sixth House :** Destruction of enemies, harmony with friends and near ones, success in litigation, gains in business, adversity to maternal uncles, and eye trouble.
7. **Seventh House :** Physical ailment, eye trouble, loss of wealth, ill health to wife, fear from foes and thieves while in travel. Benefic influences ensure professional elevation and general comforts.
8. **Eighth House :** Opposition from near and dear ones, strife at home, physical illness with much suffering, abdominal and eye disease, perineal diseases[1], loss of dignity, illness to wife and children, loss of wealth, fear from fire, and any sudden calamity.
9. **Ninth House :** If well-aspected or well-associated, it leads to virtuous deeds, benefic journey, comforts from wife, children and friends, and favours from the superiors. When under malefic influence, fall in earnings, disappointments, suffering in travel, strife with brothers and sisters.
10. **Tenth House :** Royal favours, professional elevation, gain in wealth, general progress, comforts in respect of quadrupeds and vehicles, dominance over opponents, wise decisions, success in ventures, and fulfilment of desires.
11. **Eleventh House :** Income from business and other undertakings, rise in status, inflow of wealth, harmony with friends and near and dear ones, acquisition of vehicles,

1. Diseases like piles, fistulae, fissures, etc., occurring around the anus.

inclination towards virtuous deeds. If under malefic influences, it indicates ill health to children.

12. **Twelfth House :** Eye disease, headache, abdominal discomfort, disappointments, illness to wife, excessive expenditure on treatment of illness, suffering through false allegation. If benefics influence this Sun, it indicates spending on virtuous/religious pursuits.

THE MOON

1. **Lagna :** In Aries, Taurus or Cancer, it ensures increased income, good health, favours from women and generally good results. In any other sign, especially if afflicted, it leads to loss of wealth, opposition from superiors, disappointments, eye disease, disease in the oral cavity, cough and asthmatic illness.
2. **Second House :** Acquisition of wealth, gains in business, association with good people, favours from superiors, general harmony amongst the family members. If afflicted, it leads to eye disease.
3. **Third House :** Good for brothers and sisters, inclination toward virtuous and religious deeds, fulfilment of some secret desire, and favours from women. Afflicted Moon is adverse for brothers and sisters, and inclines the native toward unscrupulous deeds.
4. **Fourth House :** Comforts from wife, friends and relatives, gain in professional status, benefit from agriculture and cattle, acquisition of vehicle, and gains from dealing it white-coloured objects. When afflicted by Rahu or Ketu, it leads to abdominal pain, and change of residence.
5. **Fifth House :** Comfort from children and wife, birth of a daughter,[2] gain of name and fame, acquisition of wealth, improved thinking, and inclination toward learning. When this Moon is afflicted, it is adverse for progeny and causes distortion of thinking.

---

2. In natal horoscopy, the Moon in the fifth house generally produces daughters as the first two issues.

6. **Sixth House :** Fear from foes, loss of favour from superiors, false allegations with consequent loss of mental peace, chest infections, cough, eye disease, and fear from water, undesired journey, and loss of money.
7. **Seventh House :** Favours from women, earnings from business and travel, elevation in profession, gain from dealings in white-coloured objects. If afflicted, it leads to illness of the native and his wife.
8. **Eighth House :** Loss of earnings and wealth, inclination toward unscrupulous deeds, grave illness and suffering, fear of drowning, dominance by opponents, mental anguish, abdominal pain, eye disease, coughs and cold, etc. Benefic influences on the Moon provide some relief.
9. **Ninth House :** Indulgence in virtuous deeds, harmonious relations with friends and relatives, comfort from wife and children, fulfilment of desires, gain of wealth through business and travel, elevation in profession. Affliction to the Moon in the ninth house causes obstacles to the fulfilment of one's undertakings.
10. **Tenth House :** Favours from superiors, professional elevation, dominance over opponents, good health, domestic harmony, fulfilment of desires, and access to comforts and wealth.
11. **Eleventh House :** Gains from dealing in clothes and white-coloured objects, rise in professional status, domestic harmony, and dominance over enemies and opponents.
12. **Twelfth House :** Eye disease, coughs and colds, increase of opponents, quarrels, mental anguish, excessive expenditure in the pursuit of good and religious deeds, and general laziness. The expenditure generally exceeds the income.

MARS

Particularly Favourable in houses 3, 6, 10 and 11 (like the Sun).

1. **Lagna :** Fear from fire, weapons and thieves, loss of money, blood disorders, fever, headache, abdominal pain, mental anguish, easy excitability, illness to wife, and proneness to accident and injury (surgical operation!).

2. **Second House :** Eye disease, loss of wealth, fear from fire, enemies and the ruler, disappointments, illness to wife, losses in business, and strife with family members.
3. **Third House :** Enhancement of status, acquisition of land, vehicles and wealth, dominance over opponents, favours from the ruler, fulfilment of desires, success through personal efforts, success in litigation. When afflicted, it causes harm to brothers.
4. **Fourth House :** Separation from friends and relatives, illness to mother, injury from weapon or fire, loss of cattle or vehicles, losses from land, lack of mental peace, and troublesome journey. The native's house may be burnt by fire.
5. **Fifth House :** Adverse for children and wife, abdominal and chest disease, loss of status, disappointments, loss of mental poise, injury from fire or weapon.
6. **Sixth House :** Annihilation of opponents, success in litigation, elevation of status, favours from the government, acquisition of wealth and vehicles, favours from women, and varied comforts.
7. **Seventh House :** Illness to wife, domestic strife, physical illness to the native, mental anguish, suffering in travel, association with unscrupulous individuals, breakdown of a marital alliance.
8. **Eighth House :** Serious illness, blood disorders, injury from weapons or accidents, surgical operation,[3] loss of wealth, domestic strife, and secret worries.
9. **Ninth House :** Loss of wealth, excessive expenditure, disappointments, frequent travel, strife with siblings, proneness to selfishness, an unwelcome transfer in job or a foreign journey.
10. **Tenth House :** Governmental favours, promotion in profession, gain in wealth and health, dominance over

3. Ketu in the eighth house acts in a similar way.

opponents, and success in undertakings. The native may become a centre of controversy.

11. **Eleventh House :** Good income, professional elevation, enhancement of dignity, gains in business, acquisition of comforts, vehicles and new dresses, and satisfaction from children, wife and friends.
12. **Twelfth House :** Loss of wealth and health, illness to children, fear from the ruler, eye disease, disappointments, injury from fire or accidents. Benefic influences on Mars mitigate the evil to a large extent.

MERCURY

Bad in houses 6, 8 and 12.

1. **Lagna :** Good health, earnings through the application of intelligence, commencement of a new business, enhancement of status, mental happiness, comforts to wife and children, and dominance over enemies. If Mercury is afflicted, it leads to domestic strife, illness and lack of comforts.
2. **Second House :** Domestic harmony, increase in income and wealth, gain of name and fame, dominance over opponents. Affliction here leads to domestic strife and loss of money.
3. **Third House :** Dominance over opponents through personal courage, peace of mind, comforts from wife and children, gain in wealth and fame, income through business, and inclination toward frequent travel.
4. **Fourth House :** Favours from superiors, domestic harmony, acquisition of vehicles, land or cattle, comfort to mother, harmony with the near and dear ones. If afflicted, it leads to illness of mother, and change of residence.
5. **Fifth House :** Earnings through the application of one's intelligence, comforts to and from children, favours from superiors, fulfilment of desires, acquisition of name and fame, higher studies, success in examination, and general comforts.

6. **Sixth House :** Increase in enemies, wasteful expenditure, quarrels, mental anguish, trouble from women, and generally ill health.
7. **Seventh House :** Comfort from wife, gain of status, comfortable journey, benefit from business transactions, and generally favourable results.
8. **Eighth House :** Eye disease, fever, chest infections, loss of wealth, excessive expenditure, and trouble from opponents. When under benefit influence, it gives excessively benefit results.
9. **Ninth House :** Fulfilment of desires, inclination toward religious deeds, good fortune, elevation of professional status, gain in wealth, birth of a child, success in undertakings, and profitable journey.
10. **Tenth House :** Professional elevation, gain of wealth and vehicles, enhanced dignity, profit from business, and inclination toward virtuous deeds. If afflicted, it causes strife with superiors.
11. **Eleventh House :** Gain of health, wealth and valour, fulfilment of desires, enhancement of status and dignity, acquisition of wealth through business and travel.
12. **Twelfth House :** Physical ailment, mental anguish, eye disease, excessive expenditure, increase in opponents, governmental disfavour. Under benefic influence, it leads to expenditure in religious and virtuous pursuits.

JUPITER

Bad in houses 6, 8 and 12.

1. **Lagna :** Generally favourable in respect of wife, children, vehicles and wealth, elevation of status (promotion in job!), gains from business, profitable association with friends, and fulfilment of desires. When afflicted, it causes ill health and worry about profession.
2. **Second House :** Good income, governmental favours, elevation of status, comforts form wife and children,

pilgrimage, acquisition of vehicles, earnings from business and travel.

3. **Third House :** Harmonious association with friends and relatives, gains from business, inclination toward virtuous deeds, gainful travel, and favourable for the siblings.[4] A sudden tragedy or loss of money may also occur.
4. **Fourth House :** Domestic harmony, good income, access to comforts and vehicles, governmental favours, monetary gains from lands and business. Good for mother. If afflicted, it leads to illness to mother and change of residence.
5. **Fifth House :** Acquisition of knowledge and learning, gain in wealth and health, increased fame and dignity, dominance over opponents, favourable for progeny, and birth of a child.
6. **Sixth House :** Frequent quarrels, increase in enemies, disappointments, mental anguish, eye disease, abdominal discomfort, general frailty, and disinclination towards religious pursuits.
7. **Seventh House :** Profitable journey, comfort from wife, sudden happiness, acquisition of vehicles, professional elevation, gain of wealth, name and fame, and development of new and fruitful associations.
8. **Eighth House :** Loss of health and wealth, injury or accident, fever, eye disease, losses in business and travel, separation from the near and dear ones, and general disappointments. On the positive side, it may lead to monetary gains to wife.
9. **Ninth House :** Pilgrimage, virtuous deeds, gain of wealth and wisdom, acquisition of land and vehicles, association with near and dear ones, profitable journey, and auspicious events.
10. **Tenth House :** Professional elevation, governmental favours, dominance over opponents, increased income, physical comforts, and auspicious events.
11. **Eleventh House :** Freedom from disease, comforts from wife, children and friends, acquisition of vehicles and wealth,

4. Affection for the siblings may increase as a result of their dire needs.

professional elevation, bestowal of honours and awards, inclination toward virtuous deeds, dominance over opponents, and fulfilment of desires.

12. **Twelfth House :** Excessive expenditure, strife with friends, disfavour from the ruler, fear from foes, fruitless journey, and physical illness. Also, expenditure on good deeds, like marriage of a child.

VENUS

Bad in houses 6, 8 and 12.

1. **Lagna :** Association with women, increase in income, fulfilment of desires, indulgence in luxuries, elevation of professional status, and domestic harmony.
2. **Second House :** Fulfilment of desires, benefit from friends, excessive wealth, success in ventures, association with women, and acquisition of vehicles.
3. **Third House :** Profitable association with friends and siblings, inclination to undertake journey, good health, gain of money, success in undertakings, association with women, and domestic harmony.
4. **Fourth House :** Acquisition of vehicles and wealth, gain from lands and business, favours from government, comfort to mother, and general material comforts. It may also cause wasteful expenditure, dissociation from near and dear ones, and instability of temper. In the case of a government servant, a posting where an office car is available to the native!
5. **Fifth House :** Gain of wealth without effort, much comfort to wife and children, fulfilment of desires, acquisition of knowledge, gain of name and fame, and dominance over enemies. It also indicates travel.
6. **Sixth House :** Fear from foes, quarrels, instability of temper, loss of wealth, secret worries, and physical illness. Also, separation from wife, or a divorce.
7. **Seventh House :** Overindulgence in sensual pursuits, marriage, gain of wealth, profit from business, success in

undertakings, earnings from travel, fulfilment of desires, and acquisition of vehicles.

8. **Eighth House :** Illness and physical suffering, affliction to wife and children, excessive expenditure, losses in business and travel, eye disease, and fear from water.
9. **Ninth House :** Elevation of professional status, gain of wealth, good health, benefit from journey, comforts from wife and children, success in undertakings, and inclination toward good deeds. Good for work connected with television.
10. **Tenth House :** Professional elevation (promotion in job!), domestic happiness, gain of wealth and dignity, dominance over opponents, acquisition of land, house, vehicles and other material comforts, and gainful journey. Good for art, culture, television.
11. **Eleventh House :** Earnings from business, gainful journey, association with friends, enhancement of status and dignity, governmental favours, comfort from wife and children, Gains from handicrafts, handloom, clothes, musical performances.
12. **Twelfth House :** Excessive expenditure, mental anguish, fear from foes, disfavour from the ruler, eye disease, and travel. When under benefic influence, it causes expenditure on religious and profitable undertakings, as also on happy events like marriage.

SATURN

Good in houses 3, 6 and 11.

1. **Lagna :** Laziness, ill health, fear from enemies, sudden calamity, disfavour from those in authority, association with the wicked and the low, illness to wife, and disappointments. When the ascendant coincides with Saturn's own sign (Capricorn, Aquarius) or with its exaltation sign (Libra), beneficial results may accrue.
2. **Second House :** Domestic strife, disease of eye, abdomen or oral cavity, false allegation, physical injury, loss of wealth, poor earnings, opposition from near and dear ones, and unwelcome travel.

3. **Third House :** Dominance over opponents, excessive enthusiasm, success in undertakings, gain in wealth, governmental favours, and strife with siblings.
4. **Fourth House :** Illness to mother, abdominal pain, fear from opponents and thieves, tensions in respect of land and vehicle, mental anguish, and travel.
5. **Fifth House :** Illness to wife, children and friends, interruption in education, distorted thinking, mental depression, loss of wealth, and abdominal ailments.
6. **Sixth House :** Good health, increased wealth, annihilation of enemies, success in litigation, relief from ailments, professional rise, gain in wealth, and fulfilment of desires.
7. **Seventh House :** Illness to wife, change of place of residence, foreign journey, suffering in travel, fear from enemies, false allegation, abdominal pain, loss of money, and association with other women.
8. **Eight House :** Serious illness (death, if the dasha running in the birth chart is adverse), loss of wealth, ill health to wife and children, false allegations, separation from near and dear ones (an unpleasant transfer!), fall in professional status, obstruction to education, and mental anguish.
9. **Ninth House :** Misfortune, loss in business, fall from virtue, disappointments, harm to elder brother and to enemies.
10. **Tenth House :** Success only through excessive effort, losses in business, fall in professional status, quarrelsome nature, travel, change of residence, and domestic strife. When strong or exalted, it leads to elevation of status, and profits through dealings in metals and dark-coloured objects (like iron and steel).
11. **Eleventh House :** Professional elevation, dominance over opponents, good health, excessive earnings, change of residence, and illness to children or to elder brother.
12. **Twelfth House :** Loss of earnings, fear from those in authority, disease of eye or chest or feet, domestic strife, unexpected calamity, and likelihood of travel.

RAHU

1. **Lagna :** Mental anguish, loss of dignity, fear from opponents, ill health to wife, excessive expenditure, distorted thinking, headache, and eye disease.
2. **Second House :** Loss of wealth, ill health, eye disease, disease of the oral cavity, fear from the ruler, losses in business and travel.
3. **Third House :** Governmental favours, good health, monetary gains, dominance over enemies and opponents, professional elevation, and success in undertakings. May prove adverse to siblings.
4. **Fourth House :** Ill health to mother, fall from status, suffering in travel, strife with friends and relatives, excessive expenditure, ill health, and some sudden calamity.
5. **Fifth House :** Intellectual deterioration, mental anguish, unfounded fears, loss of money, interruption in studies, and pain in abdomen. If under benefic influence, it may lead to the birth of a son, gain in wealth, and dominance over opponents.
6. **Sixth House :** Good health, loss of enemies, gain in wealth, access to vehicles and comforts, and rise in professional status.
7. **Seventh House :** Adverse for wife. Domestic strife, ill health, suffering in travel, fear of fire, water or poison, and some secret illness. Likelihood of separation from wife, or a divorce.
8. **Eighth House :** Varied ailments, disease in private parts of the body, abdominal pain, increase of enemies, loss of health and wealth, ill health to wife and children, unfounded fears and phobias, losses in business and travel.

9 **Ninth House :** Misfortunes, strife with near and dear ones, disappointments, fall from status, harm from animals and vehicles, travel (including foreign travel), and differences with father.

10. **Tenth House :** Loss of earnings, and physical illness. If well-associated or well-aspected, it leads to rise in professional

status, increased name and fame, and gainful business and travel.

11. **Eleventh House :** Good earnings, good health, gainful business and travel, comfort from wife and children, and elevation in professional status.
12. **Twelfth House :** Loss of wealth, physical ailment, eye disease, fear from the ruler, change of place of residence, fear from fire and thieves, and losses in business and travel.

KETU

1. **Lagna :** Ill health, loss through thefts, loss of dignity, strife with friends and dear ones, fear from fire or injury, and numerous worries.
2. **Second House :** Loss of wealth, wasteful expenditure, disease of eye or mouth, disappointments, fruitless travel.
3. **Third House :** Destruction of opponents, gainful business and travel, governmental favours, ill health to sibling.
4. **Fourth House :** Ill health to mother, vehicular accident, excessive expenditure, disfavour from the ruler, and loss of mental poise.
5. **Fifth House :** Loss of wealth, interruption in studies, lack of discrimination, illness to children, some sudden calamity, and association with the wicked.
6. **Sixth House :** Loss of enemies, increased wealth, comforts from wife, children and vehicles, professional elevation, and fulfilment of desires.
7. **Seventh House :** Illness to wife, lower abdominal ailments, frequent travel, loss in business, and unfounded worries.
8. **Eight House :** Varied ailments, heart disease, fear of injury, fire or theft, loss of money, change of residence, and fear from the ruler.
9. **Ninth House :** Opposition from friends, misfortunes, inclination toward wicked deeds, failure in undertakings, and disease of the upper limbs.

10. **Tenth House :** Fear from the ruler, change in job, loss of wealth, illness to mother, change of residence and failure in undertakings.
11. **Eleventh House :** Good health, increased wealth, domestic comforts, professional elevation, and gains in business and travel. It may also encourage one to indulge in black magic or cheating.
12. **Twelfth House :** Loss of money, fear from foes, losses in business and in travel, eye disease, decline in professional status, and much mental suffering.

HINTS ABOUT INTERPRETATION OF THE ABOVE RESULTS

As already indicated, the above mentioned results are too generalised, and cannot be applied verbatim. The following points must be borne in mind while interpreting the position of planets in various houses:

1. All good results of a planet get adversely modified when the planet producing them is under malefic association or aspect.
2. Adverse results, similarly, get favourably modified when the planet producing them obtains benefit association or aspect.
3. All planets give some or the other benefit by their location in the eleventh house, the house of gains. In practice, the association of a 'yoga' with the eleventh house or the eleventh lord ensures its fructification.
4. Planets in the twelfth house, the house of loss, generally indicate loss of money. *The benefic and malefic influences on them only indicate spending in desirable or undesirable pursuits.*
5. All planets in the eighth house give adverse results, especially affecting the health of the individual. The more malefic of them indicate more serious affliction. Benefic influences mitigate the evil to some extent.
6. In general, the natural benefics produce adverse results when located in houses 6, 8 and 12.

7. The natural malefics (Sun, Mars, Saturn, Rahu and Ketu) produce benefic results in house 3, 6 and 11. In the third house, they ensure the exercise of personal grit; in the sixth, they destroy opponents; in the eleventh, they ensure inflow of wealth through personal effort. The Sun is additionally beneficial in the tenth house where it promises a position of authority.
8. The above mentioned results get correspondingly modified as the planet in question is exalted or debilitated, retrograde or direct, combust or otherwise, and whether or not it is involved in any of the Tajika yogas.

CHAPTER X

THE YOGAS

United your resolve, united your hearts,
may your spirits be at one,
that you may long together dwell
in unity and concord!

'RIG VEDA'

The clue to successful predictions on the basis of Varshaphala lies in a proper understanding of the Tajika Yogas. Sixteen such yogas or planetary configurations are described in the Tajika texts. These yogas form as a result of specific disposition or placement of planets in relation to each other. Most of these yogas depend on the mutual Tajika aspects between planets, and on their special orbs of influence. These yogas are as appropriately applicable to the Horary chart as they are to the annual chart. The hundreds of yogas as employed in the Parashari system are generally not considered in the Tajika chart. Equally so, the Tajika yogas do not find their use generally in the analysis of the natal chart.

Recent Origin

It may be mentioned here that the sixteen Tajika yogas are a relatively later addition to the system of annual horoscopy. The various names given to these yogas have been derived from the Persian or Arabic languages. It goes to the credit of the Sanskrit writers on the Vedic astrology that the apparently alien names have been retained as such, and graciously incorporated in the Sanskrit verses or dicta on annual horoscopy. Each of these yogas will be discussed individually in the narration that follows. The original nomenclature will be retained even while an attempt will be made to denote these yogas in suitable descriptive terms where possible. It will be noted that Rahu and Ketu do not figure in the formation of these yoga.

There is generally a tendency to interpret the available astrological dicta in a restricted manner, taking into consideration only the literal meaning of the available text. Unless these dicta are boldly interpreted, astrology will not be able to keep pace with the changing times. So many of the old principles will appear to have lost their meaning in the present times unless they are seen in the light of modern times. Besides, the available principles of astrology mainly serve as guidelines. The extent of their utility, application and interpretation have to depend on the skill and experience of the individual astrologer. In the pages that follow, it will be seen that some liberty has been taken in the method of application of such principles. It is hoped that this exercise only helps to bring out newer meanings from the standard principles.

Several of the Tajika yogas may be present in any one annual chart. The correct analysis of a chart involves a balanced interpretation of the various yogas. As has been stressed only too often, a proper study of these yogas must only succeed, and not precede, a proper analysis of the birth horoscope along with the operating dasha and antardasha. Accurate results can only be arrived at by studying the birth chart and the annual chart side-by-side.

The Lagnesha and the Karyesha

These two terms are regularly used while describing most of the Tajika yogas. The lagnesha, or the lagna lord, and the karyesha, or the significator, indicate two important planets which participate in the formation of several of these yogas. The lagna lord represents the individual himself. It is understandable that the involvement of the lagna lord is essential in order to ensure the occurrence of an event to the native. The nature of this event is governed by another planet, or significator, which represents an event by its being the lord of a particular house. Thus, when the lagna lord (lagnesha) establishes some relationship with the lord of, say, the fifth house (the significator, or the karyesha, for the fifth house), some event pertaining to one's progeny (ruled by the fifth house) is likely to materialise. Similarly, when the association is between the lagna lord and the seventh house lord (the lagnesha and the karyesha respectively), the event may pertain to one's spouse (ruled by the seventh house). Thus, what events will take place during a given year is generally indicated by the lagnesha getting involved with a particular significator or karyesha.

The above strict application of the terms lagnesha and karyesha holds true in case of the 'Prashna' or the Horary chart in general. In the annual chart, however, we may extend this principle further to widen the scope of application of these yogas. Thus, any given house may be treated as a 'lagna' and the relationship of the lord of this house (the `lagnesha') with another lord (the 'karyesha') may be studied in order to know about the events pertaining to a particular house. For example, a relationship or association, through yogas, of the lord of the fifth house with that of the twelfth house may indicate some loss (the twelfth house!) in respect of one's progeny (the fifth house!). Or, a relationship between the seventh lord and the eleventh lord may indicate some gains (the eleventh house!) accruing from wife or business partners (the seventh house!). It may also be of relevance here to consider the signification of a particular planet, and consider its relationship with other planets. Thus, the involvement of the Moon in a relationship may indicate events pertaining to one's mother, or that of Mars those pertaining to one's brother. Finally, a further romantic hue to the interpretation of these yogas is provided by the actual location in the chart of the various actors in the yoga formation.

The actual interpretation of each of the Tajika yogas may thus necessitate the consideration of all of the following factors:

1. The lordship of the planets over houses.
2. The natural significatorship of planets.
3. The houses in which the yoga-producing planets are located.
4. The various planetary aspects or associations influencing the yoga-producing planets.
5. The strength of the yoga-forming planets.

In the classical texts, the terms 'lagnesha' and 'karyesha' are used to convey the strict meaning for the lagna lord and the significator. For the sake of descriptive convenience, these terms will be retained while defining the various yogas.

The Example Chart

The Example Chart already under consideration is replete with several Tajika yogas and will provide a convenient example for reference when the yogas are individually discussed. This chart refers to the forty-first year (w.e.f. August 20, 1984) of the late Mr. Rajiv Gandhi, then the youngest, and the strongest, Prime Minister of India. Since this chart will only too frequently be referred to in the discussion that follows, it is being reproduced here (see Chart X-1).

It is also appropriate here to refer to the birth chart (Chart X-2) of the native and see the promise inherent there. Any events will occur only if promised in the birth chart. A look at the birth chart reveals that the native runs the Vimshottari dasha-antar of Rahu-Jupiter from August 20, 1984 to January 1, 1987. The year in question, i.e., the forty-first year, starts right on August 20, 1984. Rahu in Cancer, according to the sage Parashara, is a Raja Yogakaraka (bestower of royal status) and must appreciably enhance the status of the individual during its dasha. The antardasha lord, Jupiter, is the lord of the fifth house in the birth chart, and forms a powerful benefic combination in the lagna in association with the lagna lord as well as all the remaining natural benefics, viz., the Moon,

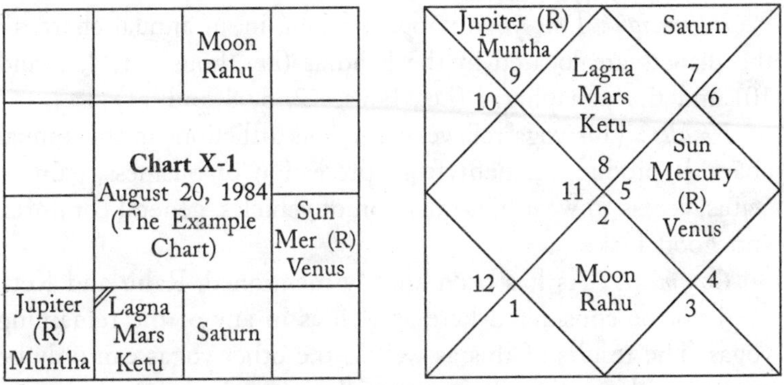

Chart X-1
August 20, 1984
(The Example Chart)

Lagna	09°26'	Mars	07°42'	Venus	21°45'
Sun	03°50'	Mercury (R)	18°20'	Saturn	17°13'
Moon	09°40'	Jupiter (R)	09°38'	Rahu	08°55'

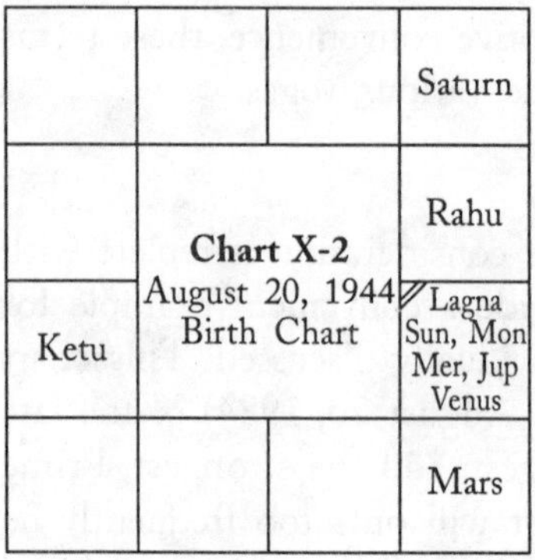

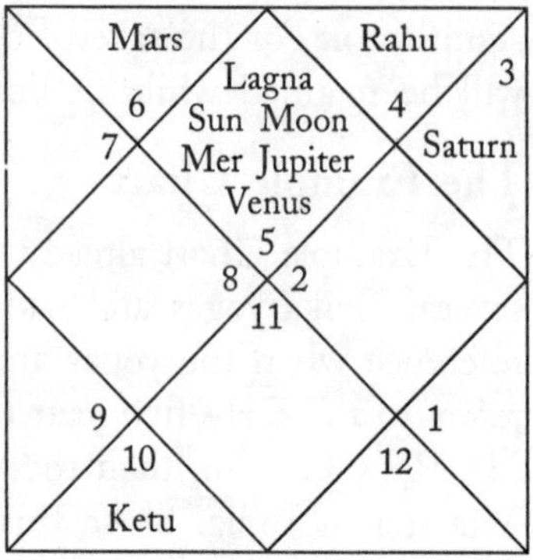

Lagna	14°36'	Mars	01°11'	Venus	18°39'
Sun	03°49'	Mercury	28°33'	Saturn	14°12'
Moon	17°08'	Jupiter	12°10'	Rahu	04°09'

Mercury, and Venus. The eighth house lordship of Jupiter instils into this configuration of planets an element of unexpected suddenness. No wonder, the native enjoyed an extra-ordinary Raja Yoga during this period, and found himself suddenly and unexpectedly catapulted to the most prestigious and coveted post of the Prime Minister of India. These events must find adequate confirmation in the annual chart for the year.

We shall now take up each of the sixteen Tajika yogas individually.

I. THE IKABALA YOGA

This is the 'yoga for good fortune'.

Definition : This yoga happens when, in an annual chart, all the planets are located in the kendras (i.e., houses 1, 4, 7 and 10) and the panapharas (i.e., houses 2, 5, 8 and 11).

Results : This yoga relieves numerous afflictions in the annual chart. It produces benefit from profession or business, gain in status, access to wealth, acquisition of vehicles, general comforts, and good luck.

Comments : As has been already mentioned, Rahu and Ketu need not be considered here as well as in any of the remaining yogas. The results of this as well as the other yogas can only be applied with caution. It is essential to correlate the occurrence of this yoga with the dasha-antardasha in the birth chart. Again, the various results accruing from the yoga as described include gain of wealth, vehicle, status, rise in profession, etc. All these results may not occur in the same proportion. A lot will depend on the strength of the lagna lord in the annual chart. A weak lagna lord generally does not permit the benefits of this yoga to manifest fully. In the presence of a strong lagna lord, this yoga has the potential to promote the name and fame of a person, and to increase his material comforts and possessions. When most of the planets are strong in the annual chart, this yoga produces excellent results. When the lagna lord and the other key planets in the horoscope are weak, the native suffers setbacks.

Another important point is the actual houses where the planets are located. If most of the planets are placed in the eighth house, the results will not necessarily be favourable.

The strength of the tenth lord along with that of the lagna lord determines the extent to which the native gains in respect of his profession and status when this yoga is present. When both these lords are strong, the native gains dignity and recognition. In the Example Chart, with Scorpio ascendant, all the planets, *except Saturn,* are placed in either the kendras or the panapharas. *The yoga thus applies partially.* However, in the Panchavargiya chart, the Vishwa Bala (or the numerical strength) of the lagna lord, Mars, is 14:10:00 units (or 14.016 units), and that of the lord of the tenth house, the Sun, is 14:20:15 units (or 14.337 units). Thus, both the lagna lord and the tenth lord are very strong. The Sun also happens to be the Varshesha. This explains the remarkable rise that the native experienced during this year.

The above situation may be compared with the annual chart cast for the forty-sixth year of the native, commencing on August 20, 1989 (Chart X-3). All the planets are located in the kendras and the panapharas. *The Ikabala yoga applies here fully.* However, it was during this particular year that the native lost the premiership of India, and his party was defeated in the general elections.

Note that the lagna lord, Saturn, is relatively weak (V.B. 7:52:30 units, or 7.875 units) according to the Pancha-vargiya Bala. The tenth lord, Mars, is equally weak (V.B. 7:24:15 units/ 7.404 units). Most of the other planets are also weak The Muntha

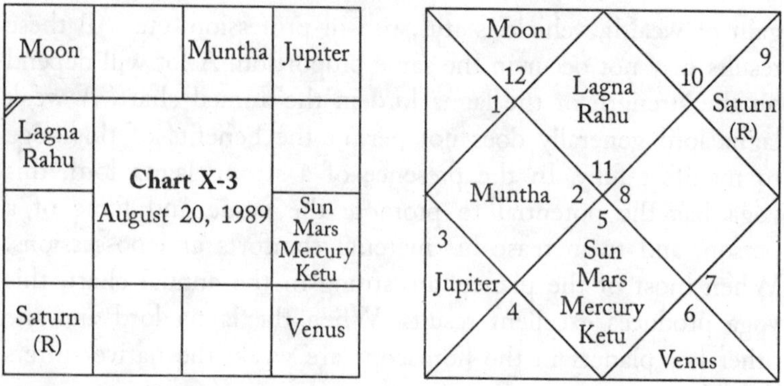

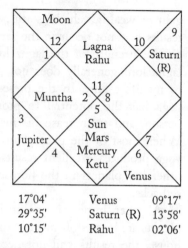

Lagna	23°36'	Mars	17°04'	Venus	09°17'
Sun	03°49'	Mercury	29°35'	Saturn (R)	13°58'
Moon	21°17'	Jupiter	10°15'	Rahu	02°06'

is in the adverse fourth house, with its lord in the most adverse eighth; it is thus unhelpful. The Ikabala yoga, however, did give him some consolation in that he individually won his election and was the 'leader of opposition' in the Lok Sabha, the Indian 'lower house', having a rank equivalent to that of a cabinet minister. Note that during this year of relative decline, the Sun was very strong, happened to be the Varshesha, and had a favaourable relationship with the lagna lord.

II. THE INDUVARA YOGA

This is the 'yoga for misfortune' (literally, 'Idbara' means 'misfortune').

Definition : This yoga happens when all the planets are located in the apoklima houses (i.e., houses 3, 6, 9 and 12).

Results: This yoga is considered inauspicious. It leads to disappointments, fall in status, illness, mental worries, and fear from opponents.

Comments : Planets are considered auspicious when they are located in the kendras and panapharas. They are deemed inauspicious when located in the apoklimas. It may not be very frequent to see an Induvara yoga in full form, with all the planets in the apoklimas. In general, when a majority of planets (five or more) fall in the apoklimas, with only one or two planets escaping into the kendras/panapharas, the Induvara yoga may be said to be, at least partially, present.

In Chart X-4, five planets, viz., the Moon, Mars, Jupiter, Venus and Saturn, are located in houses 3, 6 and 12. The remaining two planets, viz., the Sun and Mercury, are in the eleventh house in the Rahu-Ketu axis. The native, a known asthmatic, had a severe exacerbation of her symptoms and was virtually on her death bed. Of course, she was running an adverse dasha/antardasha in her birth chart also.

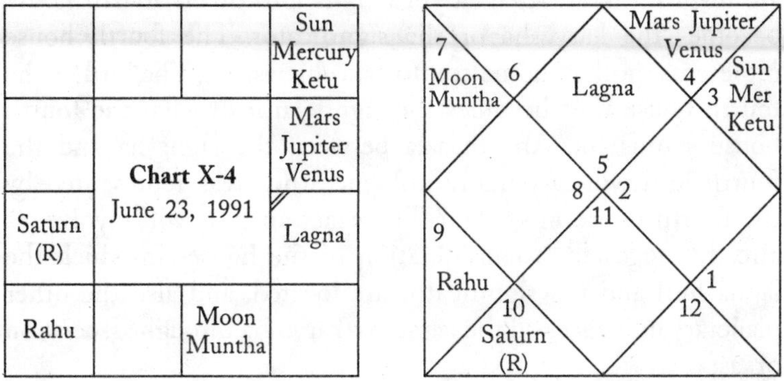

Lagna	04°20'	Mars	22°41'	Venus	22°32'
Sun	07°30'	Mercury	14°47'	Saturn (R)	12°02'
Moon	24°26'	Jupiter	19°07'	Rahu	25°16'

III. THE ITHASALA YOGA

This, literally 'the yoga of intermixing', is the most important of the Tajika yogas. It signifies an exercise of mutual influence between the planets participating in the formation of this yoga. Also called as the 'Muthsil' yoga, it provides the key to the understanding of several other yogas that follow. In this yoga, a faster-moving planet transmits its 'radiance' or strength to a slower-moving planet. In the process, both the planets share the benefit. The yoga necessarily involves two planets for its formation. The Ithasala yoga is generally considered to be a beneficial yoga. In practice, however, it may not always be beneficial. The beneficence or otherwise of this yoga depends largely on the house ownership of the involved planets, as also on their inherent nature or on their significatorship. The presence of this yoga signifies the fulfilment of some event.

The Ithasala yoga is technically described to be forming between the lagnesha and the karyesha, i.e., the lagna lord and the significator. As has already been discussed, these terms need not be applied strictly, and some flexibility in their application is necessary in order to permit an extended interpretation. The reason for retaining these terms while defining the various yogas has already been referred to.

The results of the Ithasala may be analysed thus. Let us assume that the lagna lord and the lord of the fourth house ate involved in an Ithasala yoga. This lord of the fourth house becomes the karyesha or the significator. The fourth house represents mother, home comforts, vehicles, etc. The lord of the fourth house thus becomes the significator of what the fourth house stands for. An Ithasala between the lagnesha and the fourth lord will favourably influence the areas represented by the fourth house in general. The exact analysis will involve, as already suggested, a consideration of the houses in which the lagna lord and the significator are located, and also the other planetary influences on the lagnesha/karyesha through association or aspect.

The Essentials of an Ithasala Yoga

The following basic information must be assimilated before understanding the formation of an Ithasala yoga.

1. *The Relative Motion of Planets*: As has already been indicated, in an Ithasala yoga, a fast-moving planet transmits its influence to a slow-mover. Different planets have their different velocities. The Moon, for example, moves the fastest of all while Saturn happens to be the slowest. If a slow-moving planet is ahead of a fast-moving planet, the latter is potentially capable of approaching, and finally overtaking, the former. This would permit a mutual interaction which is the essence of an Ithasala. A slow-moving planet behind a fast-moving one has no chance of overtaking the latter. Thus, an Ithasala, which literally means an 'intermingling', is only possible between two planets when the slower-moving of the two is ahead of the faster-moving one.

What is meant by 'ahead' and 'behind'? A planet is said to be 'ahead of' or 'behind' another planet depending on its degrees of longitude in a given sign. How far a planet is advanced in a giving sign is decided by taking into account only the degrees of longitude after deleting the completed rashis. In the Example Chart, for instance, the longitude of the Sun is 123°50', while that of the Moon is 39°40'. Reduced into signs, the longitudes of the two will be $4^s3°50'$ and $1^s9°40'$ respectively. After deleting the completed signs (4 in case of the Sun and 1 in case of the Moon), we get 3°50' for the Sun and 9°40' for the Moon. Thus the Moon, at greater number of degrees in a sign, is ahead of the Sun.

The planets Moon Mercury, Venus, Sun, Mars, Jupiter, and Saturn are considered to be progressively slower in motion in this order, with Saturn being the slowest of all. In the instance quoted above, the relatively slower Sun is behind the faster-moving Moon and thus has no chance of joining, or overtaking, the Moon. An Ithasala yoga will thus not be possible between the two.

2. *Mutual Aspect* : Along with the pre-requisite of a fast-moving planet being behind the slow-moving planet, the other requirement is that of a mutual aspect between the participants in an Ithasala yoga. Planets not aspecting each other generally do not constitute an Ithasala yoga. *The nature of mutual aspect (friendly or inimical) does not affect the existence of an Ithasala yoga though it may influence it qualitatively.*

3. *The Orbs of Influence* : Each planet has been assigned a particular orb over which it exerts its influence. This orb extends on either side of a planet (i.e., both ahead and behind) for a specific number of degrees. This orb of influence is called the *Deeptamsha* (literally, 'orb of radiance'). Beyond its individual orb or Deeptamsha, the planet loses its influence. An Ithasala yoga materialises only when planets fall within the orbs of each other. The Deeptamsha values of various planets have been shown in Table X-1.

Thus, the Sun exerts its influence for 15 degrees on either side of itself; the Moon does so for 12 degrees, and so on.

4. *Application of the Deeptamsha Range* : When the orbs of two planets come in contact with each other, a mutual influence comes into existence. The closer the two planets are degree-wise, the greater this influence on each other. The Ithasala yoga, however, does not commence when the outer orbs of the two planets meet. For Ithasala to occur, a mean of the individual Deeptamshas of the two planets is to be considered.

Table X-1
Deeptamshas of Planets (in degrees)

Planets	Sun	Mon	Mar	Mer	Jup	Ven	Sat
Deeptamshas	15	12	8	7	9	7	9

Let us refer to the Example Chart for clarification. Here, Mars, the lagna lord, is at 7°42' in the lagna itself. The Sun, the lord of the tenth house, is at 3°50 in the tenth house. The Sun is the faster of the two and is behind Mars when we consider the degrees of these two planets in their respective houses. These two (the Sun and Mars) are in a mutual (though hostile) aspect. As already stated, the presence of a mutual aspect is of essence here and not the nature of the aspect. Thus there is a possibility of an Ithasala yoga forming between the Sun and Mars.

Now we consider the Deeptamshas of the Sun (15°) and Mars (8°). The mean of the two values (i.e., 15 + 8, divided by 2) comes to be 11.5°. Mars has to be within 11.5° from the Sun to have an Ithasala with the Sun. Here, Mars is 3°52' (Mars-Sun, or 7°42' - 3°50' = 3°52') ahead of the Sun. The two are thus located well within their Deeptamsha range. They are, therefore, in Ithasala. Thus, for the purpose of the Ithasala yoga, the term Deeptamsha range means a mean of the individual Deeptamshas of the two planets participating in an Ithasala. An Ithasala between the lagna lord and the lord of the tenth house is highly desirable, and indicates rise in one's profession and favours from the government.[1] The yoga is further beneficial since it involves houses one and ten (i.e., the planets forming it are not only the lords of the first and the tenth houses, they are also located in these houses). The closer the two participants are in an Ithasala yoga, the more intense are the results. In addition, the results also depend on the individual strength of the planets according to the Pancha-vargiya Bala. Weak planets causing an Ithasala yoga can only produce ordinary results.

1. In Parashari astrology, the conjunction of the lagna lord and the tenth lord in the lagna or the 10th house is a combination for great fame.

Types of Ithasala Yoga

Three types of Ithasala yoga are described.

1. *The Vartamana Ithasala* (or 'the Ithasala-in-operation'). When the term Ithasala is applied, it is generally the Vartamana Ithasala that is meant. The example of the Ithasala yoga clarified above in relation to the Deeptamsha range is an example of the Vartamana Ithasala only. This yoga, as already clarified, is said to occur between two planets subject to the following conditions:

(i) Mutual aspect between the lagnesha and the karyesha (i.e., the participants in the yoga);

(ii) The fast-moving planet is at lesser number of degrees of longitude (after excluding the completed signs) than the slow-moving planet;

(iii) The two planets fall within their Deeptamsha range (i.e., half of the sum of their individual Deeptamshas).

The Rashi-Anta Muthsil (or the Ithasala involving a planet at the end of a sign): The *Rashi-Anta* (or *Rashyanta)* is the end of a sign or rashi. A planet located at 29° or more in a rashi is considered to be in the Rashyanta. A Planet in Rashyanta extends its influence to the next house also. The Rashyanta Ithasala is a type of Vartamana Ithasala where the two planets are not in Ithasala according to the definition of Ithasala as given above, because the faster-moving planet is at Rashyanta, and when it enters the next house it would immediately establish Ithasala with the slow-moving planet.

In Chart X-5, the Moon is in Rashyanta. Being faster than both Mercury and Venus, and also being far advanced compared to both of them, it does not establish Ithasala with either of them. Being in Rashyanta, however, it also functions from the beginning of the next house, from which position it will be behind both Mercury and Venus, still maintaining mutual aspects with them, and falling within the Deeptamsha ranges of both Mercury and Venus. This is an example of Rashyanta Muthsil. Here, the Moon being the 10th lord operating from the eighth house and establishing an Ithasala with the eighth lord Venus indicates an obstruction or interruption to the native's Karma or function. Mercury as lord of the twelfth house in this chart, is the eighth lord in the birth chart and, therefore, none too good to associate with for the Moon. Mercury and Jupiter form another Ithasala of the Vartamana type as described above. Incidentally, the Moon and Mars falling on the same degree also form a type of Ithasala soon to be described. Mars here is also on Rashyanta. Mars does not establish a Rashyanta yoga with either Mercury or Venus, since being slower than both of them it does not qualify for Ithasala. Besides, considering it to be operating from the next house, i.e., the fourth, it loses aspect on Mercury located in the fifth house.

2. *The Poorna Ithasala* (or 'the perfect' Ithasala). This yoga is subject to the following conditions:

(i) Mutual aspect between the lagnesha and the karyesha (or the two participants).

(ii) The fast-moving planet is behind the slow-moving planet, but within one degree.

In the example quoted above (Chart X-5), the Moon and Mars are in Poorna Ithasala. The Poorna Ithasala may be said to exist, in practice, even if the slow-moving planet has lagged behind the fast-moving one but is still within one degree from the fast-mover. However, as the fast-moving planet separates from the slow-moving one, the intensity of the yoga rapidly

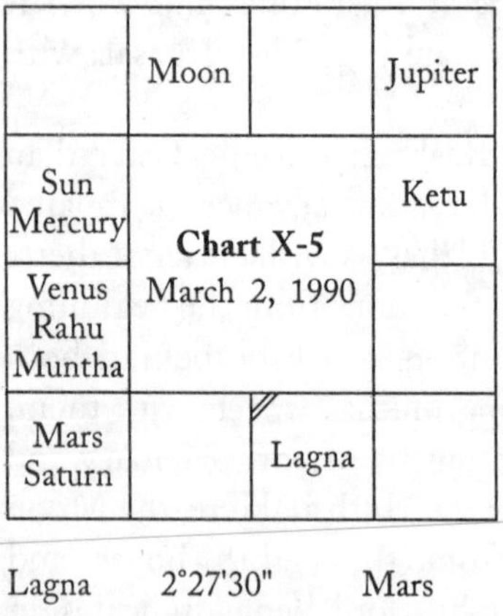

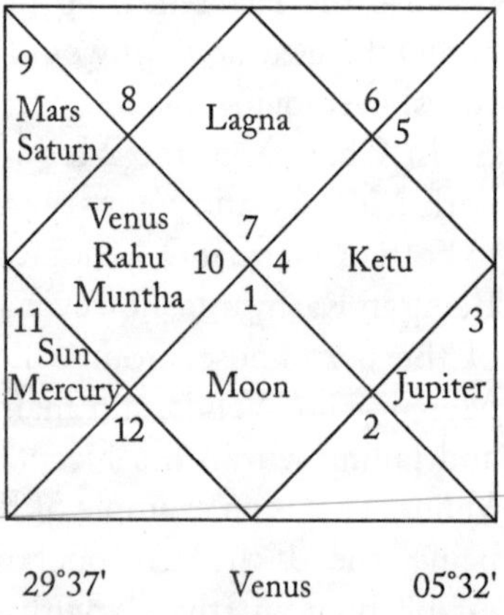

Lagna	2°27'30"	Mars	29°37'	Venus	05°32'
Sun	18°05'	Mercury	04°30'	Saturn	28°32'
Moon	29°17'	Jupiter	07°08'	Rahu	22°30'

declines till it comes to naught as the two separate by more than one degree, yielding place to an adverse yoga to be described later.

Chart X-6 needs to be considered in greater details:

(i) The lagna lord Mercury is in Vartamana Ithasala with the eighth lord Mars in the fourth house. In the birth chart, Mars is the lagna lord and Mercury the eighth lord. This does not augur well for the health of the native. He is a known case of heart disease.

(ii) There is a Poorna Ithasala between Mars, the eighth lord (inheritance), and Venus, the second lord (wealth) involving houses two and four (land, house, vehicle). The lagna lord in the fourth house also establishes Ithasala with the fourth lord, Jupiter, in the twelfth house (distant land), and with the second lord, Venus, in the second house. The native had the opportunity to derive benefit from inherited wealth (both land and money) long lying in a far off place, and long forgotten. He also acquired a house in Delhi.

(iii) Ithasala between Jupiter (the fourth lord, signifying vehicles) and Venus (the Karaka or significator for vehicles) involving houses two and twelve, along with their individual Ithasala with the lagna lord situated in the fourth house ensured the acquisition of a vehicle from the money he inherited.

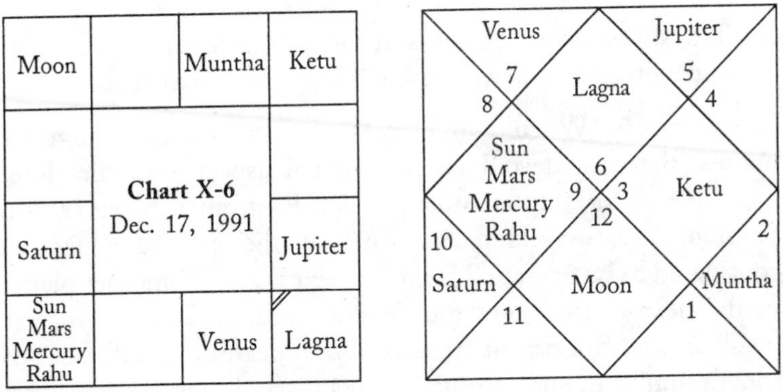

Lagna	24°02'	Mars	18°59'	Venus	18°34'
Sun	00°37'	Mercury	14°24'	Saturn	10°29'
Moon	29°32'	Jupiter	20°33'	Rahu	16°20'

(iv) The Moon at 29°32' is in Rashyanta. Being a fast-moving planet far advanced in a sign, it cannot establish Ithasala with any planet. However, being in Rashyanta, it may be considered to be operating from the next house where it will be in the beginning of the sign, and capable of causing a Rashyanta Ithasala with the Sun as well as Saturn. An Ithasala Between the eleventh lord (the Moon) and the twelfth lord (the Sun) further confirms sudden, unexpected gains from a far off place. An Ithasala Between the fifth and eleventh lords is good for children.

(v) The birth lagna sign, Scorpio, falls in the third house signifying something significant in respect of the sibling during the year. The lord of the third house, Mars, is placed in the fourth house (second from the third) in Ithasala with the tenth (eighth from the third) lord, Mercury. Mars is also in Poorna Ithasala with the ninth and second lord (seventh and twelfth lord from the third), Venus. It is in close proximity to the RKA. The native lost his brother during this year. Mars is not only the third lord but also the Karaka for brother.

3. *Bhavishyat Ithasala* (or 'the Ithasala-to-be') : This is subject to the following conditions:

(i) The fast-moving planet is at the end of a sign (29° or more; i.e., in Rashyanta);

(ii) The slow-moving planet is in the beginning of the next sign and within the Deeptamsha range of the two planets.

Comments : When two planets are situated in contiguous houses, they are devoid of any mutual aspect and, therefore, incapable of forming an Ithasala. The Rashyanta, however, is a different situation. Here, a planet at the end of a sign is considered to be operating from the next house. If another planet in the next house is not too far advanced, an Ithasala yoga is possible. The Bhavishyat Ithasala also indicates the fulfilment of some promise though it usually takes place during the later part of the year.

In Chart X-7, the Moon (twelfth lord) and Mercury (eleventh and second lord) are involved in Poorna Ithasala, the two being within one degree and are mutually aspecting. During the year in question, the native suffered losses (twelfth house : loss; eleventh house : income; second house : wealth) through theft. Mercury is also on the last degree of Sagittarius. The lagna lord, the Sun, is in the next house, in Capricorn, at 11°9'. The Deeptamsha range of the Sun and Mercury (15+7, divided by two) is 11°. The slow-moving Sun is just beyond their Deeptamsha range. This may in practice be taken as an example of the Bhavishyat Ithasala. Thus, Mercury the lord of the houses of income and wealth, establishes a relationship with the twelfth lord on the one hand, and the lagna lord in the sixth house on the other. The loss of earnings and wealth occurred through theft (indicated by the sixth house). The lagna lord, the Sun, is also involved in an Ithasala with the sixth lord Saturn in the sixth house.

The results of the Bhavishyat Ithasala generally occur during the later part of the year. It will be interesting to note that in the case of the above native, one theft occurred in the beginning of his year (indicated by the Poorna Ithasala, which indicates early accomplishment) and the other just before the year concluded (indicated by the Bhavishyat Ithasala suggesting delay). *This makes it amply obvious that an Ithasala generally indicates the accomplishment of an event which need not necessarily be favourable.* The actual nature of results will depend on both the planets as well as the houses involved.

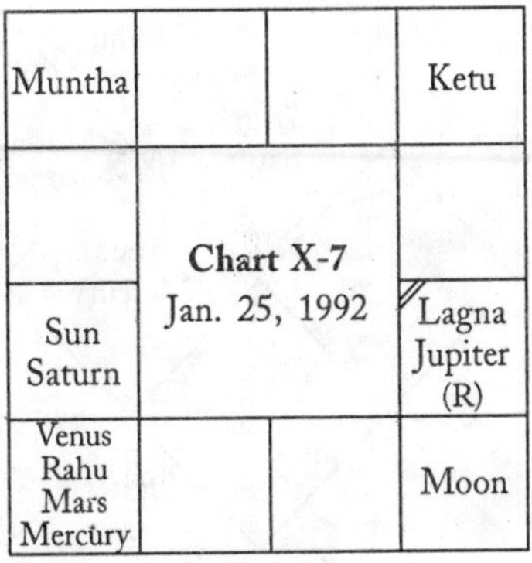

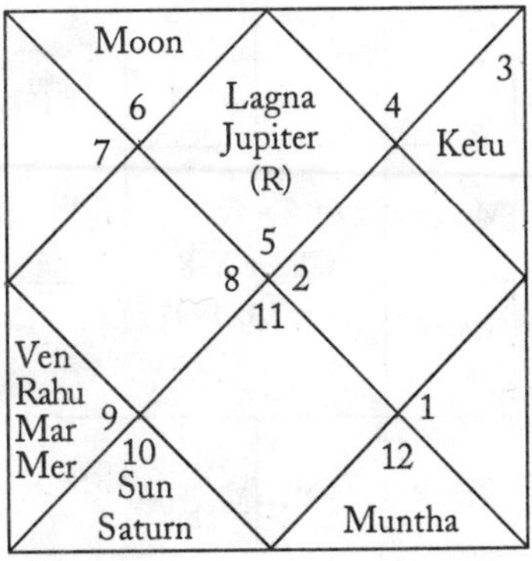

Lagna	20°47'	Mars	18°22'	Venus	06°41'
Sun	11°09'	Mercury	29°29'	Saturn	14°58'
Moon	28°57'	Jupiter (R)	19°50'	Rahu	15°50'

The Bhavishyat Ithasala has been mentioned above as occurring between two planets placed in contiguous houses, hence not mutually aspecting, with the fast-moving planet at the end of a sign in the preceding house, and the slow-moving planet in the beginning of a sign in the succeeding house. How then about a situation in which the fast-moving planet is at the end of a sign in the succeeding house, with the slow-moving one is the beginning of a sign in the preceding house? For, though the two planets are not mutually aspecting if considered in contiguous houses, they will establish aspect if the fast-moving planet is considered to be operating from the following house for reason of its being in Rashyanta. The only difference here will be that the two planets will influence each other by aspect while in the actual definition as given above they would do so by conjunction.

In Chart X-8, the Moon in the eleventh house in Rashyanta has no apparent relation with Mars in the preceding, i.e., the tenth, house at 3°56' in Libra. When the fast-moving Moon is considered operating from the twelfth house, the slow-moving Mars falls just ahead of the Moon within their Deeptamsha range, and mutually aspecting. This must produce results equivalent to a Bhavishyat Ithasala. Mars, the lord of the fourth and the eleventh houses, is in the tenth in Ithasala with the lagna lord Saturn in the lagna. The Moon in the eleventh house, about to enter the twelfth and thus establishing a sort of a Bhavishyat Ithasala with the fourth lord Mars ensured the acquisition of a

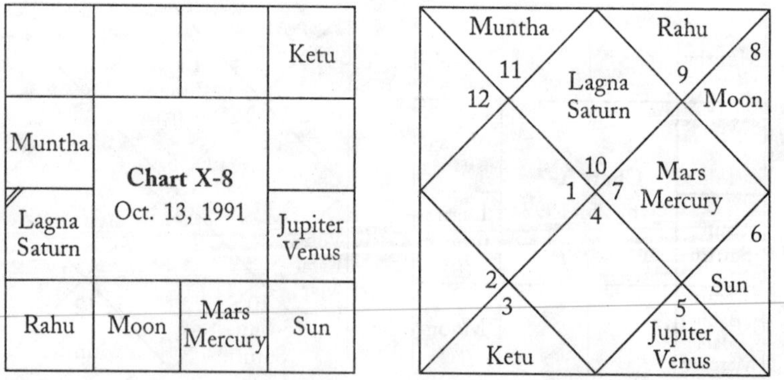

Lagna	27°50'	Mars	03°56'	Venus	11°02'
Sun	25°42'	Mercury	20°38'	Saturn	06°30'
Moon	29°56'	Jupiter	12°30'	Rahu	19°55'

vehicle toward the end of the year. The Moon is the seventh lord, of travel, entering the twelfth house, of distant or overseas journey, linking with the fourth lord. On acquisition of the vehicle, the native along with her parents, went on tour to a neighbouring state by the recently acquired vehicle. What was the 'aqueous connection' in this journey, was my question. The Moon, a watery planet, is operating from the twelfth house. This visit, I was told, was to Udaipur, the 'city of lakes', in Rajasthan where the native did a lot of boating, and enjoyed.

Note : Another situation of Bhavishyat Ithasala has been said to arise when the following conditions apply :

(i) Two planets mutually aspecting each other;

(ii) The slow-moving planet is ahead of the fast-moving planets;

(iii) The slow-moving planet, however, is beyond the Deeptamsha range.

When this sort of a Bhavishyat Ithasala is being considered, the additional points to be noted are:

(a) For this yoga to fructify, the difference between the two planets must be *more than the individual Deeptamshas of the fast-moving planet.*

(b) When the slow-moving planet is ahead of the fast-moving planet by *more than the sum of their individual Deeptamshas,* the yoga may be said to be non-existent.

Let us refer to the Example Chart (Chart X-1). The Moon, at 9°40' is aspecting Venus at 21°45'. The difference between the two is thus 12°5'. The Deeptamsha range of Moon-Venus, i.e., the mean of their individual Deeptamshas, is 9°30'. Venus has thus gone beyond the range necessary for an Ithasala. It is also located beyond the 12 degrees which are the individual Deeptamshas of the Moon. There is thus a Bhavishyat Ithasala between the Moon and Venus.

In the same chart, let us consider the relationship of the Sun (3°40') and Saturn (17°13'), which aspect each other from the tenth and the twelfth houses respectively. The slow-moving

Saturn is 13°23' ahead of the Sun, and beyond their Deeptamsha range of 12 degrees. Saturn is, however, within the 15 degrees which happen to be the individual Deeptamshas of the fast-moving Sun. There is thus no Bhavishyat Ithasala here. This definition of the Bhavishyat Ithasala needs wider application and empirical testing.

Important Points for Consideration

A few important points, particularly in regard to the direct or retrograde motion of planets, need special consideration while dealing with the Ithasala yoga. They are:

1. *A retrograde fast-moving planet at lesser number of degrees of longitude does not produce Ithasala* since its motion is in opposite direction to that of the more advanced slow-moving planet, and the two are moving away from each other. Thus, in the Example Chart, there is no Ithasala between Jupiter and Saturn although the fast-moving Jupiter is behind the slower Saturn, the two are mutually in aspect, and they are also within their Deeptamsha range, because the fast-moving Jupiter is retrograde.

2. *A slow-moving retrograde planet at greater number of degrees of longitude increases the intensity of the Ithasala.* Thus, in the Example Chart again, the Sun and Jupiter are in Ithasala, and the retrogression of Jupiter, slow-moving and ahead of the Sun, only increases the intensity of the Ithasala.

3. When both the lagnesha and the karyesha are retrograde, debilitated, combust, or otherwise weak, the Ithasala yoga generally does not fructify.

IV. THE ISHRAFA YOGA

This is the 'yoga of separation'. The word *Israf* indicates expense or wastage. It is also known as the 'Mushrif yoga'.

Definition : The Ishrafa yoga obtains when:

(i) The fast-moving planet is one degree or more ahead of the slow-moving planet; and

(ii) The two are mutually aspecting.

Results : This yoga is the reverse of the Ithasala. It indicates obstacles and failures.

Note : An Ishrafa yoga involving benefics only tends to hamper work but is not considered to be too harmful. Caused by malefics, it is particularly bad, and not only causes failure in undertakings but numerous additional troubles and disappointments.

Comments: With the fast-moving planet ahead of the slow-moving planet, the two have no chance of meeting each other, and thus there is no likelihood of their sharing each other's strength. This yoga of separation starts operating as soon as the slow-moving planet and the fast-moving planet separate by more than one degree. The yoga tends to lose in intensity as the difference between the two planets goes on increasing, until it ceases to exist as they separate by more than their Deeptamsha range (arrived at by halving the sum of individual Deeptamshas of the two planets).

In the Example Chart, the Moon is ahead of the slower-moving lagna lord Mars, and is located in the RKA in the seventh, a maraka, house. The Moon is the karaka for mother. The native lost his mother. The same Moon also has an Ishrafa with the Sun. These two planets are lords of the ninth and the tenth houses, and are located in the seventh and the tenth houses respectively. This situation indicates the development of such new associations (or the cessation of such older ones!) in the pursuit of one's *Karma* (the tenth house), which could eventually prove only unfortunate or harmful to one's career (Ishrafa between the ninth and the tenth lords). While putting forth this sort of analysis, it is important to bear in mind that the Sun and the Moon are benefic planets for the Scorpio ascendant and their Ishrafa may not prove to be too bad for the native. In addition, there is a highly beneficial Vartamana Ithasala between the tenth lord, the Sun, and the lagna lord, Mars, both quite powerful according to the Pancha-vargiya Bala. This would more than neutralise any minor obstructive influence (like the Ishrafa yoga in question) on the tenth house.

In this same chart, Saturn at 17°13' also establishes Ishrafa with Mercury at 18°20', and with Venus at 21°45'. While the Saturn-Venus Ishrafa is easy to understand, the Saturn-Mercury is rather difficult to interpret. In the latter case, the fast-moving Mercury is ahead of the slow-moving Saturn, but this Mercury is retrograde. Does it then mean an Ithasala between the two since they are proceeding towards each other? Or does it mean a more intense Ishrafa since the distance between the two is gradually decreasing? Should we also consider the likely astronomical possibility of the retrograde planet eventually joining the direct planet and creating a situation like a Poorna Ithasala, or that of the retrograde planet resuming direct motion before closing up on the slow-moving planet and thereby retaining the situation of an Ishrafa? *A large number of charts with such situations will have to be examined before formulating any conclusions.*

Another situation of an Ishrafa yoga arises when the slow-moving planet, behind the faster-moving one, is retrograde. In Chart X-9, there is an Ishrafa between the lagna lord and the eighth lord, invoking houses 3 and 7. The slow-moving eighth lord, Saturn, is retrograde. An Ithasala between the lagna lord and the eighth lord is generally adverse; an Ishrafa is worse. Is it still worse with the slow-moving planet retrograde? The native lost his life as a consequence of a bomb explosion. Note the aspect of Mars (explosions, ammunition), lord of the sixth house (enemies, accidents), on the lagna lord, from the twelfth house (departure from the world).

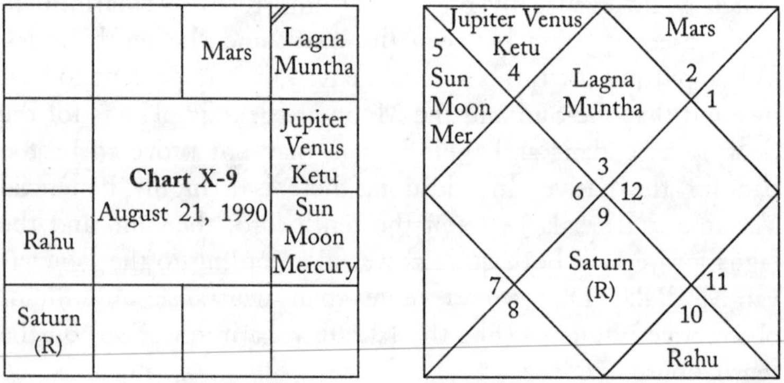

Lagna	07°15'	Mars	00°30'	Venus	14°46'
Sun	03°50'	Mercury	28°50'	Saturn (R)	25°50'
Moon	08°02'	Jupiter	06°48'	Rahu	13°31'

V. THE NAKTA YOGA

This is the 'yoga with a fast linkage'.

Definition : The necessary conditions for this yoga are :

(i) No mutual aspect between the lagnesha and the karyesha;

(ii) A faster-moving planet is located between the lagnesha and the karyesha, in mutual aspect with both, encompassing them both within its individual Deeptamshas.

Result : Accomplishment with the help of someone.

Comments : When two planets are not in mutual aspect, there is a lack of relationship between them. The intervening planet provides the necessary link. This intervening planet transmits the strength (the actual term used is *Teja or glow*) from the planet behind (the faster of the lagnesha and the karyesha) to the one ahead (the slower of the two). While an Ithasala indicates the accomplishment of a job by the native himself, a Nakta necessitates the intervention of another.

The important point in the Nakta yoga is the absence of any mutual aspect between two planets, and a link provided by a third one. This intervening planet must aspect both the mutually non-aspecting planets. Either of the two non-aspecting and, therefore, unrelated planets must lie within the individual Deeptamshas of the intervening planet. This intervening planet has to be faster than both the unrelated planets to ensure a smooth accomplishment of a purpose. *It goes without saying that a Nakta yoga cannot form with the Moon as one of the non-aspecting participants,* since there is no other planet which is faster than the Moon so as to qualify for the intervening link.

Must the faster of the two mutually non-aspecting planets be behind the slower one so as to effect a Nakta yoga? Perhaps it is preferable.

As has already been stated, the terms 'lagnesha' and 'karyesha' are being quite freely employed even when it is not always the lagna lord that is being taken to be meant by 'lagnesha'.

Likely variations of the Nakta yoga: The standard Nakta yoga demands that a faster planet should be located between the two non-aspecting slow-moving planets, and the latter two should be within the range of individual Deeptamshas of the fast-moving planet. There is a possibility of the faster planet establishing an Ithasala with one slow mover and an Ishrafa with the other slow mover though not necessarily so. The faster planet acts as a link between the mutually non-aspecting lagnesha-keryesha. We have, however, also seen that if the faster planet is behind both the slow movers and not between them, while both the slow movers remain within the individual Deeptamshas of the fast mover, with the possibility of the latter forming an Ithasala with both, the fast mover still provides a link between the two. Further, even if the fast mover has gone beyond the degrees of both the lagnesha-karyesha while still aspecting the latter two from within its individual Deeptamshas, with the possibility of an Ishrafa yoga with both, some sort of a link between the lagnesha and karyesha is still in existence. We may thus have three different variations of the Nakta yoga as follows:

(i) *Nakta yoga with double Ithasala* : In the Example Chart, there is no mutual aspect between Mars, the lagna lord, and Jupiter, the lord of the second house, since the two are placed in 2/12 from each other. They have, therefore, no direct link with each other. However, the tenth lord, the Sun, aspects both of them from the tenth house. The Sun is faster than both Mars and Jupiter, and related with them through an Ithasala yoga. In any case, both Mars and Jupiter fall within the individual Deeptamshas of the Sun. Thus Mars and Jupiter become involved in a Nakta yoga through the Sun. This appears to be the best form of the Nakta yoga since a two-way Ithasala is effected.

Chart X-10 is another example of a Nakta yoga involving a double Ithasala. Here, the lagna lord, Venus, located in the eleventh house, has no relation with the fourth and fifth lord, Saturn in the fourth house. However, the tenth lord, the Moon, located in the eighth house, establishes Ithasala with the lagna lord and with the fourth/fifth lord. Thus, a Nakta yoga is formed between the lagna lord and the fourth/fifth lord. A similar yoga obtains between the seventh lord, Mars, and Saturn again with the help of the Moon. Between the lagna lord and the seventh lord, both located in the eleventh house, there is an Ishrafa since the fast-moving Venus is situated ahead of the slow-moving

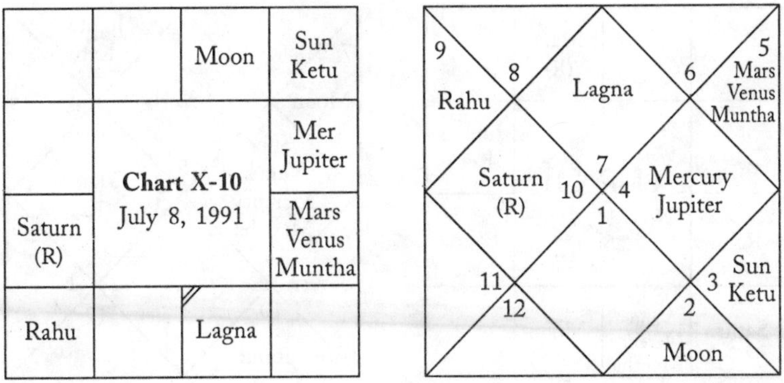

Chart X-10
July 8, 1991

Lagna	16°04'	Mars	01°45'	Venus	04°17'
Sun	21°47'	Mercury	12°52'	Saturn (R)	11°07'
Moon	01°00'	Jupiter	22°03'	Rahu	25°12'

Mars. This mutual Ishrafa has a neutralising factor in the Moon which is in Ithasala with both Mars and Venus. The native, who had to separate from his wife and children, finally united with them thanks to a Nakta yoga. The location of the tenth lord in the eighth house caused fluctuations in career but the involvement of the eleventh house did not permit any lasting damage.

Let us look at this chart for his wife, with the seventh house taken as lagna. The tenth (and eleventh) lord, Saturn, is in the tenth house in Ithasala yoga with the fourth lord, the Moon, and in a Nakta yoga with the eighth lord (and lagna lord), Mars, located in the fifth house. She had to temporarily discontinue her job in order to pursue higher studies (fifth house !). Yogas involving the eleventh house or eleventh lord generally produce benefic results in the long run. Those involving the eighth house or eighth lord generally produce obstructions or discontinuity, which may be damaging or beneficial depending upon other, attendant factors.

(ii) *One Ithasala-one Ishrafa* : This is the standard Nakta yoga as described in the classics. In Chart X-11, there is no aspect between Jupiter (lord of the fifth and the eighth houses, in the twelfth house) and Saturn (lord of the sixth and the seventh houses, in the fifth house). However, the faster-moving Moon is located in the third house and aspects both Jupiter

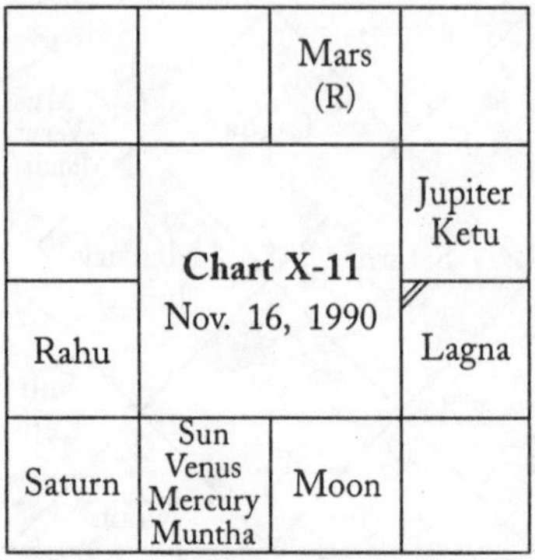

Chart X-11
Nov. 16, 1990

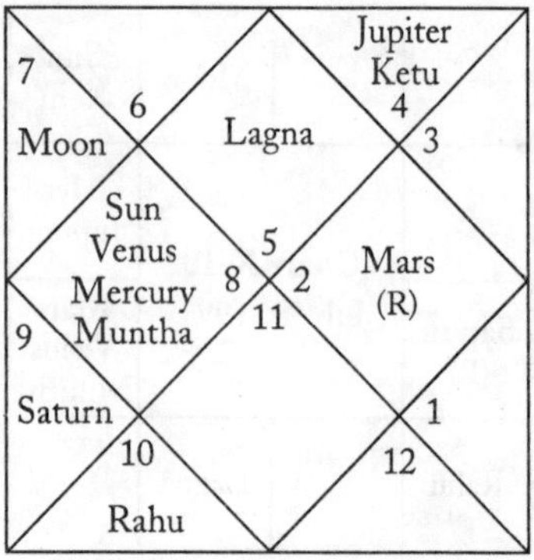

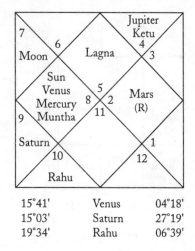

Lagna	28°08'	Mars (R)	15°41'	Venus	04°18'
Sun	00°30'	Mercury	15°03'	Saturn	27°19'
Moon	24°48'	Jupiter	19°34'	Rahu	06°39'

and Saturn. The Moon at 24°48' establishes Ithasala with Saturn at 27°19', and Ishrafa with Jupiter at 19°34'. Thus a link is established between Jupiter and Saturn through the fast-moving Moon. The 'Ishrafa' link probably reduces the quality of the Nakta yoga, and the malefic lordship of all the three participants in this yoga makes it distinctly malefic. It was during this particular year that the native had to separate from his wife and child, and undergo tremendous suffering, including imprisonment, with his father-in-law (third house; ninth from the seventh) being an active ingredient in a mixture of malefics.

(iii) *Nakta yoga with double Ishrafa* : In Chart X-12, Jupiter, the lord of the eighth house in the lagna, at 14°26', has no relation with Mercury, the lord of the second and the eleventh in the eighth house, at 15°24'. However, the twelfth lord, the Moon, at 19°46', aspects both Mercury and Jupiter, and establishes a link between the two. However, the faster-moving Moon is located ahead of both Mercury and Jupiter. Thus, it establishes an Ishrafa with Jupiter on the one hand and with Mercury on the other. Such a Nakta yoga has to be qualitatively inferior to the other two varieties mentioned above since the link involves two Ishrafa yogas. During this particular year, the native of this annual chart lost her valuables and earnings repeatedly, and suffered ill health. This

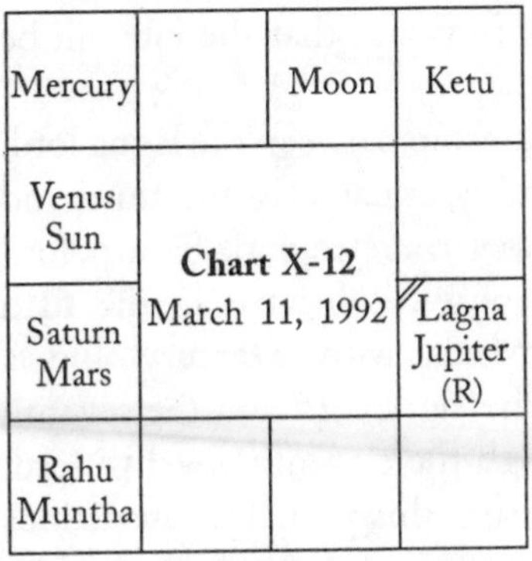

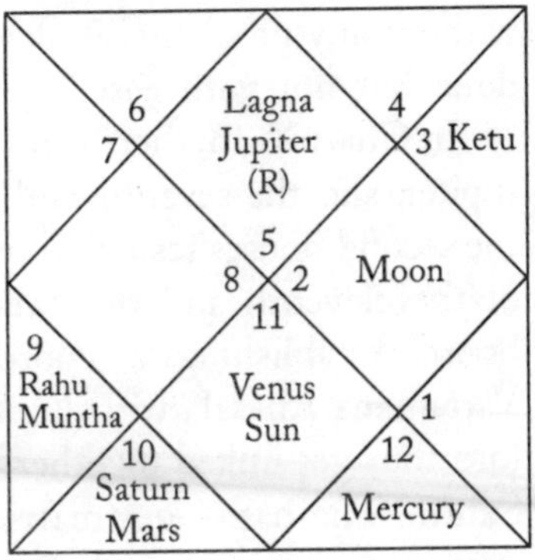

Lagna	20°20'	Mars	23°25'	Venus	02°40'
Sun	27°25'	Mercury	15°24'	Saturn	20°14'
Moon	19°46'	Jupiter (R)	14°26'	Rahu	12°48'

is in keeping with the lordship of planets (Jupiter : eighth lord; Mercury eleventh and second lord; and the Moon : twelfth lord), and the houses involved (lagna, eighth, and tenth).

A Nakta yoga, like the Ithasala, thus need not be always beneficial. An analysis of a given yoga necessarily involves the consideration of the lordship as well as the house occupation of planets.

VI. THE YAMAYA YOGA

This is the 'yoga with a slow linkage'.

Definition : A Yamaya yoga forms when:

(i) There is no mutual aspect between the lagnesha and the karyesha; and

(ii) An intervening slow-moving planet aspects both the lagnesha and the karyesha from within its Deeptamshas.

Results : Fulfilment of a promise with the help of someone, but with some difficulty.

Comments : The Yamaya yoga resembles the Nakta with the difference that here the link between the two mutually non-aspecting planets is provided by a slow intervening planet. As in the Nakta, so in the Yamaya, the presence of a link indicates the role of an intermediary in the fulfilment of a promise. When the linking planet is strong, the accomplishment is quick and without any problems. A slow link indicates that the job will be done but not with ease.

In Chart X-13, there is no relationship between the lagna lord, Jupiter, and the seventh lord, Mercury, situated in the third and the second houses respectively. However, a retrograde Saturn, lord of the eleventh and the twelfth houses, is located in the fifth house, establishing a Poorna Ithasala with Mercury and a Vartamana Ithasala with Jupiter. The lagna lord and the seventh lord thus get linked together through the eleventh/ twelfth lord, Saturn. The native got married during this year. The auspicious event was accomplished through the help of the native's elder sibling (the eleventh lord!) as well as her husband's maternal aunt (the twelfth lord, sixth from the seventh or husband!). The additional points that may be noted are that Jupiter, the significator for children, is in Ithasala with the eleventh lord in the fifth house, while the seventh lord is within one degree of the fifth lord, the Moon, and in aspect with it. A pregnancy resulted soon after marriage. However, both the seventh lord and the fifth lord are in Ithasala with Mars in the twelfth house. The result was a termination of pregnancy.

It may be pointed out that the example quoted here does not conform to the standard definition of Yamaya where the slower planet should lie between the two non-aspecting planets. The reader is advised to go back to our comments on the Nakta yoga.

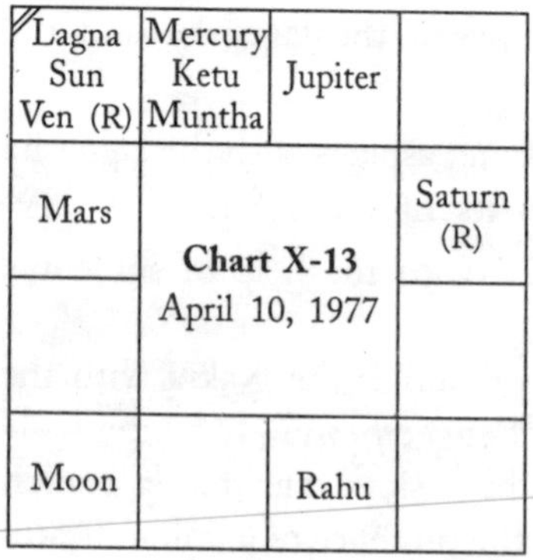

Chart X-13
April 10, 1977

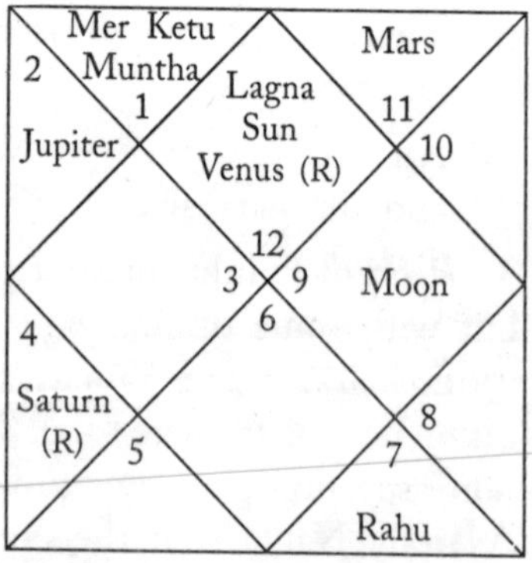

Lagna	14°35'	Mars	22°15'	Venus (R)	20°30'
Sun	26°28'	Mercury	15°44'	Saturn (R)	16°25'
Moon	16°05'	Jupiter	07°43'	Rahu	00°42'

The quality of the Yamaya may also be adversely affected when the intervening linking planet is handicapped by being combust or retrograde. In Chart X-14, there is no link between Mars, the lord of the fourth house, and the Moon, the lord of the seventh house, since the two are located in 6/8 from each other. But a retrograde lagna lord, Saturn, in the lagna is situated between the two and aspects them both. The Moon and Mars are both within the individual Deeptamshas of Saturn. A Yamaya yoga is formed. There is a Poorna Ithasala with Mars and an Isharafa with the Moon. The native (lagna) is busy attempting a rapprochement between the mutually indifferent mother (fourth lord) and wife (seventh lord). The uphill task continues.

The Yamaya yoga obviously cannot form with Saturn as one of the non-aspecting participants since there is no planet slower than Saturn to qualify for the intervening link.

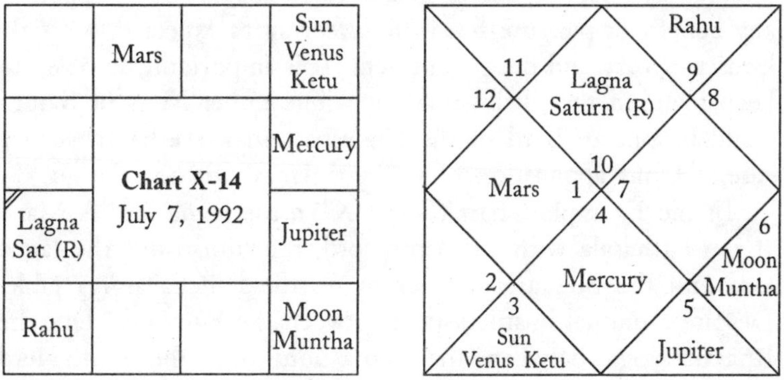

Lagna	13°34'	Mars	22°53'	Venus	28°30'
Sun	21°58'	Mercury	17°58'	Saturn (R)	23°30'
Moon	28°27'	Jupiter	17°01'	Rahu	06°51'

VII. THE MANAU YOGA

This indicates an 'Ithasala at naught'.

Definition : This yoga arises when the following conditions are met :

(i) Lagnesha and karyesha are in Ithasala;

(ii) A malefic (either Mars, or Saturn, or both) is either conjunct with or inimically aspects the faster-moving of the lagnesha/karyesha, from within its individual Deeptamshas.

Result : Fear from enemies, failure in undertakings, involvement in debts, quarrels, and loss of money.

Comments : This yoga signifies a destruction of the Ithasala yoga. Mars and Saturn tend to absorb the strength of a planet which they either inimically aspect or associate with. While their association with the faster-moving of the two (i.e., lagnesha and karyesha) has been stated to be harmful, some authorities attribute the same results to them when they are associated with or inimically aspect either of the two participants in an Ithasala yoga irrespective of its relative velocity. The affected planet must be within the individual Deeptamshas of either Mars or Saturn. It does not matter whether Mars or Saturn is behind or ahead of the affected planet. This yoga nullifies the results which are likely to accrue from an Ithasala yoga. Thus, for example, an Ithasala yoga between the lagna lord and the fifth lord, when afflicted by Mars or Saturn as described above, does not permit any benefit or pleasure from the offspring as expected, but only leads to worry and disappointment. It is important, however, to keep in mind. the likely situation where either Mars or Saturn could be one or both of the lagnesha and karyesha In such a case, a blind application of this yoga may not be relevant.

In the Example Chart (Chart X-1), the lagna lord is Mars. It is in Ithasala with the tenth lord, the Sun. Both the lagna lord and the Sun are very strong in the Panchavargiya table. Despite a mutual hostile aspect between the Sun and Mars, the Ithasala yoga between the lagna lord and the tenth lord manifested fully, conferring on the native an extra-ordinarily prestigious position. Saturn's aspect on the Sun has not rendered the Ithasala yoga defunct. Saturn's aspect here is a friendly aspect, and not inimical.

VIII. THE KAMBOOLA YOGA

The Kamboola is a 'yoga of potentiated Ithasala'.

Definition : This yoga is produced as follows:

(i) Ithasala between lagnesha and karyesha.

(ii) The Moon joins either or both of the above by Ithasala.

Result : This yoga improves the results indicated by an Ithasala yoga and enhances the signification of the houses involved. The results manifest according to the strength or weakness of the lagnesha, the karyesha, and the Moon.

Comments: Kamboola is a distortion of the word *Makbool* meaning 'highly desirable'. The association of the Moon with an Ithasala yoga enhances the status of the Ithasala yoga and speeds up its fruition. It is a highly desirable yoga. For the results to be desirable, however, both the Moon as well as the participants in the Ithasala yoga (i.e., the lagnesha and the karyesha) must be strong. When both the sides are strong, a very powerful yoga is produced. When, however, the yoga has weak constituents, the combination proves to be little more than a wastage. *Sixteen different types of the Kamboola yoga are described, depending upon the strength or weakness of participants in the yoga.*

The disposition of planets for the purpose of the Kamboola yoga may be described as follows:

(a) *Excellent* ('Uttama'), when a planet is exalted or in its own house.

(b) *Good* ('Madhyama'), when it is in its own Hudda, its own Drekkana, or its own Navamsha. Since the Moon does not own any Hudda, its being in its own Drekkana or Navamsha only is to be considered good.

(c) *Inferior* ('Adhama'), when it is placed in its sign of debilitation or in the sign of an enemy.

(d) *Mediocre or neutral* ('Sama'), when none of the above mentioned qualifications apply, i.e., when the planet is neither exalted nor debilitated, nor in its own Hudda, Drekkana or

Table X-2
Different types of the Kamboola yoga.
A shift downwards and to the right in the table indicates progressive decline in the quality of the yoga

		Lagnesha/Karyesha			
		Excellent	Good	Mediocre	Inferior
M	Excellent	Exc-Exc	Exc-Good	Exc-Medi	Exc-Inf
O	Good	Good-Exc	Good-Good	Good-Medi	Good-Inf
O	Mediocre	Medi-Exc	Medi-Good	Medi-Medi	Medi-Inf
N	Inferior	Inf-Exc	Inf-Good	Inf-Medi	Inf-Inf

Navamsha, and is located in the house of a planet neutral to it.

A combination of the above mentioned four states of the Moon on the one hand, and the lagnesha-karyesha on the other, produces sixteen different combinations as shown in Table X-2.

When it is an Excellent-Excellent Kamboola-yoga, the Ithasala yoga fructifies to the fullest extent. As we proceed downward and to the right in the table, the quality of the Kamboola yoga declines progressively, and the benefic effects dwindle, so that at the Inferior-Inferior combination the yoga loses all its potency. In between, the yoga permits fructification with effort.

In Chart X-15; the lagna lord is exalted in the tenth house, an excellent condition for rise in profession. The lord of the tenth house is in the eighth house in Ithasala with the lagna lord. This indicates a discontinuity (eighth house) in a job (tenth house) yielding place to another one of a superior nature. The presence of an Ithasala of both the lagna lord and the tenth lord with Mars in the eighth house causes the Manau yoga (yoga no.7, vide supra) which indicated the neutralisation of an Ithasala. However, there is the strong Moon, the seventh lord in the seventh house establishing Ithasala with the exalted lagna lord in the tenth house. A powerful Kamboola yoga (Excellent-Excellent type) exists here. The native had to give up his current job, but attained a better and higher position in his profession. Mars is

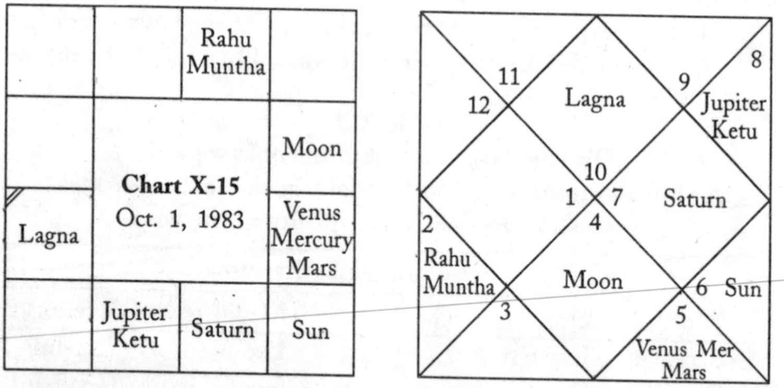

Lagna	27°06'	Mars	06°07'	Venus	03°55'
Sun	14°03'	Mercury	26°12'	Saturn	10°05'
Moon	04°57'	Jupiter	13°06'	Rahu	24°57'

also the lord of the eleventh house. *Seldom do yogas involving the eleventh house or the eleventh lord prove defunct.*

In Chart X-16, there is an Ithasala between the lagna lord, Venus, and the ninth (and tenth) lord Saturn, involving houses seven and nine. The ninth house signifies *Bhagya* (loosely and inadequately translated as 'good fortune'). The Moon involves both the lagna lord and the ninth lord in an Ithasala yoga, thus producing a Kamboola yoga. While the ninth lord is in it own house, the Moon is debilitated. This gives rise to an "Inferior-Excellent" variety of the Kamboola yoga, indicating only a mixed fortune. The ninth house is also an alternate house for progeny. Some hope of begetting progeny was aroused during this year following sustained medical treatment, though it was not successful eventually. There are other adverse features in the chart which do not permit the fulfilment of a cherished desire. They include:

- the recurrence of the birth ascendant (Taurus) in the annual chart;
- the Muntha located in the twelfth house;
- the Muntha lord in the eighth house;
- no Ithasala between the lagna lord and the fifth lord; and
- an Ishrafa between the fifth lord and the eleventh lord (denying progeny).

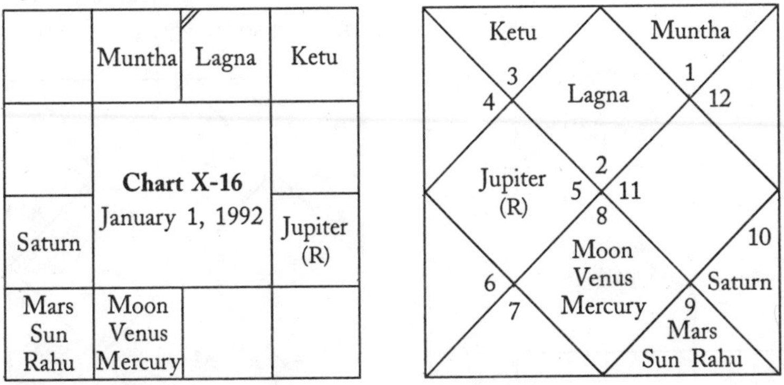

Lagna	11°53'	Mars	00°20'	Venus	07°10'
Sun	16°28'	Mercury	24°42'	Saturn	12°09'
Moon	04°52'	Jupiter (R)	20°53'	Rahu	16°06'

IX. THE GAIRI-KAMBOOLA YOGA

A 'Kamboola through intervention'.

Definition : This happens as follows :

(i) Lagnesha and karyesha in Ithasala.

(ii) An *unqualified Moon* on the last degree of a sign.

(iii) On entering the next sign, the Moon establishes Ithasala with:

(a) Lagnesha/karyesha; and

(b) Some powerful planet.

Results : Accomplishment through the help of someone else.

Comments : A planet is unqualified when it is neither exalted nor debilitated, nor aspected/associated, nor in its own Hudda, Drekkana or Navamsha.

Chart X-17 depicts a hypothetical situation where the lagna lord, Mars, located in the seventh house is in Ithasala with the Sun in the ninth house. The Moon in the second house is unqualified, and at Rashyanta (29°). On entering the next, i.e., the third, house the Moon enters into Ithasala with Saturn in its own house. It also gets involved in Ithasala with the lagna lord as well as the tenth lord. This yoga leads to the fructification of results through the help or intervention of someone else. It may be pertinent to note here that a mere Ithasala yoga between the lagnesha and the karyesha does not produce desirable effects unless it involves desirable houses, and is in some way potentiated

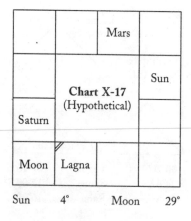

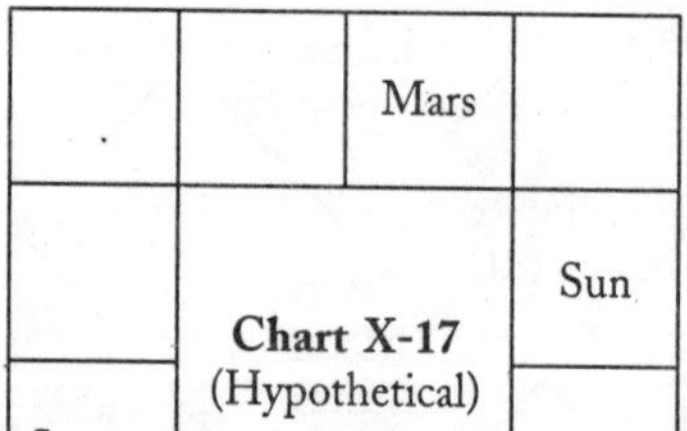

Chart X-17
(Hypothetical)

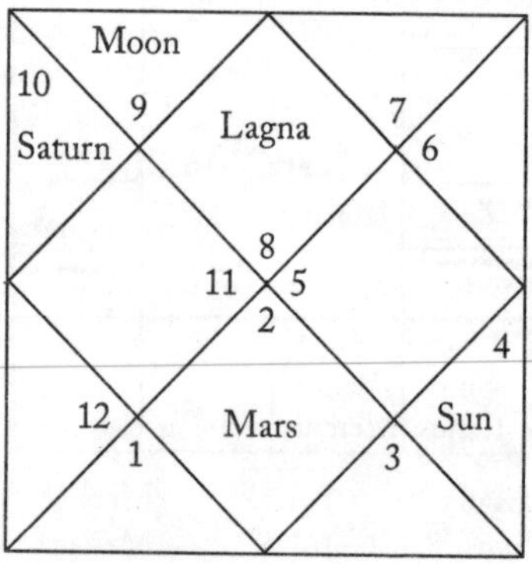

Sun 4° Moon 29° Mars 6° Saturn 7°

by the Moon. The Gairi-Kamboola yoga does not yield results if the unqualified Moon, on entering the next house, establishes Ithasala only with a weak planet.

X. THE KHALLASARA YOGA

This is a 'negation of the Ithasala yoga'.

Definition :

(i) Lagnesha and karyesha in Ithasala.

(ii) Unqualified Moon, neither associated nor in Ithasala with either the lagnesha or the karyesha.

Results : Destruction of the results of a Kamboola yoga.

Comments : The results of this yoga are mentioned to be 'destruction of the Kamboola yoga'. In fact, however, the Kamboola yoga does not arise at all since the Moon does not get involved here. And since the Moon is not even in Rashyanta, it cannot produce a Gairi-Kamboola yoga also. So, what is left behind is a plain and simple Ithasala yoga. This in a way means that an Ithasala alone is not productive of desired results unless it gets some potentiation through the Moon.

XI. THE RUDDA YOGA

Another 'negation of the Ithasala'.

Definition :

(i) Lagnesha and karyesha in Ithasala.

(ii) Either of the two above is retrograde, or combust, or debilitated, or in houses 6, 8 or 12, or occupies an inimical house, or is in conjunction with or aspected by a malefic.

Results : Destruction of the results indicated by the Ithasala yoga.

Comments : This yoga of the negation of Ithasala needs some clarification here. The qualities of retrogression, combustion, debilitation, etc., as mentioned above are considered as handicaps in the fruition of results. When such disqualifications are applicable to the faster-moving of the two participants in the Ithasala, the Rudda yoga is more likely to occur. In any case, when, in an Ithasala, a slow-moving planet is retrograde it increases the intensity of the Ithasala, and the Rudda yoga does not apply. When the fast-moving planet is retrograde, there is no Ithasala anyway. Retrogression thus does not seem to be of much significance in the consideration of a Rudda yoga. Combustion, debilitation, an adverse location or an adverse association are certainly important factors. A very weak planet participating in an Ithasala yoga also neutralises the effects of Ithasala, since a weak planet is functionally useless.

Two specific distinctions are also mentioned in relation to a Rudda yoga depending upon the placement of the two planets forming the Ithasala. When the fast-moving planet, placed in a kendra, establishes Ithasala with a slow-moving planet in an apoklima house, it gives good results in the beginning, which get spoilt finally. On the other hand, a fast-moving planet in an apoklima house, establishing Ithasala with a slow-moving planet in a kendra, causes eventual improvement in a situation which has been in a bad shape earlier.

XII. THE DUHPHALI-KUTTHA YOGA

Definition :

(i) Lagnesha and karyesha in Ithasala.

(ii) The slow-moving planet is (a) in exaltation, (b) in own house, or (c) otherwise strong.

(iii) The fast-moving planet is (a) weak, ((b) not exalted, and (c) not in its own house.

Results : Realisation of the desired effect.

Comments : The fast-moving planet in this yoga is required to be weaker than the slow-moving planet. The strength must be judged from the Pancha-vargiya table. According to the classical description, the yoga does not fructify if the fast-moving planet is retrograde or combust. This yoga appears to be nothing more than a simple Ithasala yoga between a stronger slow-moving planet and a relatively weaker fast-moving planet. We can't figure out why this yoga must at all be mentioned as a separate combination. The stipulation that the fast-moving planet should not be retrograde also does not seem to be of much relevance since an Ithasala has already been described to be non-existent when the fast-moving planet happens to be retrograde (see page 126).

XIII. THE DUTTHOTTHA - DAVIRA YOGA

Definition :

(i) Lagnesha and karyesha are weak (whether or not they are in Ithasala!)

(ii) One of them (i.e., lagnesha or karyesha) is in Ithasala with another strong planet which is either exalted or in its own house.

Results : Realisation of the motive with the help of some one else.

Comments : Ithasala with a strong planet renders a weak planet also strong. In the yoga under consideration, a weak lagnesha and a weak karyesha are rendered strong by associating with a strong planet through Ithasala. The lagnesha and karyesha may not be mutually involved in an Ithasala, but must be in mutual aspect to derive any benefit from a third strong planet.

XIV. THE TAMBIRA YOGA

Definition :

(i) Lagnesha and karyesha are not in mutual aspect or Ithasala.

(ii) The karyesha (i.e., the significator) is in Rashyanta.

(iii) On entering the next house, the karyesha establishes Ithasala with the lagnesha, and with another planet which is strong or in its own house.

Results : Accomplishment through the help of someone, generally after some delay.

Comments : According to some authorities, either of the lagnesha and karyesha may be at the end of a sign, and establish Ithasala with a strong planet as also with the lagnesha/karyesha as appropriate, on entering the next sign. This yoga is also called as the Shubha-Tambira yoga.

XV. THE KUTTHA YOGA

Definition :

(i) Lagnesha and karyesha are powerful and posited in the kendras or the panapharas.

(ii) Presence of benefic aspects, and absence of malefic aspects.

Results: Generally favourable results, success, auspicious events.

XVI. THE DURAPHA YOGA

Definition : Lagnesha and karyesha are weak, posited in the Trika houses (i.e., houses 6, 8 and 12), and combust and retrograde.

Results : Failures, inauspicious events.

Comments : This and the preceding yogas are mutually antagonistic. The simple rule is that the lagnesha and karyesha in benefic houses with benefic association/aspect are productive of good results. Otherwise, they lead to disappointments and failures.

Table X-3 provides a glimpse of the Tajika yogas mentioned above.

GENERAL HINTS AT INTERPRETATION

The Tajika yogas as mentioned above represent a very important area of annual horoscopy. The most important amongst these is, of course, the Ithasala yoga since it affords an understanding of most of the yogas and is an important constituent of many of these. It is a manipulation of the Ithasala yoga in essence, in various ways, that provides important clues to the events during the year.

The mere presence or absence of the yogas is not the only factor of significance, however. The strength of planets participating in a yoga is also important. A weak planet is incapable of performing any fruitful function. As in the birth chart, so also in the annual chart, the strength of the lagna lord is of paramount importance. If the lagna lord is weak, most of the yogas which involve it also lose their potence.

Some people hold the lord of the year to be as important as the lagna lord itself. All the Tajika yogas may also be considered from the year lord in addition to the lagna lord.

The Time of Fructification of the Yogas

The various yogas manifest themselves in the dasha-antardasha of planets participating in the yogas. The most important dasha system is the Mudda dasha, the equivalent of the Vimshottari dasha in the birth chart. In general, a Poorna Ithasala gives results during the earlier part of the year while a Bhavishyat Ithasala does so in the later part of the year.

The Importance of the Parashari System

While analysing these yogas, the Parashari principles must always be taken into consideration. Thus, the lords of the houses 6, 8 and 12, when involved in these yogas, render them crippled. Relation of the tenth lord with the eighth afflicts profession. Involvement of the third or sixth lords increases struggles during the year. Yogas involving the eleventh house or eleventh lord generally give fruitful results, while those involving the twelfth house or twelfth lord prove harmful or expensive.

The promise in the birth horoscope is also of significance. An Ithasala yoga promising progeny will not bear fruit if the birth chart does not show any promise of progeny. Similarly, the dasha-antardasha operating in the birth chart must be considered and co-ordinated with the analysis of the annual chart.

Table X-3
Yogas at a glance

S.No.	Yoga	Definition	Results
1.	Ikabala	All planets in kendras or panapharas.	Benefit from profession, access to wealth, gain in status, good luck.
2.	Induvara	All planets in apoklimas.	Disappointments, fall in status, ill health, worries.
3.	lthasala		
	(a) Vartamana	(i) Mutual aspect between lagnesha and karyesha. (ii) The fast-moving planet behind the slow-moving planet. (iii) The lagnesha and the karyesha within their Deeptamsha range.	Fulfilment of a promise indicated by the karyesha (or significator).
	(b) Poorna	(i) Mutual aspect between the lagnesha and the karyesha. (ii) The fast-moving planet behind the slow-moving planet, but within one degree of it.	(Generally, immediate) fulfilment of a promise.
	(c) Bhavishyat	(i) The fast-moving planet at the end of a sign. (ii) The slow-moving planet at the beginning of the next sign, within their Deeptamsha range.	Fulfilment (generally toward the end of the year).

Contd

Table X-3 (Contd.)

S.No.	Yoga	Definition	Results
4.	Ishrafa	(i) The fast-moving planet one degree or more ahead of the slow-moving planet. (ii) The two are in mutual aspect.	Failure in undertakings, disappointments.
5.	Nakta	(i) No mutual aspect between the lagnesha and the karyesha. (ii) A faster-moving planet is located between the lagnesha and the karyesha, aspecting them both from within its individual Deeptamshas.	Fulfilment with the help of someone.
6.	Yamaya	(i) No mutual aspect between the lagnesha and the karyesha. (ii) An intervening slow-moving planet aspects them both from within its individual Deeptamshas.	Fulfilment with the help of someone, but with some difficulty.
7.	Manau	(i) The lagnesha and the karyesha in Ithasala. (ii) A malefic (Mars/Saturn) either conjunct with or inimically aspecting the faster of the lagnesha/karyesha.	Failures and disappointments. Destruction of the Ithasala.

Contd...

Table X-3 (Contd.)

S.No.	Yoga	Definition	Results
8.	Kamboola	(i) The lagnesha and the karyesha in Ithasala. (ii) The Moon joins either or both of the above by Ithasala.	Improves the results indicated by the Ithasala. The strength or weakness of the Moon on the one hand and lagnesha/karyesha on the other determines the quality of the Kamboola Yoga.
9.	Gairi-Kamboola	(i) The lagnesha and the karyesha in Ithasala. (ii) An unqualified Moon on the last degree of a sign. (iii) On entering the next sign, the Moon forms Ithasala with: — lagnesha/karyesha; and — some powerful planet.	Fulfilment through the help of someone.
10.	Khallasara	(i) The lagnesha and the karyesha in Ithasala. (ii) Unqualified Moon, neither conjunct with nor aspecting either the lagnesha or the karyesha.	Negation of the results indicated by the Ithasala.
11.	Rudda	(i) Ithasala between the lagnesha and the karyesha. (ii) Either of the two is retrograde, or combust, or debilitated, or in houses 6, 8 or 12, or under malefic influence.	Negation of results indicated by the Ithasala.

Table X-3 (Contd.)

S.No.	Yoga	Definition	Results
12.	Duhphali-kuttha	(i) Ithasala between the lagnesha and the karyesha. (ii) The slower-moving planet is either in exaltation, or in its own house, or otherwise strong. (iii) The faster moving one is weak, not exalted nor in its own house; it should, however, not be retrograde or combust.	Realisation of the desired effect.
13.	Dutthottha-Davira	(i) The lagnesha and the karyesha are weak (whether or not in lthasala). (ii) One of them is in Ithasala with another strong planet which is either exalted or in its own houses.	Realisation of the motive with the help of someone else.

Contd...

Table X-3 (Contd.)

S.No.	Yoga	Definition	Results
14.	Tambira	(i) The lagnesha and the karyesha are not in mutual aspect or Ithasala. (ii) The karyesha (significator) is at the end of a sign. (iii) On entering the next house, the karyesha establishes Ithasal with the lagnesha, and with another planet which is strong or in its own house.	Fulfilment through the help of someone, generally after some delay.
15.	Kuttha	(i) The lagnesha and the karyesha are powerful and posited in kendras or panapharas. (ii) Benefic influences on the lagnesha/karyesha, sans malefic influences.	Generally favourable results during the year.
16.	Durapha	The lagnesha and the karyesha are weak, posited in the Trika houses, combust or retrograde.	Generally unfavourable.

CHAPTER XI

THE SAHAMS

Heaven and Earth and the space in between
Have set me in a wide expanse!
Fire, the Sun, the Waters, the Gods,
have joined to give me inspiration.

'ATHARVA VEDA'

The Sahams are sensitive points arrived at by a certain manipulation of the longitudes of various planets and the mid-point of the ascendant (or, sometimes, of other houses). Different, though specific, manipulations yield different Sahams. Each Saham then holds sway over one particular event of life during the year indicated by the annual chart. Thus, such varied events as marriage, child birth, fame, travel, illness, death, and the like, are each ruled by a specific Saham.

The number of Sahams recommended for application to an annual chart varies from one author on annual horoscopy to another. Thus, whereas Venkatesha describes forty-eight Sahams, Keshava makes a mention of only twenty-five, while Neelakantha (of the *Tajika Neelakanthi* fame) describes fifty Sahams. More recent practitioners of annual horoscopy have even considered using the extra-Saturnine planets (Uranus, Neptune and Pluto) to determine certain sensitive points although there is generally little reason to go into such diversions which, certainly, are not a recognised part of Vedic astrology.

It is generally not necessary to calculate all the Sahams described in the texts, in a given annual chart. The practitioners of the Tajika pick up only the relevant Sahams pertaining to a particular year of life of a native, and analyse them. An already married man, for example, has no use for a Saham indicating marriage. Or a child of tender years has no use for a Saham indicating progeny.

Since the Sahams are manipulations of the longitudes and the mid-points respectively of planets and houses, it is essential that these are calculated accurately. In the account that follows, the formulae for the calculation of some of the important Sahams, based mainly on the Tajika Neelakanthi, are being given.

1. **Punya Saham** (or the Saham for general auspiciousness). This is arrived at in the following manner

   (a) Varshapravesha during the day (i.e., between sunrise and sunset)
   Moon - Sun + Ascendant
   (i.e., longitude of the Moon, minus the longitude of the Sun, plus the mid-point of the ascendant).

   (b) Varshapravesha during the night (i.e., between sunset and sunrise)
   Sun - Moon + Ascendant

2. **Guru Saham** (or the Saham pertaining to the preceptor).

   (a) Day : Sun - Moon + Ascendant

   (b) Night : Moon - Sun + Ascendant
   The Guru Saham is thus the reverse of the Punya Saham in calculation.

3. **Vidya (or Jnana) Saham** (Saham for knowledge/higher education). The calculation for the Vidya Saham is the same as for the Guru Saham. This is because the Guru and Vidya (the preceptor and knowledge) go hand in hand.

4. **Yasha Saham** (Saham for fame).

   (a) Day : Jupiter - Punya Saham + Ascendant

   (b) Night : Punya Saham - Jupiter + Ascendant

5. **Mitra Saham** (Saham for friends).

   (a) Day : Guru Saham - Punya Saham + Venus

   (b) Night : Punya Saham - Guru Saham + Venus

6. **Mahatmya Saham** (Saham for fruits of virtuous living).
   (a) Day : Punya Saham - Mars + Ascendant
   (b) Night : Mars - Punya Saham + Ascendant
7. **Asha Saham** (Saham for hope/anticipation).
   (a) Day : Saturn - Venus + Ascendant
   (b) Night : Venus - Saturn + Ascendant
8. **Samarthya Saham** (Saham for capability).
   (a) Day : Mars - Lord of the Ascendant + Ascendant
   (b) Night : Lord of the Ascendant - Mars + Ascendant
9. **Bhratri Saham** (Saham for siblings).
   Jupiter - Saturn + Ascendant
   (Same for day as well as night Varshapravesha).
10. **Gaurava Saham** (Saham for dignity).
    (a) Day : Sun - Moon + Jupiter
    (b) Night : Moon - Sun + Jupiter
11. **Pitri (or Taata) Saham** (Saham for father).
    (a) Day : Saturn - Sun + Ascendant
    (b) Night : Sun - Saturn + Ascendant
12. **Raja Saham** (Saham for kingship or royal dignity). Same as the Pitri Saham.
13. **Matri Saham** (Saham for mother).
    (a) Day : Moon - Venus + Ascendant
    (b) Night : Venus - Moon + Ascendant
14. **Putra Saham** (Saham for progeny).
    Jupiter - Moon + Ascendant
    (Same for day as well as night Varshapravesha).
15. **Jeeva Saham** (Saham for life).
    (a) Day : Saturn - Jupiter + Ascendant
    (b) Night : Jupiter - Saturn + Ascendant

16. **Roga Saham** (Saham for disease).
Ascendant - Moon + Ascendant
(Some for day as well as night Varshapravesha).

Note: According to another authority, Roga Saham is calculated thus:

(a) Day : Saturn - Moon + Ascendant

(b) Night : Moon - Saturn + Ascendant.

We have found this latter giving better results.

17. **Karma Saham** (Saham for profession).

(a) Day : Mars - Mercury + Ascendant

(b) Night : Mercury - Mars + Ascendant.

18. **Manmatha Saham** (Saham for infatuation).

(a) Day : Moon - Lord of Ascendant + Ascendant

(b) Night : Lord of Ascendant - Moon + Ascendant

19. **Kali Saham** (Saham for strife).

(a) Day : Jupiter - Mars + Ascendant

(b) Night : Mars - Jupiter + Ascendant

20. **Kshama Saham** (Saham for forgiveness). Same as Kali Saham.

21. **Shastra Saham** (Saham for scriptures).

(a) Day : Jupiter - Saturn + Mercury

(b) Night : Saturn - Jupiter + Mercury

22. **Bandhu Saham** (Saham for relatives).
Mercury - Moon + Ascendant
(Same for day as well night Varshapravesha).

23. **Mrityu Saham** (Saham for death).
Mid-point of Eighth House - Moon + Saturn
(Same for day as well as night Varshapravesha).

24. **Deshantara Saham** (Saham for foreign travel; Saham for distant travel).

Mid-point of Ninth House - Ninth Lord + Ascendant
(Same for day as well as night Varshapravesha).

25. **Artha (Dhana) Saham** (Saham for Finance/wealth).

Mid-point of Second House-Second Lord + Ascendant
(Same for day as well as night Varshapravesha).

26. **Paradara Sahara** (Saham for adultery).

Venus - Sun + Ascendant
(Same for day as well night Varshapravesha).

27. **Anya-Karma Saham** (Saham for additional/alternate vocation).

(a) Day : Moon - Saturn. + Ascendant

(b) Night : Saturn - Moon + Ascendant

28. **Vanika Saham** (Saham for trade).

Moon - Mercury + Ascendant
(Same for day as well as night Varshapravesha).

29. **Karya-Siddhi Saham** (Saham for success in a venture).

(a) Day : Saturn - Sun + Lord of Sun sign

(b) Night : Saturn - Moon + Lord of Moon sign

30. **Vivaha Saham** (Saham for marriage).

Venus - Saturn + Ascendant
(Same for day as well as night Varshapravesha).

31. **Prasava Saham** (Saham for delivery of a child).

(a) Day : Jupiter - Mercury + Ascendant

(b) Night : Mercury - Jupiter + Ascendant

32. **Santaapa Saham** (Saham for sorrow).

Saturn - Moon + Mid-point of Sixth House
(Same for day as well as night Varshapravesha).

33. **Shraddha Saham** (Saham for devotion).

Venus - Mars + Ascendant
(Same for day as well as night Varshapravesha).

34. **Preeti Saham** (Saham for love).

Vidya Saham - Punya Saham + Ascendant
(Same for day as well as night Varshapravesha).

35. **Jadya Saham** (Saham for stupidity).

(a) Day : Mars - Saturn + Mercury

(b) Night : Saturn - Mars + Mercury

36. **Vyapara Saham** (Saham for business). Somewhat equivalent to the Vanika Saham, vide no. 28 supra.

Mars - Mercury + Ascendant
(Same for day as well as night Varshapravesha.

37. **Paneeya-Paata Saham** (Saham for falling in water/ drowning).

(a) Day : Saturn - Moon + Ascendant

(b) Night : Moon - Saturn + Ascendant

38. **Shatru Saham** (Saham for enemies).

(a) Day : Mars - Saturn + Ascendant

(b) Night : Saturn - Mars + Ascendant

39. **Jalapatha Saham** (Saham for sea-voyage).

(a) Day : Cancer 15° - Saturn + Ascendant

(b) Night : Saturn - Cancer 15° + Ascendant

40. **Bandhana Saham** (Saham for imprisonment).

(a) Day : Punya Saham - Saturn + Ascendant

(b) Night : Saturn - Punya Saham + Ascendant

41. **Labha Saham** (Saham for monetary gains).

Mid-point of Eleventh House - Eleventh Lord + Ascendant
(Same for day as well as night Varshapravesha).

Note : One method of calculating a Saham for any of the twelve houses is:

Mid-point of the House-Lord of the House + Ascendant

An Essential Consideration

A Saham involves three different factors (let us call them a, b, and c). Any given Saham can be represented by the formula:

$$a - b + c$$

Here, see whether 'c' falls between 'b' and 'a'. If it does, the value obtained by the formula 'a - b + c' indicates the Saham specified. If, however, 'c' does not fall between 'b' and 'a', then add one sign to the result obtained above (i.e., $a - b + c + 1^s$)

That will provide the value of the Saham in question.

Let us consider the *Punya Saham* (Saham no. 1) in the Example Chart (Chart X-1). Here, since the Varshapravesha is during day time, the Punya Saham is obtained by :

Moon - Sun + Ascendant

i.e., $1^s9°40'$ - $4^s3°50'$ + $7^s9°26'$, or $4^s15°16'$.

Here, the ascendant falls between the Sun and the Moon when counted in the regular order in the annual chart. Therefore, the value obtained above, i.e., $4^s15°16'$, represents the Punya Saham.

Let us now consider the Raja Saham (Saham no. 12) for the same native. Here, a - b + c is represented by :

Saturn - Sun + Ascendant

i.e., $6^s17°13'$ - $4^s3°50'$ + $7^s9°26'$, or $9^s22°49'$.

However, here, the ascendant ('c') does not fall between the Sun ('b') and Saturn ('a'). Therefore, we add one sign to the value already obtained. The Raja Saham will, therefore, be $10^s22°49'$.

Sahams in the Birth Chart

While the Sahams find their mention only in the Tajika texts and are generally applied only to the annual charts, their results cannot be appropriately analysed unless they are considered simultaneously in the birth chart. It is thus desirable that the various Sahams as mentioned above are calculated in the birth chart as well. During a given year, only those Sahams which are relevant to the native at that time need be considered and analysed in the background of similar Sahams in the birth chart. Only those Sahams which are strong in the birth chart can produce results during a given year when they are strong in the annual chart as well. There is generally little relevance in trying to analyse those Sahams in the annual chart which are devoid of strength in the birth chart.

The Strength of Sahams

Having calculated the various Sahams, it is important to see how strong or weak they individually are. This is decided according to the following guidelines:

1. *A. Strong Saham*: A Saham becomes strong when the following conditions obtain:
   (a) The Saham lord is exalted, or in its own house in the rashi chart as well as in the vargas, or is located in benefic houses or in those belonging to its friends; or
   (b) The Saham is associated with a friend or with a natural benefic, or with the year lord; or
   (c) The Saham lord aspects the Saham or conjoins it, or aspects the lagna.
2. *A weak Saham*: A Saham becomes weak when the following conditions obtain:
   (a) The strength of the Saham lord is less than 5 units according to the Panchavargiya Bala; or
   (b) The Saham lord lacks strength according to the Harsha Bala; or
   (c) The Saham lord does not aspect the Saham nor does it conjoin the Saham; or
   (d) The Saham is associated with inimical planets or natural malefics.

   Note:

   (i) A strong and a weak Saham give benefic and harmful results respectively during the dasha of their lords.

   (ii) According to some, the Shatru, Roga, Kali, and Mrityu Sahams (i.e., Sahams for enemies, disease, strife, and death) are not good if they are strong. They are considered best when in debility.

(iii) A Saham located in the sixth, eighth or twelfth house is handicapped, and generally gives adverse results.

(iv) A Saham related by conjunction or by Ithasala with its own eighth lord or with the eighth lord of the annual chart becomes weak.

Special Significance of the Punya Saham

A strong Punya Saham ensures general auspiciousness, and promotes the performance of virtuous deeds and acquisition of money during the year. With a weak Punya Saham, both wealth and virtue are at stake. The following points must be borne in mind when the results of the Punya Saham (as also of any of the beneficial Sahams) are being analysed.

1. Punya Saham located in the sixth, the eighth or the twelfth house in annual chart causes loss of name, fame and wealth.

2. Association or aspect of benefic planets brings in fortune and fame. The benefic results accrue mainly during the later half of the year.

3. Malefic association or aspect produces its results mainly during the earlier half of the year.

4. Benefic association or aspect on the Punya Saham located in the sixth, eighth or twelfth house may bring in some relief in the form of income and fame during the concluding part of the year.

5. Malefic association and benefic aspect on the Punya Saham produces ill effects during the first half of the year, and beneficial results during the second half.

   Benefic association and malefic aspect brings in benefic results during the first half of the year, and malefic results during the second half.

   Association thus takes precedence over aspect.

6. Malefic association and malefic aspect make the whole year adverse. Benefic association and aspect have the opposite influence.

7. The Punya Saham takes precedence over the rest of the Sahams. If the Punya Saham is extra-ordinarily strong, the other Sahams even in debility cannot produce any harm.

   A Punya Saham in debility neutralises any benefic effects that might be indicated by other Sahams is strength.

8. It is essential to consider the Punya Saham (as also all the other Sahams) in the birth chart also. A Punya Saham in the sixth, eighth or twelfth house in birth chart, when ill-associated/ill-aspected in the annual chart, along with a weak Punya Saham lord, indicates loss of wealth and virtue.

9. Strong, well placed Punya Saham in the birth chart as well as the annual chart ensures wealth, success, and virtuous deeds.

Examples of the Punya Saham

Let us apply the Punya Saham to our native, Mr. Rajiv Gandhi.

(a) *Punya Saham in the Birth Chart* (Chart X-2)
Moon - Sun + Ascendant (for day birth).
or $4^s17°8'$ - $4^s3°49'$ + $4^s14°33'$
or $4^s27°52'$

Since the ascendant (Leo 14°33') falls between the Sun (Leo 3°49') and the Moon (Leo 17°8'), there is no need to add one sign to the value obtained above. The Punya Saham for birth is thus Leo 27°52'.

This Punya Saham falls in the lagna of the native. It is associated with the lord of the Saham (i.e., the Sun) and with all the natural benefics (viz., the Moon, Mercury, Jupiter and Venus). The Punya Saham is thus extremely strong in the birth chart.

(b) *Punya Saham for the Forty-first Year of the Native* (Chart X-I). This refers to the Example Chart, and has been discussed under 'An Essential Consideration', vide supra.

Once again, the Punya Saham (Leo 15°16') is very strong here, being associated with its own lord as well as two benefits, Mercury and Venus, in the tenth house. The lord of the Punya

Saham, the Sun, is very strong and happens to be the year lord. It establishes Ithasala with the strong lagna lord, Mars, as well as with another strong benefic, Jupiter, the lord of the second and fifth houses. The Punya Saham is very strong here, and ensured success and status to the native throughout the year.

(c) *Punya Saham for the forty-sixth year* (from August 1989 onwards): See Chart X-3. The Varshapravesha being after sunset, the Punya Saham is obtained by

Sun - Moon + Ascendant
or $4^s3°49'$ - $11^s21°17'$ + $10^s23°36'$, or $3^s6°8'$.

Here, the ascendant does not fall between the Moon and the Sun. Therefore, we add one sign to the above value. *The Punya Saham will thus be $4^s6°8'$ (or Leo 6°8')*

The Punya Saham here too is associated with its own lord as also with Mercury. It is, however, not as strong as in the earlier case, since it occurs in the seventh house, and both the Saham as well as its lord (the Sun) are associated with a malefic Mars, and are in the Rahu-Ketu axis. During this year, the native lost his prime- ministership following general elections though he did gain the humbler status of 'the leader of the opposition' in the Parliament, equivalent to the status of a cabinet minister. The malefic associations of the Punya Saham ensured adverse results during the first half of the year.

(d) *Punya Saham for the Forty-seventh year* (from August 1990 onwards). See Chart X-9, under 'The Yogas'. Once again here, the Varshapravesha occurred during the night. The Punya Saham (Sun - Moon + Ascendant) will thus be :

$4^s3°50'$ - $4^s8°2'$ + $2^s7°15'$, or $2^s3°3'$.

Here, the ascendant falls between the Moon and the Sun when the counting is done in the direct manner from the Moon onwards. No addition of one sign is, therefore, required. The Punya Saham for this year thus is $2^s3°3'$ (or Gemini 3°3').

The Punya Saham is not too strong here. It is inimically aspected by the eighth lord Saturn. The lord of the Punya Saham receives the aspects of malefics, Mars and Saturn (the sixth and eighth lords), and is associated with another malefic, the Sun. The Saham lord has an Ishrafa yoga with the eighth lord. There is no benefic aspect on it. The native lost his life during this year.

Analysis of Sahams - Some More Hints

1. *The Karya-Siddhi Saham* associated with or aspected by benefics or in Ithasala with benefics ensures dominance over opponents and increase of name and fame. Malefic influences cause obstacles in undertakings.

2. *The Kali Saham* associated with or aspected by benefics as well as malefics, and in Ithasala with malefics, leads to death following strife and quarrel. Purely benefic influences on this Saham ensure dominance over opponents.

3. Marriage is likely when *the Vivaha Saham* is aspected by or associated with or in lthasala with benefics. Influence of both malefics and benefics causes marriage through difficulty. When associated with malefics only, and in Ithasala with the eighth lord, it denies the native the chance of getting married.

4. Lord of *the Yasha Saham* in the eighth house aspected by or associated with malefics deprives one of one's long sustained dignity and status. If a malefic influencing such a Yasha Saham is combust, it leads to loss of dignity and respect accumulated and enjoyed by one's ancestors also. Benefic influences, through association, aspect or lthasala, on a well-placed Yasha Saham ensure name, fame, wealth and dignity.

5. If the lord of *the Roga Saham* is itself a malefic, and is associated with or aspected by malefics, it produces illness. In Ithasala with the eighth lord, it can lead to death. If the lord of the Roga Saham is very weak, along with the affliction mentioned above, the death is accompanied by much suffering. When associated with its own lord, influenced by benefics only, and not located in houses 6, 8, or 12, a Roga Saham ensures good health.

6. *The Artha Saham* ensures riches and wealth when well-placed, well-associated, and well-aspected. Contrarily, malefic influences lead to loss of accumulated wealth during the year.

7. *The Putra Saham* under benefic influences ensures the birth of a son (or daughter) or an auspicious event (e.g., marriage) pertaining to an offspring. Malefic influences on this Saham cause suffering through progeny, or suffering to progeny.

   Lord of the Putra Saham, if weak and in Ishrafa with a malefic, leads to separation from the offspring. If the lord of the Putra Saham is also the lord of the fifth house of the birth chart, and is associated with or aspected by benefics and friendly planets, it leads to the birth of a son.

8. *A Pitri Saham* under benefic influences enhances the dignity and the financial status of the father. A weak or combust lord of the Pitri Saham, when placed in the eighth house in the annual chart, and in Ithasala with a malefic, leads to harm (death!) to father. When such a Saham is in a movable sign, it causes death in a foreign land. In a fixed sign, the death occurs in one's own country. When the lord of the Pitri Saham is in full strength and under the influence of benefics, it ensures royal favours and professional elevation for the native.

9. *The Matri Saham* should also be analysed in the same manner as the Pitri Saham. Benefic influences on this Saham ensure happiness and good health to the mother. Adverse influences indicate the reverse.

10. When *the Bandhana Saham* is associated with or aspected by its own lord, it does not lead to imprisonment. When, however, malefics influence this Saham by association, aspect or Ithasala, the native gets imprisoned.

11. *The Gaurava Saham,* when under benefic influence, leads to varied comforts, material pleasures, new clothes, etc. Under malefic influence, it causes reversals in job and fall of status.

12. When *the Karma Saham,* lord of the Karma Saham, tenth house, and the lord of the tenth house are all strong, well-associated or well-aspected, and in Ithasala with benefics, there is gain in wealth, land, vehicle and status. Lord of the Karma Saham in Ithasala with malefics, especially Saturn, renders all efforts fruitless during the year.
13. As in the case of the Punya Saham, so also in the case of other Sahams, the results indicated by association take precedence over those indicated by aspect. Benefic association-malefic aspect thus produces good results during the first half of the year and adverse results during the second half. On the contrary, malefic association-benefic aspect produces adverse results during the first half of the year and benefic results during the second half.

    However, the Shatru (enemy), the Roga (disease) and the Mrityu (death) Sahams must be interpreted in the reverse manner. With these Sahams, malefic association-benefic aspect produces benefic results during the first half and malefic results during the second half of the year. Similarly, benefic association-malefic aspect produces adverse results during the first half of the year and benefic results during the second half.
14. Authorities on the Tajika Shastra have devised additional Sahams for additional specific purposes. While Sahams constitute a brilliant area of the Tajika system, they do not give results consistently, and a lot of research is required to be done before they can be employed with infallible results. Besides, many of these have to be re-interpreted so as to give them a more modern meaning and ensure a flexible application.
15. It will be noted that in the consideration of various Sahams, the *Karkatva* or the significatorship of planets holds sway.

Some Illustrations

1. *The Example Chart* (Chart X-1). The Punya Saham in the chart has already been discussed.

In the earlier part of this chapter (under 'An Essential Consideration'), the Raja Saham (Saham no. 12; Saturn - Sun

+ Ascendant, for day Varshapravesha) for the native was calculated to be $10^s22°49'$. Referring to this chart, we find that the Raja Saham falls in the fourth house. The lord of the Raja Saham, i.e., Saturn, is exalted in the ninth house from the Raja Saham and is beneficially aspected by the year lord, the Sun, as well as by the benefics Mercury, Jupiter and Venus. Saturn is the strongest planet in the annual chart according to the Panchavargiya Bala. The native attained the most powerful status, equivalent to the ruler, in a democratic set up during the year.

Let us now consider the *Matri Saham* (no. 13) in the same chart. The Matri Saham (Moon - Venus + Ascendant for day Varshapravesh) falls in Cancer ($1^s9°40'$ - $4^s21°45'$ + $7^s9°26'$ = $3^s27°21'$). The lord of this Saham, the Moon, though exalted in the seventh house, is very close to Rahu. It is also aspected by Mars, also fairly close in degrees. The native's mother was shot dead by her own Sikh bodyguards. It may be noted here that the lord of the Matri Saham receives no friendly aspect from anywhere, and is particularly weak according to the Panchavargiya Bala.

2. *Fall from power*: In Chart X-3 (again belonging to Mr. Rajiv Gandhi, for his forty-sixth year starting from August 1989), the Raja Saham (Sun - Saturn + Ascendant) falls in Libra ($6^s13°27'$) in the ninth house. The lord of the Saham is debilitated in the eighth house, in the twelfth from the Raja Saham, and in Poorna Ithasala with the sixth lord of the Saham. The Saham lord is relatively weak in the Pancha-vargiya Chart also. The native fell from power following elections during this year.

In Chart XI-1, for the year starting from November 1976, *the Raja Saham* (Sun – Saturn + Ascendant) falls in the fourth house in Sagittarius ($8^s18°26'$). Although there is a benefic ninth lord, Venus, posited in the fourth house, from the Raja Saham this Venus is the sixth lord. The lord of the Saham is retrograde, in the sixth from the Saham. Thus there is an exchange between the lord of the Raja Saham and its sixth lord. The only aspects on this Saham are those of the Moon (the eighth lord from this Saham), Rahu and Ketu. The lord of the Saham does not get involved in any useful yoga. The

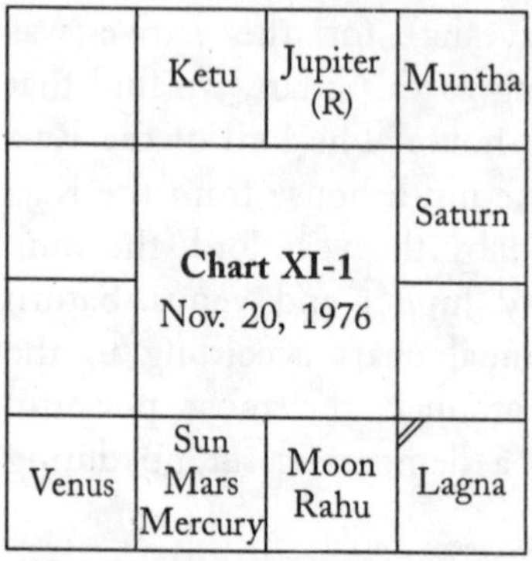

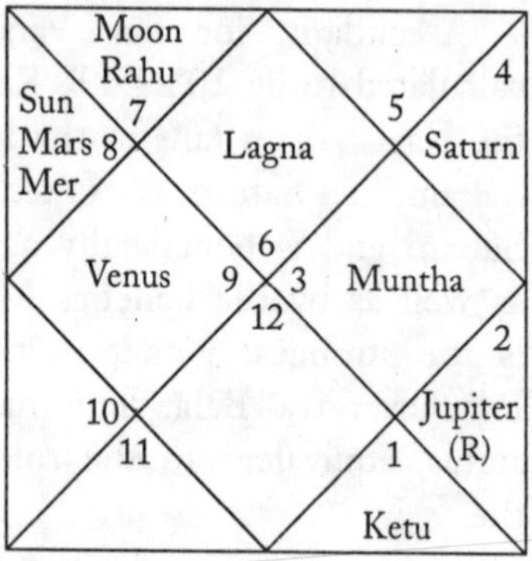

Lagna	07°36'	Mars	05°39'	Venus	12°59'
Sun	04°07'	Mercury	11°14'	Saturn	23°17'
Moon	09°05'	Jupiter (R)	02°23'	Rahu	09°57'

native fell from power during this year following the general elections in India.

3. *Chart VII-1* (page 81). The *Vivaha Saham* (Venus - Saturn + Ascendant + 1^s) falls in Cancer ($3^s13°24'$). While the Saham is occupied by Ketu, its lord is in the lagna, with Jupiter, and in the seventh from Venus and Saturn. Venus is the Karaka for marriage as also the fifth lord, while Saturn is the seventh lord of the birth chart. The native got married during this year. With its Panchavargiya Bala of 12:28:15 units, the lord of the Vivaha Saham is the strongest of the office-bearers in the chart. It may be noted, however, that the Saham lord, the Moon, being a fast-moving planet, is just a little too far advanced so as to deny the native any useful Ithasala yoga. The marriage did not proceed the harmonious way that it should have.

4. *Chart X-11* (page 131). In this chart, the *Putra Saham* (Jupiter - Moon + Ascendant + 1^s) falls in the eleventh house, in Gemini ($2^s22°54'$). The lord of the Putra Saham establishes Ithasala with Jupiter, the Karaka for progeny. The native begot a son during this year. However, the lord of the Saham is in the sixth from the Saham, while Jupiter is in the twelfth house, in the RKA.

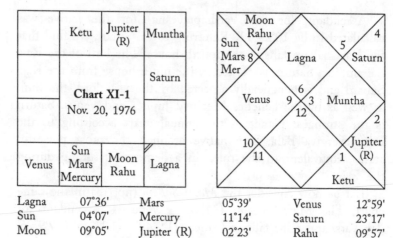

The Vivaha Saham (Venus - Saturn + Ascendant) for this year falls in Cancer ($3^s5°6'$), in the twelfth house, too close to Ketu. Jupiter, the lord of the eighth house of the annual chart, is located here, establishing an Ishrafa yoga with the lord of the Saham, the Moon. The Moon also establishes Ithasala with Saturn, lord of the sixth house from the ascendant, and of the eighth house from the Vivaha Saham, located in the sixth house from the Saham. The native lost his wife during this year, and also had to part with his son.

For the same native, *the Punya Saham* (Sun - Moon + Ascendant + 1^{s}) falls in Libra ($6^{s}3^{\circ}50'$). The Moon, the twelfth lord, is situated here, while the Saham lord is combust in the fourth house. The Punya Saham is weak.

The Bandhana Saham (Saham no. 40; Saturn - Punya + Ascendant + 1^{s}) falls in Sagittarius ($8^{s}21^{\circ}37'$) where the sixth lord of the annual chart and the eighth lord of the birth chart, Saturn, is situated, establishing Ithasala with the twelfth lord, the Moon; this Moon is the eighth lord from the Saham. The lord of the Bandhana Saham is in the twelfth house, in the eighth from the Saham, in the Rahu-Ketu axis. The native suffered imprisonment during this year.

5. *More about Bandana Saham.* In Chart XI-2, *the Bandhana Saham* falls in the second house, in Capricorn ($9^{s}24^{\circ}35'$). While the lord of the Saham is in the Saham itself, the lord of the eighth from the ascendant, the Moon, is also located there, establishing an Ithasala with the Saham lord. The lord of the Bandhana Saham is in Poorna Ithasala with the sixth lord of the annual chart placed in the twelfth house. The native suffered a brief spell of imprisonment during this year.

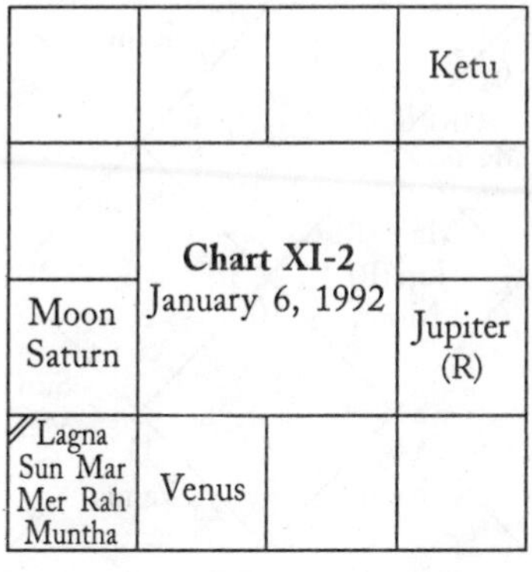

Chart XI-2
January 6, 1992

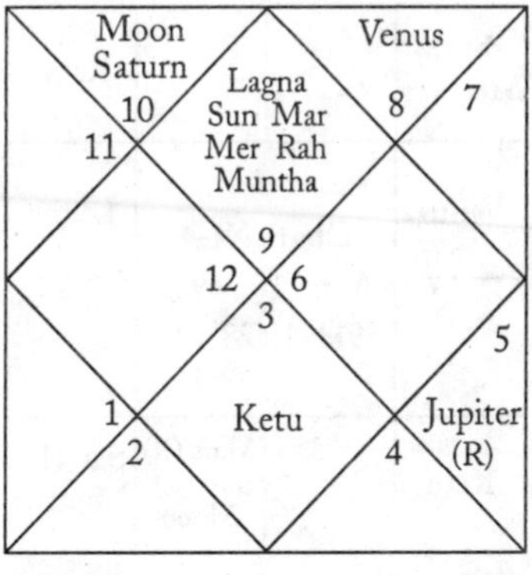

Lagna	19°20'	Mars	03°47'	Venus	12°49'
Sun	21°14'	Mercury	00°46'	Saturn	12°40'
Moon	03°09'	Jupiter (R)	20°49'	Rahu	16°06'

In the following year too, the native was imprisoned for some time. The Bandhana Saham in this chart (Chart XI-3) falls in Scorpio ($7^s29°34'$), in the eighth house, in the Rahu-Ketu axis. The lord of the Saham is retrograde, and in the eighth house from the Saham itself. Houses 6, 8, and 12, along with their lords, and malefic influences on them, indicated imprisonment.

6. *Foreign travel* : In Chart XI-4, *the Deshantara Saham* (Mid-point of the Ninth House - Ninth Lord + Ascendant + 1^s) falls in Sagittarius ($8^s18°19'$) in the sixth house, with Ketu

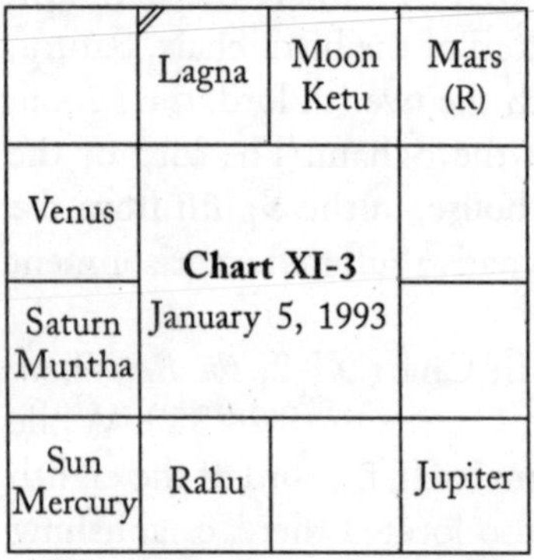

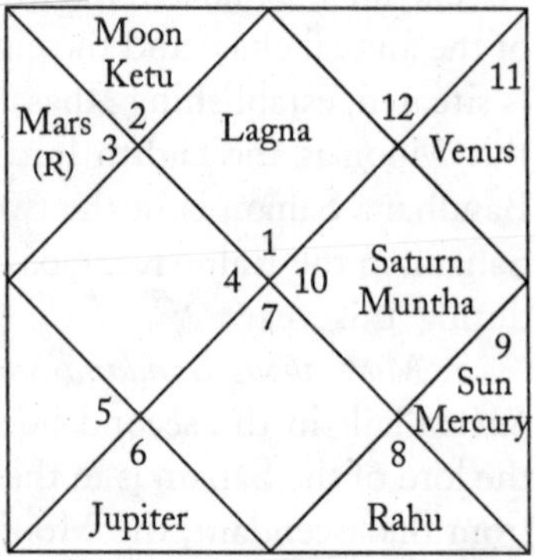

Lagna	17°06'	Mars (R)	24°57'	Venus	07°42'
Sun	21°14'	Mercury	10°23'	Saturn	23°03'
Moon	09°39'	Jupiter	20°03'	Rahu	27°38'

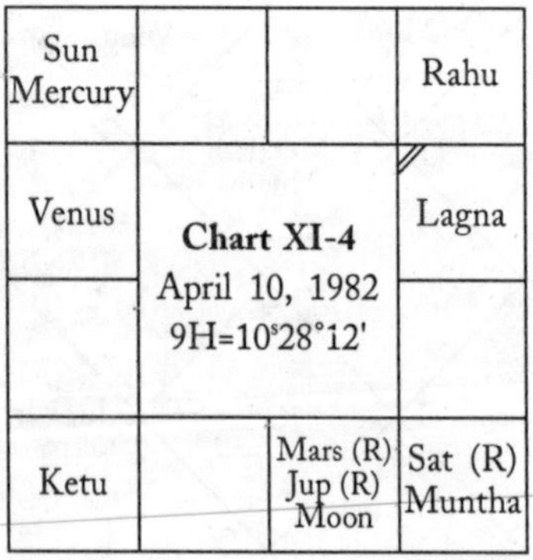

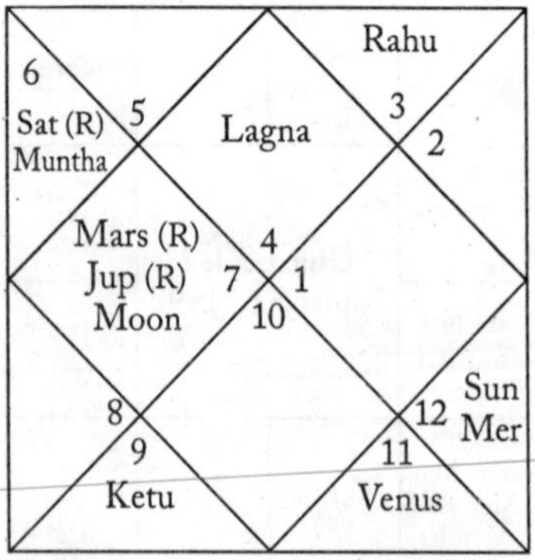

Lagna	03°55'	Mars (R)	13°01'	Venus	10°17'
Sun	26°30'	Mercury	24°57'	Saturn (R)	25°13'
Moon	18°25'	Jupiter (R)	13°48'	Rahu	24°06'

in it. The lord of the Saham, Jupiter, is in the fourth house, in Poorna Ithasala with Mars. Here, Mars is the Yoga-karaka, being the lord of the fifth and the tenth house, and is also the lord of the fifth house as well as the twelfth house from the Deshantara Saham. The native left India for a middle east country during this year.

7. *Mrityu Saham.* In Chart XI-5, *the Mrityu Saham* (Mid-point of Eighth House - Moon + Saturn + 1^{s}) falls in Gemini ($2^{s}5^{\circ}14'$), in the seventh house. There is a lot of malefic influence on the eighth house from the Mrityu Saham, viz., that of Mars, Saturn, and Rahu. The lord of the eighth from the Mrityu Saham, Saturn in this case, is in the eighth house from the year lord, Jupiter. The native died after a surgical operation.

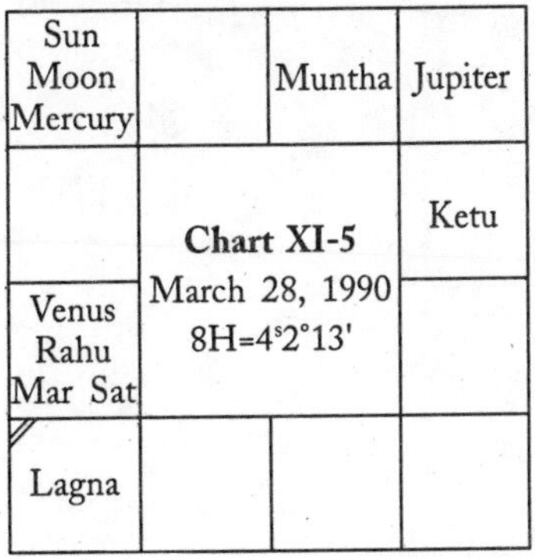

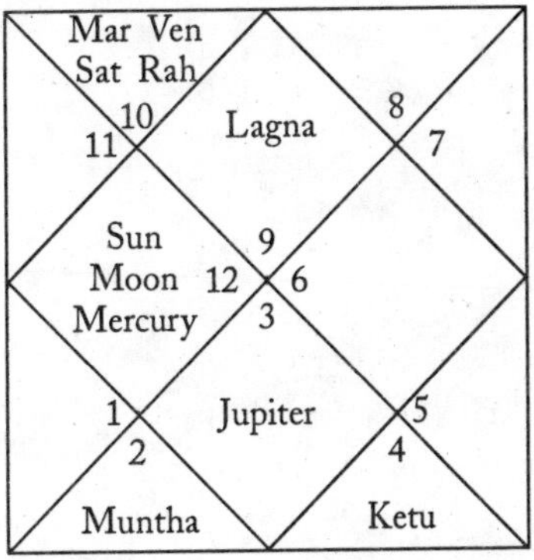

Lagna	29°07'	Mars	18°17'	Venus	26°45'
Sun	13°10'	Mercury	22°04'	Saturn	00°27'
Moon	27°26'	Jupiter	08°37'	Rahu	21°30'

In Chart X-9 (page 128), the mid-point of the eighth house is $9^{s}4^{\circ}12'$. The *Mrityu Saham* falls in Taurus ($1^{s}22^{\circ}0'$), in the twelfth house with Mars, the sixth lord of the annual chart, in it. The eighth from the Mrityu Saham is occupied by Saturn which is the eighth lord of the annual chart and the sixth lord of the birth chart. The eighth lord from the Mrityu Saham is in the third house, in the Rahu-Ketu axis, and in Ishrafa with Venus which is the lord of the Saham as well as the sixth lord from it. The native met with a violent end.

A Note of Caution

The Sahams are a highly remarkable feature of the annual horoscopy. They, however, are not the final word in themselves. They must be analysed along with the birth chart. The annual chart must also be analysed in respect of the yogas, the dashas, and other aspects already mentioned. Making a prognostication on the basis of the Sahams alone, without considering other relevant features in a horoscope, is doomed to failure.

As has already been pointed out, the Sahams have not been sufficiently worked and researched on. Unless they are applied to thousands of annual charts, their analysis may not yield the required accuracy.

CHAPTER XII

ANALYSIS OF DIFFERENT HOUSES

She wakes to action all who repose in slumber.
Some rise to labor for wealth, others to worship.
Those who saw little before now see more clearly.
Dawn raises to consciousness all living creatures.

'RIG VEDA'

Each house of the annual chart must be analysed first individually, and then jointly with other houses. The placement of planets in the various houses, their associations and aspects, the formation of various yogas in the chart, as also the relevant Sahams, must all be carefully analysed before reaching at any conclusion. It goes without saying that any conclusions must be arrived at only against the background of the promise already existing in the birth chart.

The analysis of the annual chart deeply intermingles with that of the birth chart. Some of the factors that frequently require a joint attention are :

(1) Placement of the birth ascendant in the annual chart.

(2) The signs occupied by the different planets in the birth chart and their placement in the annual chart.

(3) Position of the natal lagna lord in the annual chart.

(4) Location of the Muntha as well as the Muntha lord in relation to the ascendant in the annual chart and the ascendant in the birth chart.

(5) Recurrence of the birth ascendant as the ascendant in the annual chart.

(6) The Sahams in the birth as well as the annual chart.

The Role of the Office-Bearers

The five office-bearers in the annual chart have an important role to play. Their strength and weakness reflects the inherent strength and weakness of the annual chart. One of them, the Varshesha, as has already been pointed out, assumes almost the same significance as the lagna lord. Some of the results attributed to these office-bearers are as follows:

(1) *The Lagna Lord*: When *fully strong* (strength above 10 units in the Panchavargiya chart), it ensures comforts, good health, wealth, and peace of mind. When *of medium strength,* it reduces the intensity of benefic results. When *weak,* the whole year proves troublesome.

(2) *The Sun* as one of the office-bearers, when weak, leads to skin diseases, itching, eye disease, along with lack of enthusiasm.

(3) *The Moon* as one of the office-bearers, when weak, leads to impairment of vision, penury, subjugation, strife at home, and lack of mental peace.

(4) *Mars* as one of the weak office-bearers leads to cowardice, and lack of stability in general.

(5) *Mercury* as one of the weak office-bearers distorts one's thinking as well as reasoning.

(6) *Jupiter* as a weak office-bearer deviates one from the path of virtue.

(7) *Venus* as an office-bearer, when weak, causes loss of mental peace, and strife with women.

(8) *Saturn* as a weak office-bearer produces trouble from servants, and windy ailments.

Thus, when any of the planets holding an office is weak, its significations suffer. On the other hand, when these planets are strong, the events and objects signified by them prosper.

The Strength of a House

A house prospers when it is:

(i) associated with its own lord; or

(ii) aspected by its own lord; or

(iii) associated with natural benefics; or

(iv) aspected by natural benefics; or

(v) under the association or aspect of the year lord, or the lagna lord, or a strong or exalted planet.

On the other hand, the indications of a house suffer when it is :

(i) under the influence (aspect/association) of malefics; or

(ii) under the influence of weak or debilitated planets; or

(iii) bereft of the influence of its own lord, or the lagna lord, or a strong planet.

When both benefic and malefic influences operate on a particular house, mixed results are indicated.

Some of the classical combinations in respect of the various houses shall now be discussed. Some overlap in the influence of one house over another is inevitable here. In addition, certain events of life which may extend beyond the domain of a particular house may have been discussed under one particular house for the sake of convenience. For example, combinations for child birth have been discussed under the fifth house, while those for marriage have been dealt with under the seventh house, even though all the combinations mentioned may not fall under the said house.

THE FIRST HOUSE

A strong lagna lord in the lagna or in a kendra or in a trikona ensures good health throughout, and dominance over opponents.

The Moon, strong, in a Kamboola yoga involving the lagna lord is good for health and for peace of the mind.

The lagna under the influence (association/aspect) of malefics, bereft of any benefic influence, leads to varied troubles, quarrels with people, ill health, and unpalatable meals.

When the lagna lord of the birth chart, the lagna lord of the annual chart, the Muntha lord, the lord of the eighth house of the annual chart, as well as the lord of the year, are all strong and placed in houses other than 6, 8 or 12, the whole year passes in comfort, and is characterised by good health and access to wealth and fame. When they are weak. in houses 6, 8 or 12, and bereft of benefic influence, the whole year proves troublesome and may coincide with death in case an adverse dasha operates in the birth chart during the year.

A strong benefic in the ascendant, aspected by the ascendant lord, also ensures good health and wealth.

Jupiter as the lagna lord located in the lagna ensures favours and honour from those in power, and gain is wealth.

A malefic, in a kendra in the birth chart, falling in the lagna in the annual chart, produces adverse results.

A malefic, happening to be the lagna lord in the birth chart, casting inimical aspect on the lord of the year (or on the lord of the lagna of the annual chart) indicates illness. Any additional malefic influences may lead to troubles equivalent to death.

When the sign falling in the eighth house of the annual chart is identical with the lagna in the birth chart, it indicates illness.

The Dwi-Janma Year (The year of second birth) :

When the birth lagna recurs as the lagna in the annual chart, it is *referred to as the Dwi-janma year.* Such a year is generally adverse and leads to illness, disappointments, reversals, monetary loss, loss of name and fame, etc. The following points must be noted in this regard.

(a) If the degree of the lagna in the annual chart is identical with that of the lagna at birth, the whole year proves troublesome.

(b) If the birth nakshatra (i.e., the nakshatra occupied by the Moon in the birth chart) too recurs in the annual chart, along with the ascendant, and if the Moon and Jupiter are weak or in house 6 or 8, and under malefic influence, the year proves very bad. If the birth chart too shows an adverse dasha, the year may prove fatal.

(c) The Moon in the sixth house and Jupiter in the eighth house, during a Dwi-janma year, may cause serious illness or death.

(d) When the lord of the year, the lagna lord of the annual chart, and the Muntha lord are strong, much of the blemish is taken out of the Dwi-janma year.

(e) Much of the adverse influence of the Dwi-janma year is lost if Jupiter and the Moon are strong in the year chart, and if they are well placed. If Jupiter and the Moon fall in the sixth or the eighth house, adverse results are ensured.

Some Additional Adverse Combinations

Placement of the lagna lord in the eighth house of the annual chart, aspected by Mars, causes injury by weapon, or accidents.

The lagna lord, the lord of the eighth house, and the Muntha together in the fourth, eighth or twelfth house may lead to death.

When the lagna lord and the Muntha lord are combust and under inimical aspect of Saturn, there occur numerous calamities, ill health and even death.

The lord of the year establishing Ishrafa yoga with natural malefics causes illness.

Debilitated Jupiter and Venus, in inimical Navamshas, deprive the native of all comforts during the year. If in addition there is an exchange of the lagna lord with the eighth lord, there may ensue death.

When the sign falling in the eighth house of the birth chart becomes the lagna in the annual chart, it leads to ill health.

A direct planet in the twelfth from the lagna and a retrograde planet in the second house causes illness. Such a situation arising in relation to the year lord, or the lagna lord of the birth chart, or the lagna lord of the annual chart, can lead to imprisonment, if the birth chart too indicates this.

The Moon in houses 4, 6, 7, 8 and 12 from the lagna in the annual chart is also considered adverse for health.

No benefit can accrue from the year lord Mercury which is conjoined or aspected by malefics. Combust Mercury as the year lord becomes an obstacle in intellectual pursuits.

Jupiter as the lord of the year, conjoined or aspected by malefics, placed in the lagna, leads to loss of wealth, and displeasure of those in power.

Cancellation of Adverse Influences

No adverse effects should be pronounced unless factors causing their cancellation are also taken into consideration. Some of such relieving factors are being mentioned hereunder.

- A strong lagna lord under benefic influences (aspect/association) in a kendra or a trikona (i.e., houses 1, 4, 7, 10, 5, 9).
- A strong Jupiter under benefic influence, bereft of malefic influence, in a kendra or a trikona.
- Jupiter and the seventh lord under benefic influence, bereft of malefic influence.
- Malefics in houses 3, 6 and 11, and benefics in the kendras or trikonas.
- Strong lords of the Muntha, the birth ascendant and the annual ascendant, in kendras, trikonas, the second house or the eleventh house.
- Exalted Jupiter, Venus and Saturn establishing Ithasala with benefics.

Chart X-7 has Leo ascendant which is the same as that at birth. There is thus a recurrence of the birth lagna in the annual chart. The Muntha is located in the eighth house, the worst house for the Muntha. The ascendant is occupied by a retrograde eighth lord. The lagna lord is located in the sixth house along with the sixth lord Saturn. A Bhavishyat Ithasala occurs between the tenth lord Venus and a retrograde eighth lord Jupiter; from the Muntha too, Jupiter and Venus happen to be the tenth and the eighth lords. The native had every thing going wrong for him during the year. He had to quit his job (the tenth lord-eighth lord link) under compulsion, and narrowly escaped arrest. Twice during the year, he lost all his possessions due to thefts at his residence. His health too suffered during this year.

The above chart may be suitably compared with Chart X-12. Here again, the sign Leo rises with a retrograde eighth lord, Jupiter, located in the lagna. The birth lagna happens to be Pisces which coincides with the eighth house of the annual chart. The Muntha in Sagittarius is in the Rahu-Ketu axis while its lord Jupiter is retrograde, and located in the sixth house from the birth lagna. The sixth lord is with the fourth lord Mars in the sixth house indicating losses, thefts, accidents, domestic strife. The owner of this chart happens to be the wife of the native referred to in Chart X-7. She too underwent a lot of suffering along with her husband. These charts show that similar destinies tend to run in families.

Chart XII-1 belongs to the late Mrs. Indira Gandhi, the former Prime Minister of India, for her sixty-seventh year, the year of her death, commencing on November 20, 1983. The adverse factors in this chart may be listed as under :

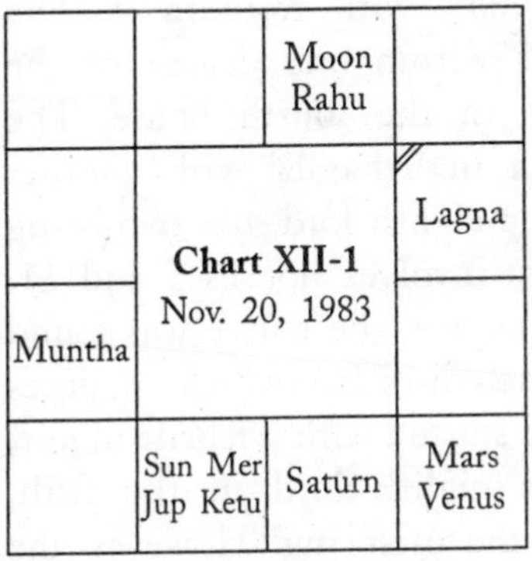

Chart XII-1
Nov. 20, 1983

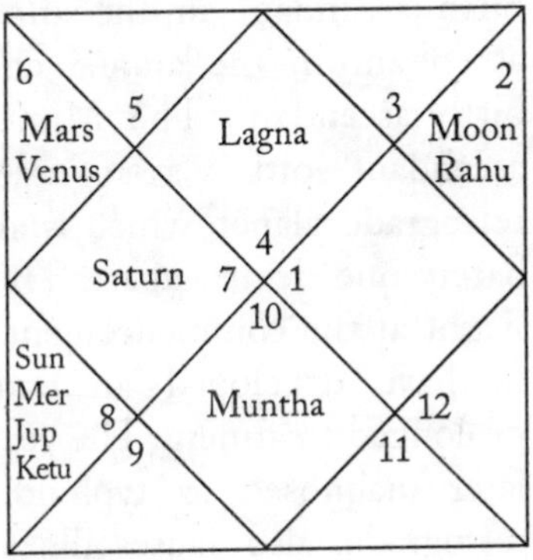

Lagna	01°56'	Mars	07°41'	Venus	18°29'
Sun	04°07'	Mercury	16°00'	Saturn	16°03'
Moon	05°51'	Jupiter	22°58'	Rahu	22°21'

1. Recurrence of the birth lagna Cancer.
2. The lagna lord in the Rahu-Ketu axis.
3. No benefic in kendras, and the only planet posited in a kendra is the malefic Saturn which is the lord of the seventh as well as the eighth house.
4. The Muntha is in the adverse seventh.
5. The Muntha Lord is in the adverse fourth.
6. Saturn is also the lord of the year. The significance of the year lord, as already indicated, is no less than that of the ascendant lord. From such a Saturn, the Moon, which is the

lagna lord of the annual chart as well as the birth chart, is located in the eighth house in association with Rahu.

7. The year lord is placed between malefcs. In the twelfth from it is Mars while in the second house are the Sun and (a retrograde) Ketu.

The native was assassinated by her own body guards. There is affliction to the ascendant, to the ascendant lord, to the year lord and to the Moon, along with an adverse location of the Muntha and the Muntha lord. When the lagna in the birth chart recurs in the annual chart, all adverse influences in the chart seem to become manifold.

Chart XII-2 shows another example of the recurrence of the birth ascendant in the annual chart, with Ketu in it. The ascendant in the annual chart is within one degree of the birth ascendant. The Muntha is in the fourth house. The ascendant lord is retrograde, and in 'Ithasala' with another retrograde planet, which is also the eighth lord, the two being barely one degree apart. The yoga involves houses 5 and 11. Right at the commencement of the year, the native was found to have developed an endocrine disorder which requires prolonged treatment. The year also started with a febrile illness, later diagnosed as typhoid. The eighth lord in the fifth, retrograde, also causes illness to the offspring. However, the tenth lord is in the tenth house, and the Ithasala already

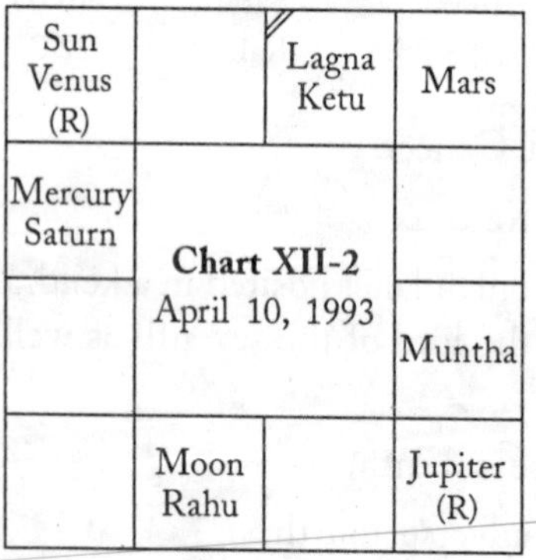

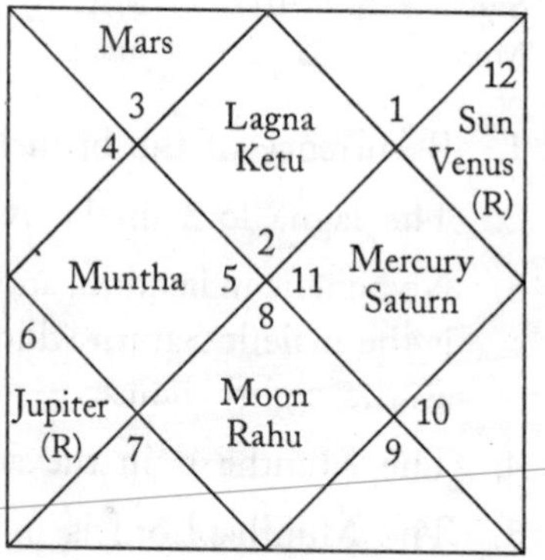

Lagna	02°41'	Mars	28°13'	Venus (R)	13°05'
Sun	26°28'	Mercury	29°10'	Saturn	03°40'
Moon	11°37'	Jupiter (R)	14°41'	Rahu	19°41'

mentioned also happens to be between an exalted lagna lord and the eleventh lord, involving houses 5 and 11. The native got a promotion in her job along with the consequent monetary benefits.

THE SECOND HOUSE

Jupiter is the significator for wealth. If Jupiter is strong and favourable, the second house prospers and inflow of wealth is ensured.

Jupiter as the second lord of the birth chart, falling in the second house of the annual chart and establishing Ithasala with the lagna lord, ensures flow of money during the year. Such a Jupiter, if in Ishrafa with planets other than the lagna lord, causes loss of wealth.

When Jupiter in the annual chart beneficially aspects the second house of birth chart, and the year lord is also strong, it ensures inflow of money without much effort.

Strong Mercury as the year lord in the second house, when well-aspected, ensures earnings through writing and intellectual pursuits.

Benefics in the birth lagna falling in the second house of the annual chart ensure good earnings during the year.

The Sun in the lagna in the birth chart, falling in the second house in the annual chart, ensures acquisition of wealth. Saturn in a similar situation causes failures in undertakings.

Jupiter in the second house in the birth chart, becoming the year lord in the annual chart, ensures benefits accruing from the house that it inhabits in the annual chart.

Mercury, Jupiter and Venus in the second house or in the Dhana Saham ensure income and wealth during the year. A strong lord of the second house, aspecting the second house of the birth chart or of the annual chart, ensures acquisition of wealth. When weak, it leads to loss of money.

When the second lord as well as the occupants of the second house in the birth chart are weak or combust in the annual chart, there is loss of accumulated wealth.

A movable sign rising in the lagna associated with or aspected by malefics leads to loss of money.

Jupiter in the second or the eighth house, associated with malefics leads to danger of punishment.

THE THIRD HOUSE

A strong Jupiter in the third house, or the third lord in Ithasala with Jupiter, indicates comforts from brothers and increase of valour.

The third lord in the third house in Ithasala with the lagna lord leads to harmony with brothers.

Harmonious relations with the siblings also result when there is benefic aspect on the third house, with Mars in the third house identical with Capricorn or Aquarius, or Mercury in the third house identical with Aries or Scorpio.

Strong Mercury or Venus as the lagna lord, in the birth chart or the annual chart, located in the third house of the annual chart, also ensure harmony with brothers and relatives.

Strong Venus in Cancer in the third house, and being one of the office-bearers, ensures the birth of a sibling.

The Sun or Venus as the year lord, bereft of malefic influence, ensure comforts from brothers and sisters. When weak or under malefic influence, there is trouble from siblings.

Strife with siblings results when (a) the third lord is also the lord of the year, and is combust; or (b) there is weak Jupiter in the third house; or (c) the Moon and Mars, bereft of Jupiter's influence, are located in the third house; or (d) the third lord is in the third house in Ishrafa with malefics.

The third lord in Ishrafa with the lord of the year causes illness, and conflicts with siblings and relatives.

Saturn in the third house identical with Aries or Scorpio leads to illness of the native or his brother.

Mars in the third house identical with Gemini or Virgo also leads to the brother's illness.

The lagna lord and the third lord together in the seventh house lead to trouble from brothers.

Bhratri Saham afflicted by malefics, or with its lord combust, proves harmful to the brother during the year.

Lord of the Bhratri Saham in house 6, 8 or 12, weak, combust or retrograde, leads to affliction to the siblings.

Exchange between the third lord and the sixth lord causes open conflict with the siblings.

THE FOURTH HOUSE

The presence of the fourth lord in the fourth house is good for both the mother and the father of the native.

A weak fourth lord in the birth chart as well as the annual chart promises no comforts to the parents.

Afflicted Sun in the fourth house causes affliction to the father.

Afflicted Moon in the fourth house causes affliction to the mother.

The Sun and the Moon together in the fourth house cause affliction to both parents.

When Saturn and Mars, bereft of benefic influence, are located in the annual chart in a sign identical with the fourth house of the birth chart, or the sign occupied by the fourth lord of the birth chart, there occurs trouble to both mother and father.

Location of the Matri Saham or the Pitri Saham in the fourth house is beneficial for both the mother and the father.

Lord of the Matri Saham or the Pitri Saham in Ithasala with the lagna lord also proves good for the mother and the father. Combust and afflicted lord of the Matri Saham in the annual chart leads to separation from the parents.

When the Matri Saham or the Pitri Saham is afflicted in the fourth house from the Muntha, there is separation from (or loss of!) parents.

Lords of the Matri Saham and the Pitri Saham in Ithasala with malefics cause trouble to parents. When, instead, there is Ishrafa with inimical planets, it is still worse and causes fear to mother and father.

The Moon in the same sign as in the birth chart leads to affliction to the mother.

Saturn conjunct the Sun causes disgrace and opposition at the hands of the father.

Saturn on the Moon's natal sign leads to strife with the mother. When it is on the Sun's natal sign, there is strife with the father.

THE FIFTH HOUSE

The fifth house primarily deals with progeny. Combinations indicating child birth generally result in auspicious or favourable events pertaining to children when the birth of children is not relevant to the native.

Jupiter's natal sign identical with the fifth house of the annual chart, and occupied by the year lord Mars or Mercury, indicates the birth of a son.

Jupiter as the year lord in the fifth house or the eleventh house ensures the birth of a son and comforts from children. The Sun, Mars or Mercury as the year lord in these houses also give progeny. Afflicted Mars or Saturn, or a weak Moon in these houses produce adverse results.

Jupiter's natal sign falling in the lagna in the annual chart indicates the birth of a son. Same result is obtained when the natal sign of Venus or Mercury falls in the ascendant of the annual chart. The natal sign of Saturn or Mars falling in the lagna or the fifth house of the annual chart indicates affliction to progeny.

The birth of a son is also indicated when (a) a strong lagna lord and fifth lord conjoin in the fifth house; or (b) an exalted Moon, Jupiter or Venus is located in the fifth house; or (c) a strong Venus as the fifth lord in the birth chart falls in the fifth house of the annual chart and establishes Ithasala with the lagna lord.

Jupiter as lord of the Putra Saham, located in the fifth house, indicates the birth of a son.

When the fifth lord or the Putra Saham are strong, or when the Putra Saham is located in the fifth house, a son is born. Punya Saham, associated with or aspected by benefics, falling in the fifth house, ensures the birth of a son.

When Jupiter, the karaka for progeny, is afflicted, there occur worries in relation to one's offspring.

Affliction to one's son occurs if the sign of natal Saturn falls in the fifth house and is inimically aspected by a malefic. Retrograde Mars in the fifth house indicates the death of a son.

Benefic influences on the fifth house or the fifth lord, and a strong fifth lord, promote the events indicated by the fifth house; the reverse holds true when there is affliction to fifth house or the fifth lord.

Combinations that promise welfare of progeny also ensure favourable results pertaining to the other significations of to the fifth house.

In Chart XII-3, the lagna lord, the Sun, is in Ithasala with the fifth lord Jupiter, involving houses 2 and 11. The native begot a child during this year. Seeing from the Muntha also, the fifth lord Jupiter is in Ithasala with the Muntha lord Mars, the houses involved being the eighth and the eleventh here. The presence of the sixth lord Saturn in the fifth house also does not speak well of the health of the new born. It may be noted that there is a recurrence of the birth ascendant in the annual chart, the ascendant degree also falling on exact degree of the natal ascendant. The lagna lord is within one degree of the sixth lord forming an Ithasala. The Muntha in the fourth house is of no help. Since no office-bearer aspects the lagna, the Muntha lord assumes the year lordship. The Muntha lord, however, is deeply combust and in Poorna Ithasala with the 6th lord Saturn. The native suffered ill health throughout the year and had several obstacles coming his way.

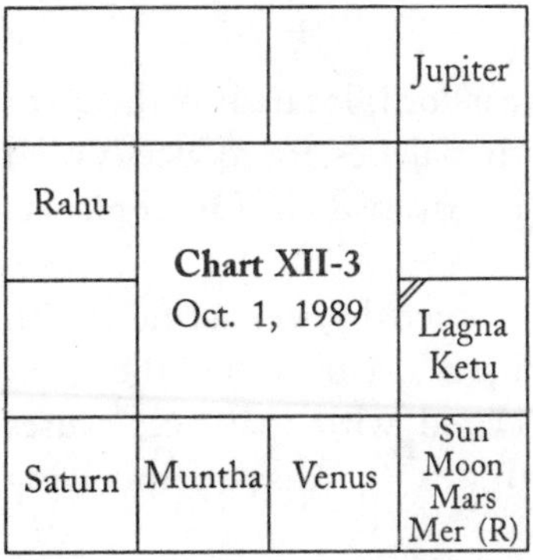

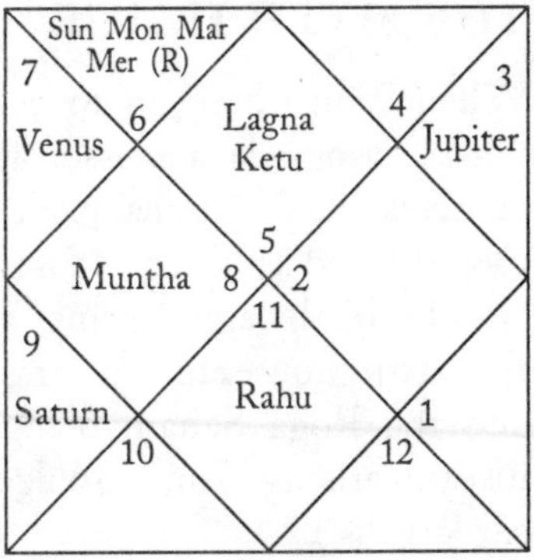

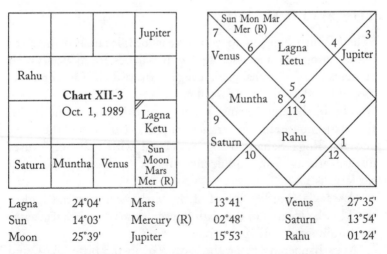

Lagna	24°04'	Mars	13°41'	Venus	27°35'
Sun	14°03'	Mercury (R)	02°48'	Saturn	13°54'
Moon	25°39'	Jupiter	15°53'	Rahu	01°24'

In Chart XII-4, there is an Ithasala between the lagna lord, the Moon, located in the tenth house conjoined with the eleventh lord Venus, and the fifth lord Mars located in the sixth

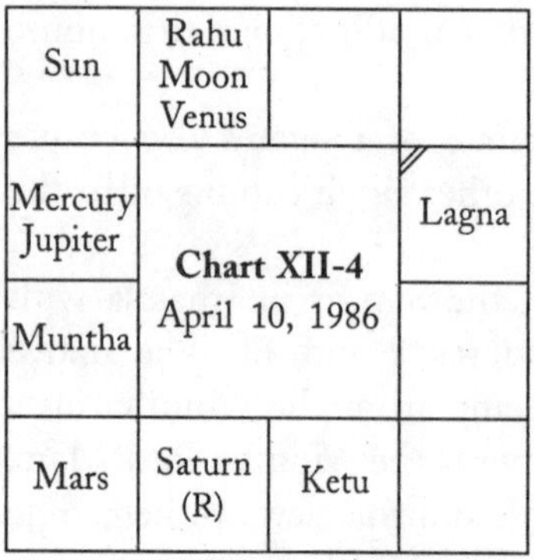

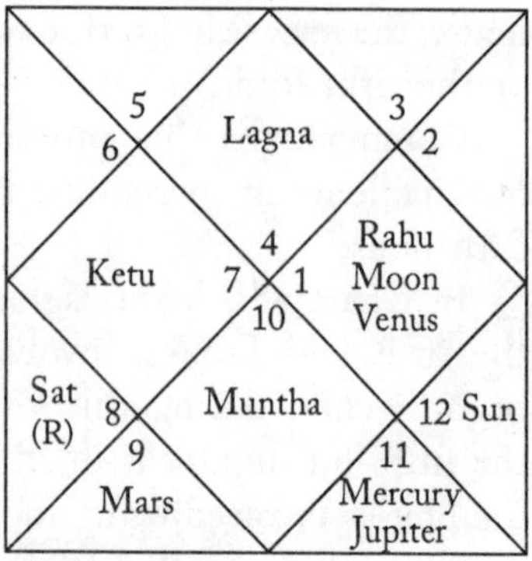

Lagna	11°43'	Mars	12°45'	Venus	16°09'
Sun	26°28'	Mercury	29°09'	Saturn (R)	15°39'
Moon	08°03'	Jupiter	17°34'	Rahu	06°24'

house. The native gave birth to a daughter during this year. It was, however, a pregnancy marked by multiple ailments like injury from a roadside accident, premature uterine contractions, urinary tract infection and low weight gain. Mars, the fifth lord, is in the adverse sixth house while the eighth lord, Saturn, retrograde, is located in the fifth house and bereft of any bencfic influence.

THE SIXTH HOUSE

When Saturn happens to be the year lord, located in the sixth house, retrograde, and associated with malefics, it produces varied ailments like abdominal pain, fever, eye disease, etc. Other planets too, afflicted similarly, cause illness.

The birth lagna, being a sign owned by Venus, falling in the sixth house in the annual chart, occupied by the Sun, and the Roga Saham being associated with malefics, causes disease arising from indulgence in sex (or disease involving sex organs!).

A weak and afflicted lord of the birth ascendant and lord of the Muntha located in the sixth house in the annual chart causes varied ailments during the year.

Mars happening to be the sixth lord in the birth chart, and falling in the sixth house of the annual chart, leads to ill health. If such a Mars is in Ithasala with a malefic, it could lead to a serious disease.

The lagna lord or the lord of the year in Ithasala with the sixth lord leads to illness as determined by the nature of the sixth lord (refer to Chart XII-3, vide supra).

A benefic in its own sign in the sixth house leads to illness caused by one's wife. (According to some, this indicates acquisition of a wife).

Placement of the sixth lord in the lagna generates enemies and opponents during the year.

The sixth lord located in the fifth house, or the fifth lord in the sixth house, causes affliction to progeny.

Placement of the ninth lord in the sixth house causes troubles in transit.

Chart XIl-5 belongs to a patient suffering from chronic myeloid leukemia, for his thirtieth year commencing from November 25, 1988. The birth ascendant (Virgo) falls in the eighth house of the annual chart. The lagna lord, Saturn, is in Ithasala with the sixth lord, the Moon, in the fifth house. The lagna is involved in the Rahu-Ketu axis. The lagna lord is in Ishrafa with Mars which is in Ithasala with Mercury, the eighth lord of the annual chart. The lagna lord, Saturn, thus establishes a direct link with the sixth lord, the Moon, and an indirect link, through Mars, with the eighth lord, Mercury. Mars, the eighth lord of the birth chart, is also indicative of bone marrow, the "factory" that synthesises blood in the body and is primarily at

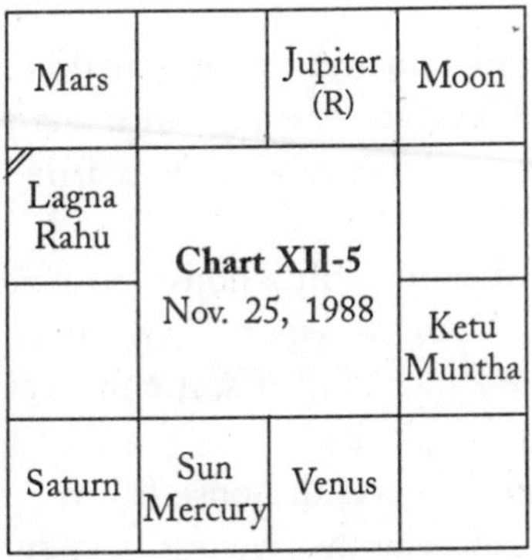

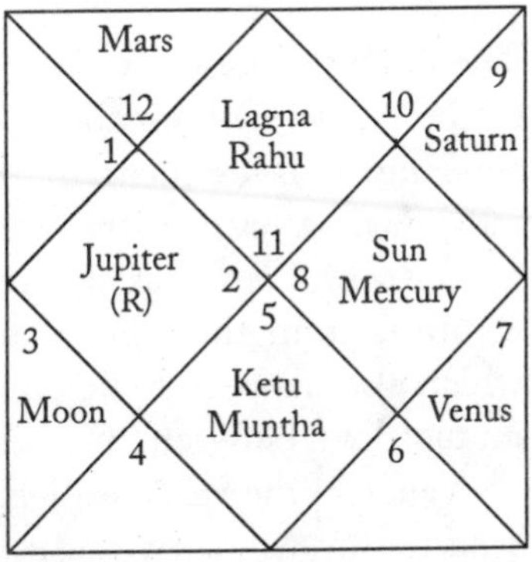

Lagna	18°48'	Mars	10°53'	Venus	08°28'
Sun	10°04'	Mercury	06°09'	Saturn	07°38'
Moon	00°58'	Jupiter (R)	06°59'	Rahu	16°20'

fault in case of leukemia. The native died of leukemia (blood cancer) in February 1989.

Some Other Indications for Ill Health

- The Sun, afflicted in the twelfth house, causes eye disease.
- The rashi of natal Saturn falling in the lagna of the annual chart, and under inimical aspect from Saturn, leads to death.
- The rashi of natal Mars falling in the lagna in the annual chart, with inimical aspect from Mars, causes inflammatory disease, and fear from fire (burns!).
- A malefic occupying a kendra in the birth chart, located in the lagna in the annual chart, leads to ill health.
- When the Sun is associated with Mercury or Ketu, and is in Ithasala with Mars, the whole year is spent in illness.
- Illness also results when the Muntha, the Muntha lord, the lagna and the lagna lord, are hemmed between malefics.
- When Mercury and Venus are weak in the birth chart and are associated with Ketu in the annual chart, again the whole year is characterised by ill health.

Note : Benefic aspects on the sixth house relieve affliction.

THE SEVENTH HOUSE

The Seventh house primarily deals with marriage and sexual life of the native. Combinations which indicate marriage in a chart generally indicate marital harmony in the case of a married individual, or even extra-marital relations.

A strong Venus as the year lord in the fifth house ensures comforts from the wife. If such a Venus is aspected by Mars, which also happens to be one of the Panchadhikaris, it enhances mutual love between the native and his wife.

Venus as the year lord located in the seventh house (a) when aspected by Mercury, causes association with a young women; (b) when aspected by Saturn, leads to association with an older women; and (c) when aspected by Jupiter, ensures progeny from one's (legitimate) wife.

The lagna lord of the birth chart when strong and located in the seventh house of the annual chart ensures comforts from women.

The lagna lord of the birth chart together with the lagna lord of the annual chart, located in the seventh house of the annual chart, again ensures favours from women.

Venus in the Hudda of Jupiter, and aspected by Mars, leads to excessive mutual attraction between man and wife. Affliction to wife occurs when the lord of the Vivaha Saham and the lord of the seventh house of the annual chart are under malefic aspect or association.

A weak Moon in the sign of natal Venus promises little comfort from one's wife.

Troubles arise from wife and children when the Muntha is located in the seventh house in association with the Sun and Mars.

The Moon, exalted or in its own sign (Cancer), in the seventh house from the Muntha, indicates foreign travel.

Combinations for Marriage

- The rashi of natal Venus falling in the seventh house, with Venus being the year lord.
- The lagna lord in Ithasala with the seventh lord.
- A strong Mars in the natal rashi of Venus proves auspicious and ensures marriage.
- Jupiter in the natal rashi of Venus, in a kendra or a trikona.
- The Muntha in the house of any of the five office-bearers, aspected by Jupiter.
- Venus as seventh lord in the birth chart, happening to be the strong seventh lord in the annual chart, in Ithasala with the lagna lord.
- Mars as the year lord aspected by Venus.
- Venus as the year lord aspected by Mars.
- Vivaha Saham aspected by Venus and Mars.
- The seventh lord of the birth chart, the Muntha lord of the

annual chart, as well as the lord of the year, together located in the seventh or the tenth house.

- The seventh lord of the birth chart happening to be the lord of the Vivaha Saham.
- A strong fifth lord in the seventh house.
- Jupiter associated with the Muntha or the Muntha lord.

Marriage, along with excessive sexual indulgence, results from the following combinations:

- Lord of the seventh house in the birth chart related, by association, aspect or Ithasala, to Venus which happens to be the year lord.
- Lord of the Hudda of the ascendant in the annual chart, in the rashi of natal Venus, and located in a kendra or a trikona.
- Lord of the Vivaha Saham in the rashi of the natal Venus, and located in a kendra or a trikona.

In Chart XII-6, there is an Ithasala between the lagna lord Saturn and the seventh lord, the Sun. The Vivaha Saham (Taurus 21°31') is beneficially aspected by Venus and Mars. The seventh lord of the birth chart (Aries ascendant) happens to be the lord of the Vivaha Saham in the annual chart. The Hudda

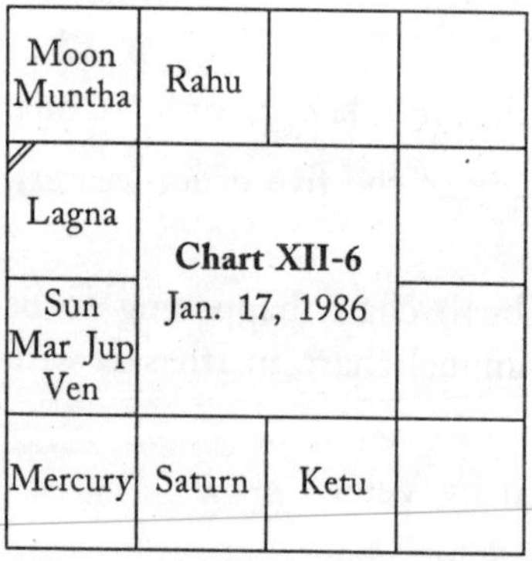

Chart XII-6
Jan. 17, 1986

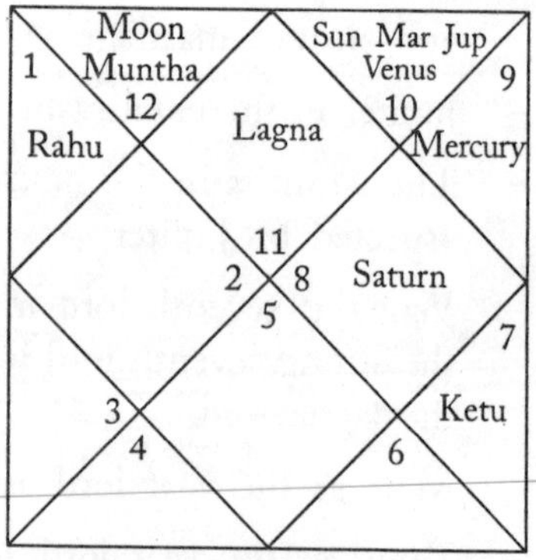

Lagna	29°35'	Mars	26°48'	Venus	05°01'
Sun	03°06'	Mercury	23°41'	Saturn	13°05'
Moon	24°56'	Jupiter	28°09'	Rahu	11°31'

lord of the ascendant (Saturn in this case) is in Scorpio which is the sign occupied by Venus in the birth chart, and is located in a kendra (tenth house). The native got married during this year.

The native of Chart XII-7 got married in February 1991. The annual chart shows Jupiter located in Cancer, which is the rashi of Venus in the birth chart, in the ninth house (a trikona). The Muntha is located in the sign identical with the birth ascendant, aspected by Jupiter. Here, Jupiter is in Poorna Ithasala with the seventh lord as well as the Muntha lord. The Hudda lord of the ascendant (Jupiter in this case) is in the rashi of natal Venus (Cancer), and is located in the ninth house (a trikona).

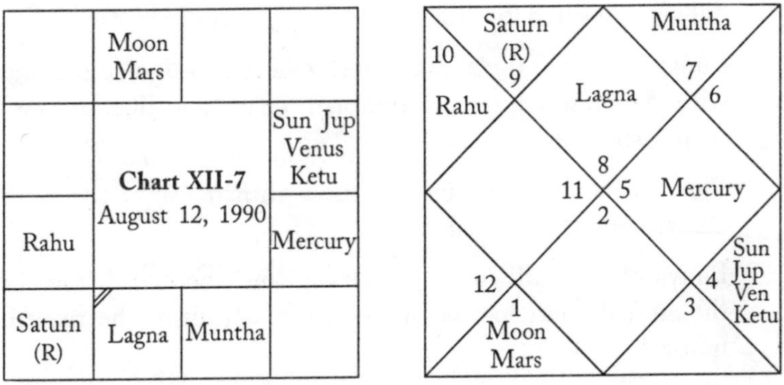

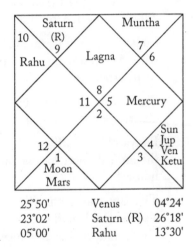

Lagna	19°52'	Mars	25°50'	Venus	04°24'
Sun	25°41'	Mercury	23°02'	Saturn (R)	26°18'
Moon	08°46'	Jupiter	05°00'	Rahu	13°30'

THE EIGHTH HOUSE

Jupiter as the lord of the year located in the second or the eighth house, aspected by malefics, causes loss of wealth.

Mars in the eighth house causes fear from fire or weapon or from the ruler.

Mars in the eighth house in the signs Aries, Leo, Sagittarius or Taurus causes injury from a sword. When this Mars is associated with the lagna lord and the lord of the eighth house, it leads to death.

The Sun and Mars in the eighth house result in fall from a height.

The Sun, Mars and Saturn located in the eighth or the tenth house lead to a fall from a vehicle.

Combinations for Death

The following combinations indicate death if there is a maraka dasha operating in the birth chart. When the birth chart does not indicate serious affliction, these combinations generally lead to ill health.

- The Sun, Mars and Mercury in the eighth house.
- The year lord associated with Mars and located in the eighth house: death or death-like trouble.
- The lord of the Punya Saham in the eighth house from the Saham, aspected by malefics.
- Punya Saham in the annual chart, falling in a sign coinciding with the eighth house of the birth chart, and ill-associated or ill-aspected.
- Punya Saham and its lord in the eighth house of the birth chart or of the annual chart.
- Punya Saham afflicted by malefics, and the eighth lord of the annual chart located in the sixth, eighth or the twelfth house.
- The lagna lord, the Muntha lord and the year lord, being also the lord of the eighth, or in Ithasala with the lord of the eighth, in the presence of a maraka dasha in the birth chart.
- A malefic in the birth lagna, falling in the eighth house of the annual chart. When a debilitated Mars aspects it, the result is a suicide.
- Saturn in the eighth house in Ithasala with the eighth lord. When there is Ithasala with benefics, the affliction gets cancelled.
- Saturn being the eighth lord in the birth chart, in Ithasala with the lagna lord of the annual chart involving a hostile aspect: immediate death.

- The lagna lord of the birth chart and the lagna lord of the annual chart together falling in the eighth house of the annual chart.
- A combust birth lagna lord in the eighth house of the annual chart: illness and fear from opponents.
- The year lord with the Moon and Mars in the sixth, eighth or twelfth house : troubles equivalent to death.
- The lagna lord in Ithasala with the eighth lord: some affliction though not necessarily death.
- The lord of the eighth house of the Shatru Saham in the eighth house of the birth chart or the annual chart.

The lord of the eighth house of the Mrityu Saham in the eighth house of the birth chart or the annual chart.

In Chart XII-8, the Moon, occupant of the eighth house of the birth chart, is located in the lagna. The Punya Saham falls in Scorpio ($7^s29°33'$), occupied by the Sun, the lord of the eighth house of the birth chart. The lord of the Punya Saham, Mars, is located in Leo, coinciding with the eighth house of the birth chart, and is in Rahu-Ketu axis. The Mrityu Saham falls in Aries ($0^s2°47'$). Its eighth lord, Mars, is in the eighth house from the birth lagna (Capricorn). The Muntha and the Muntha lord are also not favourably placed. The native died in a plane crash.

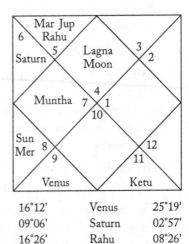

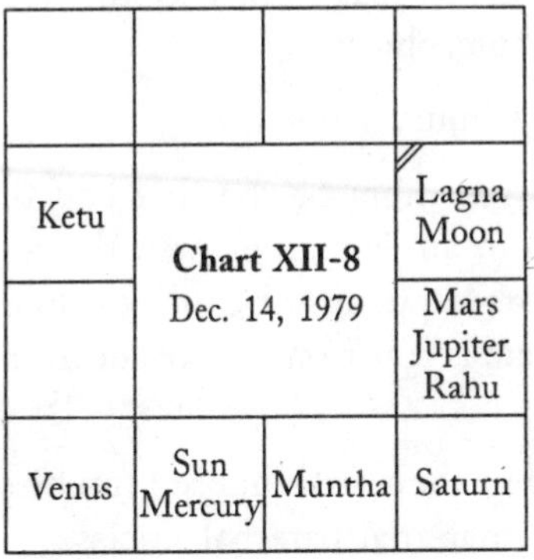

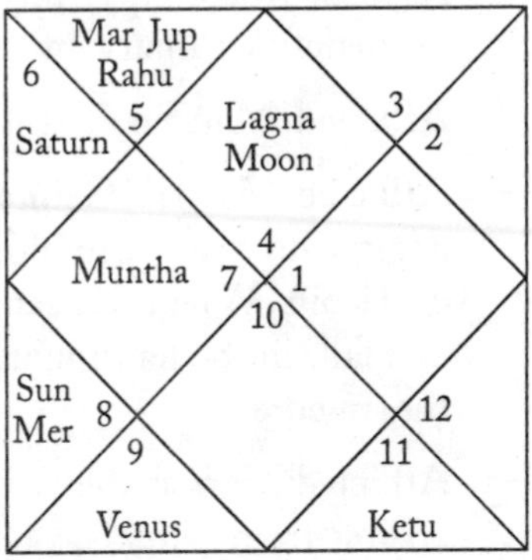

Lagna	09°59'	Mars	16°12'	Venus	25°19'
Sun	27°26'	Mercury	09°06'	Saturn	02°57'
Moon	07°52'	Jupiter	16°26'	Rahu	08°26'

Combinations for Suicide

- The birth lagna lord, with a malefic, in the eighth house of the annual chart.
- The Muntha with Saturn, aspected by the fourth or the seventh aspect of Mars. Aspect of a debilitated Mars also has the same effect.
- Saturn in the eighth house in Ithasala with the eighth lord.

Quarrels

- The Lagna lord weak, combust and ill-associated : quarrels with women.
- Jupiter in the eighth house, not holding any of the five portfolios.
- Mars as the year lord, afflicted : quarrels with relatives as well as opponents.
- The birth lagna falling in the eighth house of the annual chart, afflicted by a malefic : disease, strife.
- Afflicted Saturn in the seventh house : quarrels, false allegations, loss of fame and dignity.

Death or Disease

- A weak Mars happening to be the year lord, and afflicted by malefics : injury by a metallic object.
- Afflicted Mars in fiery signs : injury from fire.
- Afflicted Mars in Gemini, Virgo, Libra or the first half of Sagittarius : death resulting from an encounter with thieves or dacoits. When this same Mars happens to be the year lord and falls in the tenth house, there is fear from thieves or from the ruler.
- Afflicted Mars as the year lord in the fourth house : troubles arising from parents, or from maternal/paternal uncles.
- The Sun having Ishrafa with Venus *in the birth chart,* also being one of the office-bearers in the annual chart and located in a kendra : illness; fall from status.

- Mercury in a sign of Mars in the birth chart, being one of the office-bearers in the annual chart : illness. When this Mercury receives inimical aspect of Mars, there is disease involving blood. When it is combust, and afflicted by malefics, there is death or imprisonment in a foreign land.
- The Moon in the rashi of natal Mars, and being one of the office-bearers : illness; secret troubles from the superiors.
- Ill-associated Mercury in Ithasala with Mars, involving a hostile aspect : death.
- Mars in the tenth house, afflicted : fall from a quadruped; blood disorder.
- Afflicted Saturn in the tenth house : injury from a metallic object.
- A strong Saturn in the tenth house : fear or troubles from the wife.
- Mrityu Saham being weak : death-like troubles.
- Punya Saham and the Moon in the lagna, and malefics in the seventh house : death.
- A malefic each in the second house and the twelfth house : death.

THE NINTH HOUSE

Mars as the strong year lord, bereft of ill association or aspect, in the third or the ninth house, ensures a comfortable journey. A weak Mars in the ninth house indicates distant travel along with one's near and dear ones. A strong Mars in the ninth from Jupiter leads to a beneficial or auspicious journey.

The Sun as the year lord, located in the third or the ninth house, and involved in a Kamboola yoga with a strong Moon, causes a comfortable journey according to one's own desire. When this Sun is bereft of any 'office', it causes foreign journey with the help of someone.

Venus as the year lord in the third or the ninth house indicates a comfortable journey. When this Venus is combust or retrograde, journey is uncomfortable.

An unafflicted Mercury as the year lord in the third or the ninth house causes journey to auspicious places, pilgrimages, etc. When this Mercury is afflicted, the journey is painful.

Jupiter as the year lord, unafflicted, in the third or the ninth house : pilgrimages.

Weak and afflicted Jupiter and Venus in the third or the ninth house lead to an inauspicious journey.

A planet in the ninth house and in Ithasala with the lagna lord : unplanned journey.

The lagna lord in Ithasala with the ninth lord : journey.

The lagna lord/the year lord in Ithasala with the year lord/ the Muntha lord indicates journey.

Saturn, bereft of office, in the ninth house : uncomfortable journey associated with loss or theft.

Jupiter bereft of office, in the ninth house : distant travel; increase in name and fame.

The Moon or Jupiter in the ninth house in the rashi of natal Saturn : prolonged journey.

The Muntha in the seventh house and the Moon in the ninth house : foreign travel.

Mars, as the lord of the year, located in a kendra: distant travel.

The lord of the Yatra (Deshantara) Saham in the ninth house (a) under benefic influence indicates a comfortable journey; and (b) under malefic influence indicates a troublesome journey.

Mars in the ninth house in the rashi of natal Jupiter signifies fear of death in travel.

Mars in its own house in the birth chart, located in the ninth house in the annual chart coinciding with its own sign ensures a beneficial and comfortable journey.

The Muntha in the ninth house enhances the Bhagya (luck).

The ninth lord in Ithasala with the fourth lord promises benefit in respect of property.

THE TENTH HOUSE

A strong year lord in the tenth house leads to increase in status, wealth and dignity. Even when it is located in any of the other kendras (houses 1, 4, 7), it gives benefic results including promotion in job.

The Sun in the tenth house with the Muntha ensures gain in position or status, and comforts. Ill-associated and debilitated Sun here gives fall in status or punishment from the ruler.

A strong Sun in Leo in the tenth house gives favours from the ruler and an elevation of status. For Scorpio ascendant, the tenth house coincides with the sign Leo. The Sun here, establishing Ithasala with the lagna lord, indicates attainment of governmental favours depending upon its strength, or a change of job for a better one.

A strong Moon in the tenth house, falling in the sign of the natal Mars, leads to a gain in status following a change in place or job.

A strong Mars in its own sign in the tenth house indicates enhancement of status following one's own courage and efforts. A strong Jupiter here also gives similar results.

A strong Mercury in its own sign in the tenth house of the annual chart results in gain of honour and status through astrology or through other intellectual deeds.

The year lord when located in the tenth house also enhances the status of the individual. Thus Saturn as the year lord, in the tenth house, coinciding with Capricorn, Aquarius or Libra, ensures good health and leads to increased wealth. The Sun in a similar situation provides wealth through elevation of status. Mars when similarly placed gives wealth through one's own valour. Mercury here ensures wealth from medication (treatment!), Jyotisha and poetic skills.

An Ithasala involving the lords of the lagna, the year, and the tenth house bestows royal favours and status on the native. Favours from the government also accrue when the lord of the year, also happening to be the lord of the Raja Saham, is in Ithasala with the Sun.

Mars in the annual chart in the sign of natal Saturn, falling in the tenth house and in aspect with the Muntha, causes loss of wealth and status through unscrupulous deeds, theft, dacoity, etc. It also indicates punishment from the ruler.

Some other combinations affecting the *karma* of the individual are as follows :

– A strong Sun in the fourth house leads to regaining of the lost status, or regaining of status earlier held by the native's ancestors.

- A strong Sun in the eleventh house leads to association with the ruler and his ministers.
- A weak Mars in the sign of natal Saturn, combust, located in the third or the ninth house, and under malefic influence, prompts the native to indulge in sinful deeds.
- Saturn as the lord of the year, or as one of the office-bearers, located in the third or the ninth house indicates increasing religious inclinations.
- A weak Saturn, as lord of the Karma Saham and aspecting the tenth house, leads to unorthodox Karma and lack of foresight.

THE ELEVENTH HOUSE

All planets, by their location in the eleventh house, are capable of giving benefic results depending upon their Pancha-vargiya Bala.

A strong benefic in the eleventh house, bereft of any malefic aspect or association, indicates material gains, and enhancement of all that the eleventh house signifies. Malefic association or aspect leads to obstacles and losses.

A weak planet in the eleventh house causes loss of wealth.

Ithasala between the lagna lord and the eleventh lord results in excessive gains, and association with worthy men.

The lagna lord as well as the lord of the year, strong and located in the seventh or the eleventh house, indicate gain of wealth from business, trade, etc.

Mercury as lord of the year located in the eleventh house ensures good profits in business.[1,2]

A strong Muntha or the Muntha lord located in the eleventh house leads to achievements in education and intellectual pursuits.[3]

---

1. Same results accrue when Mars is located in the lagna or the second house, and involved in a Kamboola yoga with the lagna lord.
2. Mercury as the year lord located it the second house also causes profit in business.
3. Increase in income from academic and intellectual pursuits follows as a result of Mercury becoming the year lord, located in the lagna along with the Muntha, in association or aspect of benefics.

Artha Saham occupied by benefics indicates multiple gains.

Artha Saham falling in the lagna, associated with benefics, promises access to hidden and underground wealth; not so if malefics aspect or associate with it.

THE TWELFTH HOUSE

A weak lord of the lagna or a weak year lord, located in the sixth, the eighth or the twelfth house, indicates varied losses during the year. The nature of these losses depends upon the signs falling in the said houses (houses 6, 8, 12).

For example :

(a) In quadruped signs (Aries, Taurus, Leo, second half of Sagittarius, first half of Capricorn) : Losses involving cattle and pets.

(b) In biped signs (Gemini, Virgo, Libra, and first half of Sagittarius) : Loss of or through servants, subordinates and enemies.

(c) In water-related signs (Cancer, Scorpio, Aquarius, Pisces): Loss of watery animals or of possessions related to water.

The Sun as the year lord located in the sixth, eighth or twelfth house, in a quadruped sign, and afflicted, leads to losses occurring through servants and subordinates, as also to strife with them.

Mars and Saturn together in the tenth or the twelfth house indicate loss of horses, vehicles, etc. Location of the eighth lord of the annual chart in the sixth, eighth or twelfth house is also not held beneficial.

Strong Saturn as the year lord, located in the sixth, eighth or twelfth house, increases one's inclination towards religion, as well as towards virtuous deeds.

MISCELLANEOUS COMBINATIONS

Venus as the year lord ensures inflow of wealth, especially when located in the second house.

Jupiter as the year lord promotes the house that it aspects in the birth chart.

Jupiter in the annual chart, in the house owned by it in the birth chart, in Ithasala with the lagna lord, promotes all good results pertaining to that house.

Natal Jupiter's rashi as lagna in the annual chart, if well-associated, ensures good health, dominance over others, and increase in wealth.

The lagna lord of the birth chart in a kendra, trikona or the eleventh house from the lagna lord of the annual chart ensures wealth and comforts during the year.

The year lord and the lagna lord in Ithasala indicate procurement of a vehicle.

Mars as the year lord in the third or the tenth house, under benefic aspect indicates travel.

Mars involved in a Kamboola yoga indicates definite travel.

The Moon as one of the office-bearers in the birth chart as well as the annual chart, in a sign owned by Mercury and associated with malefics in the annual chart, indicates foreign travel and strife.

A debilitated Mercury in the Hudda of Mars indicates loss of wealth. If there is benefic aspect on Mercury, it leads to gains. When Mercury is weak and the sign of natal Mars coincides with the lagna in the annual chart, it indicates low thinking and a generally inauspicious year.

CONCLUSIONS

1. A planet strong in the birth chart but weak in the annual chart gives good results during the first six months and adverse results during the last six months.[4]
2. A planet weak in the birth chart but strong in the annual chart gives adverse results during the first six month and good results during the last six months.[5]
3. A strong planet in the birth chart, when weak in the annual chart, gives good results during the first half of its dasha and adverse results in the later half.

4,5 That is, to say, the birth chart takes precedence over the annual chart though the annual chart too must find expression.

4. A weak planet in the birth chart, when strongly disposed in the annual chart, gives adverse results during the first half of its dasha and favourable results during the second half.
5. A planet which promises benefic or harmful results by its particular location in the birth chart, produces similar results during the year when it is located in a similar manner (house-wise!) in the annual chart.
6. Planets strong in the birth chart as well as the annual chart produce consistently good results.
7. They produce adverse results throughout when they happen to be weak in both the birth chart as well as the annual chart.
8. When the lord of the year is in any of the houses 6, 8 or 12, and the tenth lord of the annual chart is also weak, the year proves very inauspicious.

CHAPTER XIII

THE MAASA PRAVESHA

Where do the half months and months together
proceed in consultation with the year?
Where do the seasons go, in groups or singly?
Tell me of that Support - who may he be?

'ATHARVA VEDA'

The basis of the annual horoscope, as must be amply clear by now, is the longitude of the Sun at the time of birth. The importance of the Sun in Vedic astrology has been extolled by an authority no less than the sage Parashara himself who, in his famous Sudarshana Chakra method, advocates considering the lagna, the Sun and the Moon as of equal import while analysing a horoscope. Significant variations in the position of the Sun are supposed to herald significant changes in the life of the native.

As has been already said, when the Sun approaches the same sign, degrees, minutes and seconds of longitude as at the time of birth, that moment is called as the Varshapravesha or the beginning of the new year for the native. The Sun, in one year, traverses twelve signs of the zodiac, staying in one sign for roughly one month. It will thus be seen that every month, after the Sun enters the next sign, at some moment it will pass over the same degrees, minutes and seconds of longitude as at the time of birth. This will repeat every month, roughly at intervals of one month. *The time when the Sun in any sign attains the same degrees, minutes and seconds of longitude as it had at the time of birth is called the 'Maasa-pravesha' or the 'monthly return of the Sun'.* There will thus be twelve Maasa-praveshas in a year, and the first Maasa-pravesha will be the same as the Varsha-pravesha for that year.

A horoscope cast for the moment of the Maasa-pravesha is called the *'Maasa Kundali'* or the *'monthly chart'*. A monthly chart is prepared in order to further narrow down the timing of events. Since it involves additional labour, practitioners of annual horoscopy generally resort to the monthly charts only in special circumstances.

Calculating the Maasa-pravesha and the Monthly Chart

Note the exact longitude of the Sun at birth. This is the same as the longitude of the Sun at the time of Varshapravesha for any year of life. If we add one sign to it, we get the longitude of the Sun at the next Maasa-pravesha. From the ephemeris, we work out the exact date and time when the Sun attains this longitude. This date and time is the Maasa-pravesha for the second month. Adding two signs to the Sun's natal longitude gives us the Sun's longitude for the third month, and the date and time when the Sun attains this longitude constitutes the Maasa-pravesha for the third month. Similarly, the Maasa-pravesha can be worked out for all the twelve months of a given year of native's life. The monthly charts are the horoscopes for the Maasa-praveshas thus obtained.

It may be required to cast a monthly chart only for a particular month, and not for all the months of the year. For example, Mr. Rajiv Gandhi was assassinated on May 21, 1991, during his forty-seventh year of life. In order to make a monthly chart for the month of May 1991, we first refer back to the birth chart of Mr. Rajiv Gandhi (Chapter III : Casting the Annual Chart) and find that the longitude of the Sun is Leo 3°49'4". We work out from the ephemeris for the year 1991, the date and time during the month of May (and before the date of the event!) when the Sun attains in Taurus (the sign in which the Sun will be located in the later half of May) the longitude of 3°49'4". This date and time is the Maasa-pravesha for the month in question. A horoscope is then prepared for this time. The method of working out the Maasa-pravesha for the said moment is as follows :

From the ephemeris for 1991, in the month of May, we find that:

(a) The longitude of the Sun at 5:30 AM on May 19, 1991 is $1^s3°47'57''$.

(b) The longitude of the Sun on May 20, 1991 is $1^s4°45'43''$. Thus our required degrees of the Sun (3°49'4") fall between 5:30 AM on May 19, 1991 and 5:30 AM on May 20, 1991.

(c) The movement of the Sun in 24 hours is 57'46".

We see that the Sun must move another 1'7" from its position on May 19, 1991 (5:30 AM) to reach the longitude of 3°49'4". This distance is travelled is 27 minutes and 50 seconds (calculating from the daily motion of the Sun). Adding this time to 5:30 AM (the time for which the Sun's position for May 19, 1991 is available), we find that the Maasa-pravesha comes to be 5h 57m 50s AM (IST), equivalent to 5h 19m 10s AM (LMT) for Bombay (the place of birth of the native).

The ascendant as calculated for this time will be $1^s1°24'20''$. Planetary longitudes are then calculated for this time in the usual manner.

The Muntha in the Monthly Chart

As has been already mentioned, the Muntha is in the lagna at the time of birth. It progresses by one sign every year, or 2°30' every month. For locating the Muntha in the monthly chart, first locate it in the respective annual chart. For the forty-seventh year of our native, whose birth ascendant is Leo, the Muntha will fall in the sign Gemini (denoted by the remainder after dividing by twelve the sum of completed years and the sign in the birth ascendant) in the annual chart. Since the Muntha is on the birth lagna at the time of birth, its degrees coincide with the degrees of the ascendant. The mid-point of the ascendant of the birth chart of our native is Leo 14°36'. Thus, the Muntha falls in Gemini 14°36', in the annual chart for the forty-seventh year of Mr. Rajive Gandhi.

Now we calculate the Muntha position for May 1991. The forty-seventh year of Mr. Rajiv Gandhi starts in August 1990. The number of completed months upto May 1991 (from August 1990) is nine. The progression of the Muntha in these nine months will be :

2°30' × 9 = 22°30'

Adding this value to the Muntha in the annual chart, we get :

Gemini 14°36' + 22°30' = Cancer 7°6'.

The monthly chart cast for the month of May 1991 for Mr. Rajive Gandhi will be as given below.

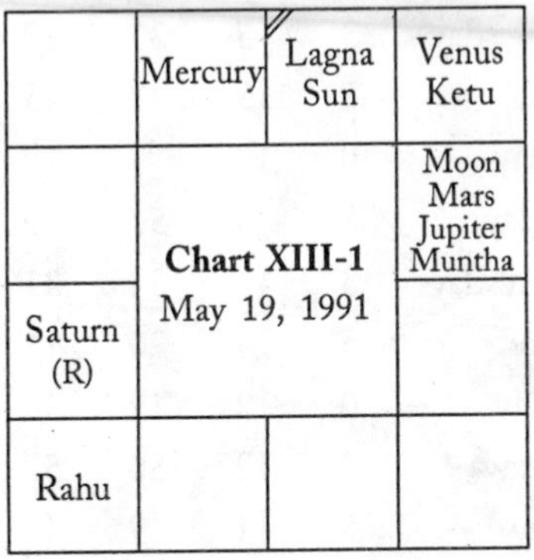

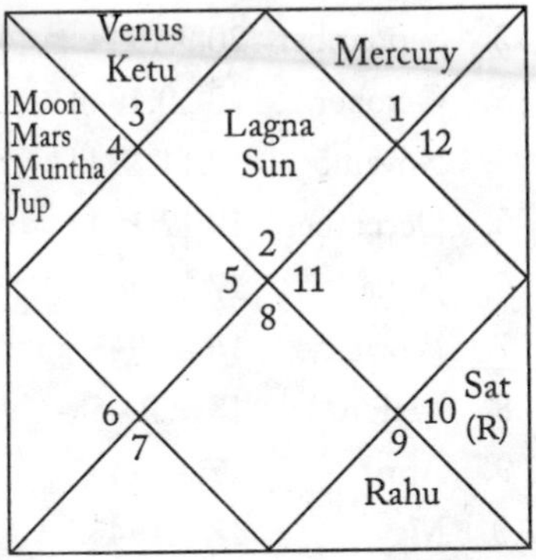

Lagna	01°24'29"	Mars	01°53'41"	Venus	17°16'17"
Sun	03°49'04"	Mercury	08°46'29"	Saturn (R)	13°06'00"
Moon	10°24'06"	Jupiter	13°21'09"	Rahu	26°30'01"

Alternative Method for Maasa-pravesha

An alternative and much simpler method of calculating the Maasa-pravesha for any given month is being described. Note the longitude of the Sun at the time of birth. For the next eleven months, find out the day and time each month when the Sun attains in successive signs the same degrees, minutes and seconds of longitude as at birth. Thus we get the Maasa-pravesha for the first twelve months of life. This may be tabulated for future use.

In order to calculate the Maasa-pravesha for any given month in any given year of life, *add the Dhruvanka (Chapter III: Casting the Annual chart) for the completed number of years* to the Maasa-pravesha for the corresponding month during the first year of life. This will give the Maasa-pravesha for the required month.

The Maasa-pravesha for the first twelve months of Mr. Rajiv Gandhi may be tabulated on next page.

Table XIII-1

Maasapravesha for the first twelve months of the native born on August 20, 1944, at 7:11 AM (IST), in Bombay.

Month	Date	Day	Maasa-pravesha d.	h.	m.	s.
1. August	20.8.1944	Sunday	0	7	11	0
2. September	20.9.1944	Wednesday	3	5	31	38
3. October	20.10.1944	Friday	5	15	48	45
4. November	19.11.1944	Sunday	0	14	3	19
5. December	19.12.1944	Tuesday	2	3	57.	9
6. January	17.1.1945	Wednesday	3	14	34	31
7. February	16.2.1945	Friday	5	4	20	11
8. March	18.3.1945	Sunday	0	2	19	36
9. April	17.4.1945	Tuesday	2	12	50	57
10. May	18.5.1945	Friday	5	11	9	45
11. June	18.6.1945	Monday	1	18	34	51
12. July	20.7.1945	Friday	5	5	31	41

By the above method, the Maasa-pravesha for May 1991 for the native under consideration may be calculated as follows :

Maasa-pravesha in May 1945 (18-5-1945) : 5d 11th 9m 45s.

Dhruvanka for 46 (i.e., completed) years : 1d 19h 1m 27s.

Maasa-pravesha in May 1991 (47th year) : 7d 6h 11m 12s, or Sunday 6h 11m 12s.

The Maasa-pravesha in May 1991 occurs on Sunday which should fall on the 18th of May (the date of the Maasa-pravesha during the first year of life) or a day before or after the said date. In 1991, the Sunday nearest to the 18th of May falls on May 19, 1991. Thus, we get the Maasa-pravesha as May 19, 1991, at 6h 11m 12s (IST). The ascendant calculated for this moment of time will be $1^s5°14'29''$.

It will be noted that the above method, though much simpler, gives a slight variation in the time of the Maasa-pravesha, with a corresponding variation in the mid-point of the ascendant. It is for the readers to judge the veracity of this method. In any case, this method deserves to be experimented with.

The Maasesha or the Lord of the Month

Five office-bearers have been already described while discussing about the lord of the year (Chapter VII : The Lord of the year). In the monthly chart, there are six office-bearers. Besides the five (the lagna lord of the birth chart, the lagna lord of the annual chart, the Muntha lord, the Tri-rashi-pati and the Dina-Ṛatri-pati) already mentioned, the lagna lord of the monthly chart constitutes the sixth officer-bearer. The strength of the office-bearers is determined on the same basis as the Pancha-vargiya Bala. The lord of the month is also decided on the basis of the same principles as are applicable to the determination of the lord of the year.

Analysis of the Monthly Chart

The monthly chart must be analysed in the same manner as the annual chart. The results of the monthly chart will obviously be applicable to one month only. The lord of the month has the same significance in the monthly chart as the year lord in the annual chart. The Tajika yogas, Sahams, and other principles applicable to analysis of houses may all be applied in order to make possible a closer timing of events. Needless to say that the monthly chart must be analysed only in conjunction with the annual chart as well as the birth chart.

THE DINA PRAVESHA

Just as the Sun's transit through one sign indicates the monthly return of the Sun, so also its transit through one degree indicates the daily return of the Sun. The Sun is supposed to cover a longitude arc of one degree in one 'day'. Keeping the minutes and seconds of the Sun's natal longitude constant, and adding one degree for each day, provides the longitude of the Sun for a given day; the time at which the Sun attains this longitude is called the *'Dina-pravesha'* or the *'daily return of the Sun'.* A Dina-Kundali or day-horoscope can be cast for this moment and analysed as usual. There can thus be 360 day-horoscopes in any given year.

CHAPTER XIV

SUMMARY

Vanished are those who in the days before us
gazed at the rising of the morning Sun.
It is we the living who now behold the Dawn,
and after us her shining others will see.

'RIG VEDA'

Chapter I explains the basis of the annual chart. The Tajika system with its special features, especially the Tajika aspects and the planetary relations, has been briefly explained. The links of the annual chart with the birth chart have been highlighted. Stress has been laid on the fact that the annual chart is essentially a transit chart of a superior nature, and must only be treated of along with the birth chart.

Chapter II explains the difference between a north Indian and a south Indian chart. Special features of various houses along with their significance, the planets, the zodiac, the rashis or signs of the zodiac, and the characteristics and significations of the rashis have been detailed here. Nature of planets, their natural relations, their significations, and such important aspects as planetary exaltation, debilitation, retrogression, combustion, Moolatrikona signs, etc., have been explained. The nakshatras and the vargas have also been briefly touched upon.

Chapter III deals in detail with the method of casting the annual horoscope. The solar cycle and the time of commencement of the year (also known as the Varsha-pravesha) have been explained. Both the modern and the ancient methods of arriving at the Varsha-pravesha have been described. The birth chart of Mr. Rajiv Gandhi, and his annual chart for the year 1984, when he became the Prime Minister, have been taken as examples.

Chapter IV deals with a very special feature of the annual horoscope called the Muntha. Locating the Muntha in a chart, its progression during the year, and the results of the Muntha depending upon its location in different houses have been described. The Muntha also gets influenced by the planets which aspect or associate with it, and by the signs in which it is located. These, as well as the results pertaining to the Muntha lord, have also been dealt with.

Chapter V explains the three main dasha systems generally employed in the annual chart in order to time the events. Methods of calculation of the Mudda dasha, the Yogini dasha and the Patyayini dasha, along with their antardashas or sub-periods, have been discussed in detail. The view of Kalidasa, the author of the Uttarakalamrita, in respect of the Mudda dasha has been discussed.

Chapter VI deals with the methods employed to assess the strength of planets. Of the three main methods, the Harsha Bala is the simplest to calculate and gives a quick view of the planetary strength. The Dwadasha-vargiya Bala consists of twelve-fold strength of planets and is the most elaborate. The Pancha-vargiya Bala, however, is the most important in annual horoscopy. This consists of five-fold strength of planets, and gives an accurate numerical value for planetary strength. One of the five factors considered here is known as the Hudda which is a very special feature of the annual chart and needs to be researched upon.

Chapter VII Concerns itself with the determination and interpretation of the lord of the year. The lord of the year is selected out of five planets, known as the five office-bearers in the annual chart. This selection makes use of the planetary strength as determined by the Pancha-vargiya method. Also discussed in this chapter are the special circumstances when the Moon, otherwise considered unsuitable for the year lordship, qualifies for the post of the lord of the year. The results of various planets as year lords have been dealt with in details.

Chapter VIII deals with a very special feature of the annual chart, the Tri-pataki Chakra, which gives an overall view of whether the year in question will be generally favourable or generally unfavourable. The basis of this is the influence or 'vedha' of various planets on the Moon. The views of late Shri Hardev Sharma Trivedi, an eminent astrologer of north India with whom the author had personal discussion, on the use of the Tri-pataki Chakra have also been incorporated in this chapter.

A detailed description of the results accruing from the location of various planets in different houses forms the substance of **Chapter IX.** Hints about the interpretation of these results, which otherwise appear too generalised, have been added toward the end of the chapter.

A comprehensive treatment has been meted to the sixteen Tajika yogas, with several illustrations from actual horoscopes, in **Chapter X.** An understanding of the Tajika yogas is essential in order to make any successful predictions on the basis of the annual horoscope. The most important of these, the Ithasala yoga, has been dealt with in great details. Stress has been laid on the fact that the basic Parashari principles of astrology must always be adhered to while analysing these yogas.

Chapter XI deals with another special feature of annual horoscopy, called the Sahams. Numerous Sahams have been described in the classical as well as modern texts. A list of important Sahams, taken out from the classics, and method of their calculation, have been detailed. Judgement of the strength or weakness of a Saham and the special significance of the Punya Saham have been highlighted. Analysis of the Sahams, along with illustrations, has been dealt with in details. The importance of the strength of a Saham in the birth chart has also been stressed.

Chapter XII details important principles and combinations pertaining to the twelve houses of the annual chart. Each house has been separately dealt with. Affliction to the annual chart, prosperity, comforts, progeny, disease, death, marriage, professional rise and fall, income and expenditure, have all been discussed in details, along with appropriate illustrations. Stress has again been laid on the importance of studying the annual chart along with the birth chart.

Chapter XIII briefly deals with the Maasa-pravesha or the monthly return of the Sun. The method of calculation of the monthly chart in order to permit a closer timing of events has been described. Location of the Muntha in the monthly chart has also been discussed. In the end, mention has also been made of the Dina-pravesha or the daily return of the Sun to permit the casting of a day-chart.

INDEX

OTHER BOOKS BY THE AUTHOR

Elements of Vedic Astrology (2 volumes)

•

Yogas in Astrology

•

Essentials of Medical Astrology

•

Subtleties of Medical Astrology

•

Predictive Techniques in Varshaphala

•

Surya the Sun God

•

Jatakalankara